South Asia

CURRENT HISTORY BOOKS

Founded in 1914, *Current History* is the oldest U.S. publication devoted exclusively to world affairs. Drawing on the best that this distinguished journal has to offer, *Current History* Books will present timely, comprehensive, and accessible overviews of regions and topics related to international affairs and policy.

South Asia
Edited by Sumit Ganguly

South Asia

EDITED BY

Sumit Ganguly

NEW YORK UNIVERSITY PRESS
New York and London

NEW YORK UNIVERSITY PRESS
New York and London
www.nyupress.org

Library of Congress Cataloging-in-Publication Data
South Asia / edited by Sumit Ganguly.
p. cm. — (Current history books)
Collected articles previously published in the journal Current history, 1995–2003.
Includes bibliographical references and index.
ISBN–13: 978–0–8147–3176–5 (cloth : alk. paper)
ISBN–10: 0–8147–3176–7 (cloth : alk. paper)
ISBN–13: 978–0–8147–3177–2 (pbk. : alk. paper)
ISBN–10: 0–8147–3177–5 (pbk. : alk. paper)
1. South Asia—Politics and government. 2. Ethnic conflict—South Asia.
3. Democratization—South Asia. 4. National security—South Asia.
5. India—Economic policy. I. Ganguly, Sumit. II. Current history. III. Series.
DS341.S635   2006
954.05—dc22   2005056235

c 10 9 8 7 6 5 4 3 2 1
p 10 9 8 7 6 5 4 3 2 1

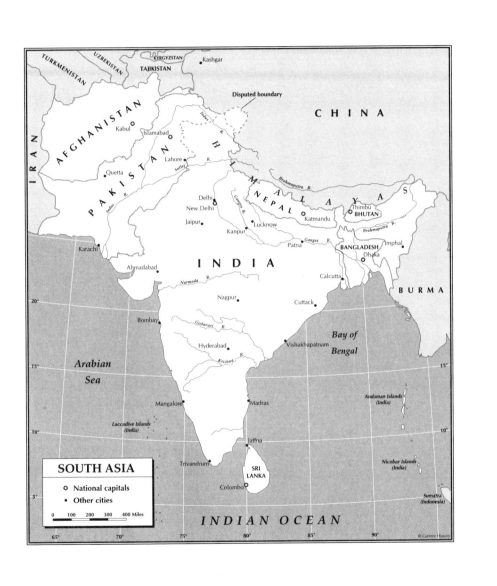

SOUTH ASIA

○ National capitals
● Other cities

0   100   200   300   400 Miles

TURKMENISTAN
UZBEKISTAN
KYRGYZSTAN
TAJIKISTAN
Kashgar

Disputed boundary

CHINA

IRAN

AFGHANISTAN

Kabul ○
Islamabad ○
Lahore ●
Quetta ●

PAKISTAN

Indus R.
Sutlej R.

H I M A L A Y A S

Brahmaputra R.

Delhi ●
New Delhi
Jaipur ●

Ganges R.

NEPAL

Katmandu ○

Thimbu ○
BHUTAN

Lucknow ●
Kanpur ●
Patna ●
Ganges R.

Brahmaputra R.

Imphal ●

BANGLADESH
Dhaka ○

Karachi ●

INDIA

Ahmadabad ●

Narmada R.

Calcutta ●

BURMA

20°

Nagpur ●

Cuttack ●

Bombay ●

Godavari R.

Vishakhapatnam ●

Bay of
Bengal

Arabian
Sea

Hyderabad ●

Krishna R.

15°

15°

Mangalore ●

Madras ●

Andaman Islands
(India)

Laccadive Islands
(India)

10°

10°

Jaffna ●

Nicobar Islands
(India)

Trivandrum ●

SRI
LANKA

Colombo ○

Sumatra
(Indonesia)

5°

INDIAN OCEAN

© Current History

65°   70°   75°   80°   85°   90°

Contents

Preface

BILL FINAN   Editor, *Current History*

South Asia's transition over the past decade from a region that attracted only marginal major-power interest to an area that has become a strategic and economic focal point is captured in the articles that make up this introductory volume in the *Current History* Books series. The essays, which range over the past 10 years, detail the major events that have turned the global spotlight on South Asia. These include the atomic tests of 1998, which saw India and Pakistan become the newest members of the group of declared nuclear weapons states; the US invasion of Afghanistan in the months after September 11, which found the United States newly attentive to Islamic radicalism and courting not just Pakistan but also India; and the stirrings of economic change in India, beginning in the early 1990s, which have led to speculation that India may be poised to become an economic powerhouse to rival China.

The economic stirrings prompted *Current History*'s editors to begin annual coverage of India and the region in the early 1990s. But it was not just the potential economic impact regionally and globally of an India determined to pursue a liberalized economic path that led to our decision to focus coverage on the subcontinent. A new strategic equation also appeared to be forming in the region, once the Soviet Union had withdrawn from Afghanistan and then withered into Russia. Teasing out the implications of these two sets of changes while also explaining them became the guiding principles by which the magazine's coverage of the region evolved.

Sumit Ganguly, this volume's editor and a contributing editor to *Current History*, helped immensely in sorting through the implications and also suggesting authors and themes for various articles during the years. His intellectual guidance has proved invaluable, and I also welcome his collegiality and the friendship he has extended as we have worked together over the years. As this book's editor he has worked diligently to ensure that this volume is representative of *Current History* itself: works of first-rate scholarship that are recognized as such by the academic community yet are accessible to the student and general reader.

India and South Asia inaugurates a series of collected works from *Current History*. Each volume will offer readers a unique focus on a region of the world or a global concern, drawing on coverage from the magazine. The articles contained in each volume will be selected by one of our contributing editors or one of our recognized specialist authors, who will also provide an introduction to the articles that follow. The selections will offer concise, analytical, authoritative essays written by leading scholars, policy makers, and journalists. These will be supplemented by a comprehensive chronology of events in the highlighted region, drawn from the Month in Review, a regular feature in *Current History*.

Mark Redmond, *Current History*'s publisher, and I have long discussed the idea of a *Current History* Book series. But it was only because of the interest of Eric Zinner, New York University Press's editor in chief, that the project became more than just a thought. His initiative, along with the interest, enthusiasm, and guidance of Press Executive Editor Ilene Kalish and the editorial support provided by *Current History* Associate Editor Alan Sorensen, has ensured the steady progress of this volume from outline to bound book. It is a good team to work with in putting together the other titles in the series planned for the coming years.

Introduction

SUMIT GANGULY

The writer V. S. Naipaul once wrote a dire travelogue about India, *An Area of Darkness*. This evocative phrase could easily be applied to the status that India and South Asia occupied on the US foreign policy agenda during most of the cold war. During the half century after the end of World War II, India and South Asia received only spasmodic and periodic attention by American foreign policy makers. Even in the immediate postwar period, when the US foreign policy establishment paid more sustained heed to political developments in the region, American interests derived from other, more global concerns, the most prominent of which was the anticommunist enterprise. In the late 1960s the United States lost almost all interest in the region as it sought to prosecute the Vietnam War in Southeast Asia. In the 1970s and 1980s the principal American concern in South Asia stemmed from broader attempts to combat the dispersion of nuclear weapons.

When the Soviet Union invaded Afghanistan in 1979, South Asia and particularly Pakistan acquired renewed significance. Yet it was not until India's embrace of economic reforms in the early 1990s that the United States found any intrinsic reasons for devoting sustained attention to South Asia. Since then, American interest in the region has grown for a number of other compelling, though still derivative, reasons. These have included the Indian and Pakistani overt testing of nuclear weapons in May 1998; the war between these two antagonists in April–July 1999; and the September 11, 2001, attacks on the United States by Al Qaeda forces based in Afghanistan.

From the vantage point of 2006 it appears that the United States will not relegate India and South Asia to the lesser reaches of its foreign and security policy concerns in the foreseeable future. Some important indicators suggest a slow but significant shift under way in American policy considerations. One of the most compelling of these indicators is a segment devoted to India in the December 2004 National Intelligence Council (NIC) report on the prospective state of the world in the year 2020.[1] Although the report did not suggest that India would become a global or regional competitor to the United States, it nevertheless made clear that within the next 15 years India would, in all likelihood, become a significant regional and global player. The report's conclusions are predicated on India's ability to solve a number of pressing demographic, economic, and political problems. It also assumes that India will be able to craft policies enabling it to address the misgivings of its immediate neighbors: Pakistan, Bangladesh, Sri Lanka, and Nepal. These key caveats notwithstanding, it is important to underscore that the NIC report was based on certain identifiable secular trends and relied on extensive scholarly expertise on India and the region.

Another key indicator of the growing interest in India and South Asia is the emergence of new academic programs on South Asia throughout the United States. Universities that once paid scant attention to the region are now inaugurating India and South Asian studies programs. Within the past few years, Harvard University has launched a major initiative to create a South Asian studies program and Johns Hopkins University's School of Advanced International Studies has begun an entirely new program on South Asia. Other institutions that had allowed their programs to fall in desuetude are rapidly recruiting new faculty and seeking to attract graduate students. Not surprisingly, positions in South Asian politics, history, anthropology, and language, among other fields, are now also opening up at a range of colleges and universities. This trend can be easily explained: contrary to popular belief, academic institutions are remarkably sensitive to prevailing political trends and intellectual currents.

Even in times when governmental and academic neglect of India and South Asia prevailed, one opinion journal, *Current History*, consistently paid heed to the region, and it has continued to do so during the tumultuous past decade. The collection of essays in this volume provides a representative sample of articles focused on key issues and developments that characterized the region over the past 10 years. These essays can provide the reader with succinct and pithy accounts of turning points and critical moments. They also offer sufficient background to illuminate the current preoccupation in American circles, both governmental and societal, with events and trends in India and across South Asia.

Recognizing India

Of course, renewed interest in the region would not have occurred in the absence of profound changes in India and its neighboring countries. Perhaps the most significant of these changes was India's decision in 1991 to jettison the "license, permit, quota" raj, a set of rules under which bureaucrats had for decades micromanaged and stultified every aspect of the economy. Faced with an unprecedented domestic and international fiscal crisis, India's leadership did not try to tide over its economic difficulties through financial sleights of hand. Instead, Prime Minister Narasimha Rao, assisted by his finance minister, Manmohan Singh (now prime minister himself), fundamentally altered the course of India's economic trajectory. They led the country fitfully but surely to an embrace of the market and put India on a path of self-sustaining economic growth.

The potentially extraordinary size of the Indian market prompted the Clinton administration to anoint India as one of "ten big emerging markets" on which the United States should focus its attention. This designation led to a flurry of visits by business professionals as well as high-level government officials. These activities presaged growing American investment in the Indian market. The volume of this investment was small in comparison to that sent to China, India's most obvious competitor. The investments were focused, however, on areas of key significance to the Indian economy, such as software, bioinformatics, pharmaceuticals, and other forms of high technology.

The last several Indian governments have with fits and starts extended the reforms initiated under the Rao-Singh regime. The results have been nothing short of dramatic. India's GDP has grown at rates ranging from 6 percent to 7 percent annually for the past several years. Although a vigorous debate has ensued regarding the degree and extent of poverty reduction, there is little question that economic growth has had some salutary effects. That said, both absolute and regional disparities have increased as a consequence of rapid and uneven growth. How present and future regimes will cope with these remains to be seen. Continuing regional disparities may contribute to intrastate tensions and thereby pose important new challenges for India's federal structure. The persistence of economic disparities may also contribute to social tensions within and across various parts of India.

Obviously, India's striking economic success over the past decade explains much of the renewed American attention to the country and the region, but other factors have also driven South Asia's growing importance. In May 1998, after maintaining postures of nuclear ambiguity for many years, both India and Pakistan crossed the nuclear Rubicon. As Samina Ahmed discusses in her contribution to this volume, "The (Nuclear) Testing of Pakistan," the initial American response to both countries' public tests was one of shock and anger; the shock stemming from the failure of American intelligence agencies to have predicted these events, the anger directed mostly at India, which despite warming relations with the United States had carefully concealed its plans for nuclear testing. Policy makers in the United States were also dismayed that the carefully woven fabric of the nonproliferation regime had been so blatantly tattered. Some of that frustration is nicely captured in Toby F. Dalton's essay, "Toward Nuclear Rollback in South Asia."

After exhibiting some public fury, the Clinton administration appointed Deputy Secretary of State Strobe Talbott to negotiate with the Indians and the Pakistanis to address American nonproliferation concerns. In the event, Talbott focused most of his energies on India, the principal player in the region. After 11 rounds of talks in which he made little progress in advancing US nonproliferation goals, Talbott concluded his negotiations with his counterpart, Indian Foreign Minister Jaswant Singh, with what he acknowledged was a far better appreciation of India's security concerns.[2] In the waning days of Bill Clinton's presidency, this newly acquired sensitivity toward India's security needs also helped to open up the possibility of a new strategic relationship. For New Delhi, nuclear weapons were not simply a symbol of status and prestige but a strategic hedge in a region with a rising power—China—with which it had a longstanding border dispute.

The new strategic relationship did not emerge, however, until the first administration of George W. Bush lifted the bulk of the Clinton-era nonproliferation sanctions on India and Pakistan. India, for its part, surprised many in the United States and elsewhere when it endorsed, albeit in a qualified fashion, the Bush administration's decision to jettison the 1972 Anti-Ballistic Missile Treaty (ABM) and pursue a national missile defense program. Washington, though utterly unprepared for this abrupt Indian endorsement, nevertheless welcomed it, especially since various long-term allies had expressed considerable dismay about the unilateral decision to terminate the ABM treaty.

Indeed, the Bush administration had signaled an interest in working with India even before Bush won the 2000 election. The administration's first national security advisor, Condoleezza Rice, in a pre-election article in

Foreign Affairs, devoted a paragraph to India's emergence as a regional power and its significance in the American foreign policy calculus.[3] The administration's interest in making India the centerpiece of its foreign policy toward South Asia was not spelled out in this brief reference, but remarks by key administration loyalists implied that the incoming government was keen on courting India because of its potentially large market, its robust democratic credentials, and its possible role as a counterweight to China.

In the Aftermath of 9/11

It is intriguing to speculate how US–South Asian relations in general and US-Indian relations in particular might have evolved had the tragic events of September 11, 2001, not transpired. In the wake of the Al Qaeda attacks, the Bush administration, without abandoning India, focused its attention on Pakistan and its military regime led by General Pervez Musharraf. In a manner markedly reminiscent of the period after the Soviet invasion and occupation of Afghanistan, when the Reagan administration chose to court another military dictator, General Mohammed Zia ul Haq, the United States felt compelled to cultivate its relationship with General Musharraf. This was hardly surprising: Pakistan had incubated, nurtured, and sustained the Taliban regime in Afghanistan,[4] and the Taliban had been the principal haven for Osama bin Laden and Al Qaeda. Pakistan's proximity to Afghanistan and the close ties of its Inter-Services Intelligence agency to the Taliban made it the logical base for operations designed to topple the Taliban regime and to eviscerate Al Qaeda.

Musharraf's regime, facing a financial meltdown thanks to the fiscal profligacy of his predecessors, saw little recourse but to accede to Bush's demand for cooperation against his military establishment's former acolytes. The general's willingness to cooperate with the United States provided his government much-needed debt relief and substantial American economic assistance. It also provided the United States virtually unfettered access to Pakistani territory and military bases in the conduct of military operations in Afghanistan.

This arrangement has been mutually beneficial but with important limitations. The United States has managed to seize several important members of the Al Qaeda hierarchy, while Pakistan has enjoyed considerable American munificence. Yet the Musharraf regime does not appear to have been entirely forthcoming in its efforts to curb the activities of the remnants of the Taliban (much of which fled to the difficult terrain and lawless provinces along the Afghan-Pakistani border). Pakistan's unwillingness to cooperate fully with the United States on this matter is not entirely surprising. It fears that the government of President Hamid Karzai in Afghanistan may not be entirely pliable and sufficiently attentive to Pakistani interests. It also fears that India, which has a cordial relationship with the Karzai regime, may be steadily extending its influence within Afghanistan, thereby undermining the Pakistani military's long obsession with strategic depth.

The United States, no doubt in an effort to elicit greater cooperation from Pakistan, has recently gone to extraordinary lengths to court Musharraf. To this end it has avoided exerting significant pressure on Pakistan to reveal the full scope of the clandestine nuclear activities run by Abdul Qadeer Khan, one of the key progenitors of Pakistan's nuclear weapons program. It has also avoided any direct criticism of Musharraf's unwillingness to set a firm date for the restoration of democracy in Pakistan.

In a striking departure from past American policy, President Bush in April 2005 agreed to sell F-16 combat aircraft to Pakistan—a deal that had been stymied by congressional sanctions for 15 years. A decision that in the past would have drawn vehement criticism from New Delhi as a dangerous escalation in the Indo-Pakistani arms race now drew only a muted adverse reaction. Since India has already developed a fairly robust relationship with the United States, and since President Bush also offered to sell F-18 aircraft to India in a possible co-production arrangement, India saw substantial benefits in downplaying its protest. It remains to be seen if the aircraft offer to India comes to fruition.[5]

Why South Asia Matters

Beyond the current exigencies of American security and foreign policy, why does South Asia matter? Once the United States disrupts the Al Qaeda network beyond repair and suppresses the last elements of the Taliban, will Pakistan again be consigned to its previously marginal status? Will the current engagement with India prosper and result in a more substantial relationship? Finally, will the United States pay much heed to the smaller, peripheral states of South Asia—Afghanistan, Bangladesh, Nepal, and Sri Lanka—when the present crises of governance that afflict these states no longer warrant a watchful American eye? Obviously, it is impossible to answer any of these questions with a degree of certainty. It is, nevertheless, possible to speculate on the future of American interests and policies toward the region based on certain ongoing concerns in Washington and some trends in the region.

One issue that appears likely to preoccupy decision makers in Washington for the foreseeable future is the rise of radical Islam in South Asia. Without adopting an excessively alarmist posture on this subject, it is still possible to argue that the rise of Islamic extremism poses a threat to American interests on a global basis. Combating and containing radical Islam may not become the basis of a second cold war, but it seems likely to focus the minds of American policy makers for the next several years, if not longer. Given the presence of Islamic religious extremists in Afghanistan, Pakistan, and Bangladesh, it is unlikely that the United States will ignore the region. If Hindu religious chauvinism again manifests itself in India, that might further arouse and inspire Islamic radicalism in the region. (David Stuligross discusses competing visions of the Indian state in his essay, "India's Vision—and the BJP's.") Thus, US policy makers will be wise to monitor radical communalist trends throughout South Asia.

How the United States chooses to deal with religious extremism remains a vital question. A security-driven agenda focused on collecting intelligence on these organizations, physically disrupting their activities, and incarcerating their members may well be a necessity. Such a strategy, however, will not uproot the basis of Islamic radicalism either in South Asia or elsewhere. To successfully undermine the attraction of radical Islam the United States may have to pursue other strategies, in particular the exercise of "soft power," described by Harvard's Joseph Nye as the exercise of economic, cultural, and moral influence. Taking advantage of soft power will require a far more adroit and sustained public diplomacy, attempts to encourage the growth of civic institutions, and a willingness to promote and uphold the values that Americans cherish and enjoy at home. This will mean slowly but surely beginning to criticize pro-American but authoritarian regimes and a greater willingness to speak out on behalf of the protection of fundamental human rights. The current silence of the Bush administration on these matters, especially as far as Pakistan is concerned, is ultimately counterproductive and a deeply flawed strategy.

The United States also needs to confront the inexorable growth of Islamic radicalism in Bangladesh. The steady erosion of state capabilities in Bangladesh and the concomitant rise of Islamic zealotry could create conducive conditions for various terrorist groups to use Bangladesh as a base for their operations. Nor should India, despite the robustness of its democratic institutions, be above criticism when it fails to protect the rights of its sizeable Muslim minority. Pogroms such as that which took place against Muslims in the state of Gujarat in February 2002 must be declared intolerable. Containing religious extremism is, of course, in India's own interest. A country that is home to substantial religious minorities cannot afford the costs associated with the rise of violent religious intolerance. The protection of the rights of religious minorities is a necessity for the maintenance of social peace.

American efforts to curb the rise of religious extremism in South Asia cannot be confined to diplomatic jawboning, either. Any viable effort to combat religious radicalism will entail increased foreign direct assistance to the states involved. Yet merely increasing funding will not be enough. The United States will have to ensure that the funds are appropriately targeted toward building institutional capacity, expanding primary education, providing access to rudimentary health care, and promoting rural development. This list, though seemingly unimaginative, encompasses acute needs throughout much of Afghanistan, Bangladesh, and Pakistan. The almost willful neglect of these critical areas of state policy in all three of these countries has contributed to the rise of radical religious movements that promise to address the failures of notionally secular, utterly corrupt, and mostly authoritarian regimes.

Economic Hurdles

Of course, combating the manifestations and sources of radical Islam hardly constitutes the complete foundation of a sound and sustainable American policy toward South Asia. There are other cogent reasons for continued and ongoing US engagement with the region. One is the steady emergence of a substantial Indian market. The long-term expansion of a trade and investment relationship with India remains fraught, however, with several potential pitfalls that could have significant consequences for the future of American policy toward the region.

As Shalendra D. Sharma notes in "India's Economic Liberalization: A Progress Report," India has, albeit with some setbacks, made impressive strides in deregulating its once hidebound economy. Since the onset of its economic reform process in 1991, it has dramatically reduced tariffs, simplified investment procedures, and addressed important infrastructure bottlenecks. Yet key hurdles, both material and legal, still need to be overcome. One of the most significant constraints is India's inadequate infrastructure. The country lacks world-class airports, its port facilities are antiquated, and its road network is poorly developed. Under the previous government an ambitious effort was undertaken to link India's four major metropolitan areas with a modern highway network. The National Highway Authority of India has started work on the project and considerable progress has been made toward this goal. The completion date, however, remains uncertain. India has already overcome one critical infrastructural hurdle—the problem of telecommunications—through technological leapfrogging. It is rapidly emerging as one of the most successful cell phone markets in the world.[6]

While the transport and telecommunications sectors show some promise, India's power sector remains a major constraint on growth and investment. Power shortfalls for both consumer and manufacturing sectors are endemic. Throughout India, with marked exceptions, power generation and distribution are the preserve of state-controlled enterprises known as the State Electricity Boards. These entities, a legacy of India's experiment with state-led industrialization, are antiquated, lack adequate and technically competent staffing, and fail to generate power sufficient to meet India's burgeoning energy needs. Despite their myriad problems, few politicians have proved willing to dismantle these boards. Their employees are unionized and all the unions are closely linked to major political parties. The political sensitivity and risk associated with any comprehensive attempt to reform these organizations have resulted in only piecemeal, incremental, and partial efforts to change their operations. Thus far, only two Indian states, Orissa and Delhi, have succeeded in fully privatizing electricity distribution. Yet, if India is to make meaningful economic progress, reform of the power sector is critical.

Another aspect of the energy sector also poses a significant barrier to India's long-term economic well-being: the national government is forced to subsidize the power sector's losses. These subsidies, in turn, constitute a major fiscal drag. And subsidies for the power sector alone do not explain India's continuing fiscal woes. A range of other subsidies to agriculture and other state-run enterprises also adds to India's ballooning fiscal deficit.

Finally, India faces a major problem with organized labor. Although it constitutes a small fraction of India's workforce, organized labor's political clout is tremendous. Closely linked with all of India's major political parties, the unions remain an almost insurmountable barrier to labor law re-

form. In the absence of reform, inefficient industries will continue to stag-
ger along, labor forces will stay bloated, and foreign investors will remain
cautious about entering the Indian market. India's ability to address all
these constraints on its economic prospects will, in considerable measure,
define the future of the Indo-US relationship.

Coddling Pakistan

Wary of Iran's regional ambitions, fearing a recrudescent Taliban, and concerned about Pakistan's nuclear arsenal, the United States will continue to
see its relationship with Pakistan as important. The manner in which it
handles this relationship will make a vital difference both for the pursuit of
American foreign policy goals and for the stability and prosperity of the region. Recent US involvement in Pakistan, unfortunately, has followed a
rather familiar and desultory course. The United States has not exerted any
great pressure on Musharraf to return his country to democratic rule, to
provide a full accounting of the covert activities of A. Q. Khan, or to end
Pakistan's support for a range of anti-Indian insurgent groups operating
from its soil.

Such reticence may well serve American interests in the immediate
term, as Musharraf provides substantial cooperation in the battle against
Al Qaeda. Over the longer term, however, the policy of coddling an un-
popular military dictator will serve both American and Pakistani interests poorly. It will inevitably generate more anti-Americanism in a wide
swath of Pakistani society. It may promote alliances among disparate
political groups ranging from besieged Pakistani liberals to more conservative religious parties because of their common hostility to Musharraf's
rule. The policy also does nothing to bring about the restoration of Pakistan's denuded political institutions. Uncritical support for the Musharraf regime will enable Pakistan's behemoth military to embed itself more
firmly in Pakistani society at the cost of civil and representative institutions.

Ahmed Rashid, in his 1999 *Current History* essay, "Pakistan's Coup:
Planting the Seeds of Democracy," thoughtfully analyzed the factors that
led to General Musharraf's coup and its domestic and international
ramifications. Sadly, most of Rashid's admonitions to the military to restore the independence of the judiciary, to protect the free press, and to
bolster human rights groups as a prelude to the restoration of democracy

have not been realized. Instead virtually all of the army's actions in these areas have been retrograde. Furthermore, contrary to American expectations, religious parties and their followers have dramatically increased their political clout under Musharraf's rule. These developments will do little to address Pakistan's chronic and debilitating problems of poverty, income and gender inequality, illiteracy, and political instability.

Across the Region

American interests in Bangladesh and Afghanistan, except for the containment of religious extremism, will remain mostly developmental and humanitarian. Craig Baxter's "Bangladesh: Can Democracy Survive?" provides a useful discussion of that country's efforts to sustain democracy. In both countries, state weakness presents a barrier to accomplishing any goals. As Marina Ottaway and Anatol Lieven suggest in their intriguing essay, "Rebuilding Afghanistan," the promotion in Afghanistan of a minimal level of governance and order may be the most compelling task. In the absence of better governance, some dent in pervasive poverty, and provisions for the protection of human rights, it is unclear how the United States can hope to prevent religious extremism from rearing its hydra head again.

No vital American strategic, economic, or diplomatic interests are directly implicated in Nepal or Sri Lanka. The United States should, however, try to prevent state collapse in Nepal and put an end to the sanguinary and fratricidal civil war in Sri Lanka, which has pitted the principal minority community, the Tamils, against the Sinhala majority since the early 1980s. The human costs of the Maoist insurgency in Nepal and the ethnic civil war in Sri Lanka have been immense. In Nepal, since the outbreak of the insurgency in 1996, some 11,000 people have perished. In Sri Lanka, the costs have been even higher: most estimates place the number of dead around 60,000 since the start of the current insurgency in 1983. The death toll continues to mount in both countries.

Current American policy toward the conflicts in these two countries is poorly conceived if the goal is to help ameliorate either situation. As a direct consequence of its preoccupation with the war on terror, the Bush administration is continuing to provide military assistance to the hapless regime of Nepal's King Gyanendra. But this is a deeply flawed position because the monarchy still seeks to curb the insurgency using primarily military instruments. India, the principal regional power, cut off military assistance following the king's dismissal of his hand-picked parliament in March 2005. The United Kingdom, which has long had ties to Nepal owing to its colonial relationship with South Asia, followed suit. Both these states, which have some understanding of Nepal's tortured history, realize that the Maoist insurgency cannot be defeated through military means alone. Accordingly, they have sought to bring pressures on the monarchy to restore some semblance of democracy. The United States would be wise to follow their lead.

Similarly, in Sri Lanka, the United States has mostly contented itself with designating the principal Tamil insurgent organization, the Liberation Tigers of Tamil Eelam (LTTE), as a foreign terrorist organization. This has had some impact on the insurgency, curbing Tiger fundraising activities in North America, but it has not eviscerated the substantial support that the group enjoys among segments of the Tamil diaspora community. As Miriam Young's analysis in her essay, "Making Peace in Sri Lanka," makes clear, even those who oppose and decry the brutal tactics of the LTTE believe that it cannot be excluded from the quest for a genuine and lasting political settlement. Again, US military assistance to the Sri Lankan government, far from ameliorating the situation, has had pernicious effects.

Terms of Engagement

It appears unlikely that the United States will easily disengage from South Asia in the foreseeable future. The terms of engagement, however, remain open to question. The relationship with India, the region's principal state, is multidimensional and growing. As long as the present trends of defense cooperation, trade and investment, and diplomatic contacts continue, the Indo-US relationship can only prosper, occasional hiccups notwithstanding.

American ties to most of the other South Asian states are more tenuous and fraught. The Bush administration, like many of its predecessors, seems almost destined to repeat the same diplomatic blunders over and over again. It appears obsessed with the quest for immediate and short-term gains rather than the pursuit of more sagacious policies that would require some difficult choices and skillful effort. For example, militarily bolstering the flagging regime of King Gyanendra may enable him to fend off the

Maoist rebels for another year or more, but it will not encourage or enable him to undertake the drastic restructuring of the Nepalese polity that is so urgently necessary. Similarly, granting Musharraf virtual carte blanche may serve the immediate purpose of obtaining access to Pakistani military bases and remote regions of that country to hunt down the remnants of Al Qaeda, but it also risks courting the growth of increased anti-Americanism and the further stultification of Pakistan's democratic institutions.

South Asia as a region, principally because of India's rising importance in the global order, cannot be ignored or dealt with in a spasmodic fashion, as was the case during the cold war. The attention it has received from the United States within the past few years has been unprecedented but telling. Perhaps the current engagement with the region will create new constituencies in the United States, both within and outside the government. The growth and development of such constituency interests may finally presage the beginnings of sustained attention to a long-neglected but significant region of the world.

NOTES

1. National Intelligence Council, *Mapping the Global Future* (Pittsburgh: U.S. Government Printing Office, 2004).

2. Strobe Talbott, *Engaging India: Diplomacy, Democracy, and the Bomb* (Washington, DC: The Brookings Institution, 2004).

3. Condoleezza Rice, "A Republican Foreign Policy," *Foreign Affairs*, Jan.–Feb. 2000.

4. Ahmed Rashid, *Taliban: Militant Islam, Oil and Fundamentalism in Central Asia* (New Haven: Yale University Press, 2000).

5. Jo Johnson, "Indians greet US declaration of strategic relationship with cynicism," *Financial Times*, April 5, 2005.

6. Ray Marcelo, "India's rural market becomes a holy grail for mobile phones," *Financial Times*, April 27, 2005.

PART I

Nuclear Weapons and Regional Security

1. India: The Nuclear Politics of Self-Esteem

December 1998

PRATAP BHANU MEHTA

India's decision to conduct five nuclear tests in the deserts of Rajasthan on May 11 and 13, and the resulting pressure on Pakistan to follow suit, have come as a revelation. Although no legal agreements were broken by these tests, and although the precise strength of the devices exploded remains a matter of some dispute, there is a palpable sense that they represent a decisive break with India's past commitments.

For many, the tests represent India's misplaced sense of priorities. Its attempts to secure great power status through military means rather than by attending more assiduously to the economic well-being of its citizens seem misguided. The nuclear tests also appear to represent a decisive break with the best moral intimations bequeathed by Gandhi and Nehru, who for all their failings articulated an idealism that could have been the basis of a more morally exemplary foreign policy. Internationally, India's tests have challenged the privileges of the established nuclear order and seem to have dealt a blow to hard-won successes to combat nuclear weapons proliferation.

It has also been argued that the compulsion behind the testing was primarily driven by domestic concerns. The Bharatiya Janata Party, the major party in the ruling coalition that assumed office in March 1998, had openly declared during the election campaign its intention to make India a nuclear power. Since coming to power, the BJP government had been struggling to find its footing. The BJP's concerted efforts to portray itself as a moderate, centrist party had left it without a clear ideological direction. Yet the political brinkmanship of many of its coalition partners seemed to pull the government in many directions at once. In such circumstances, conducting nuclear tests was a way to shore up the government's credibility and demonstrate its decisiveness.

While it is difficult to determine the government's motives, it would be a grave mistake to view India's nuclear tests simply as a product of short-term expediency. The tests had an almost 80 percent approval rating among the Indian public, and despite some protest by peace activists, enthusiasm for them seems not to have abated significantly. But the BJP has not been the electoral beneficiary of this enthusiasm and is still at the mercy of its allies. To understand their full significance, the tests must be placed in the broader context of recent Indian history.

Goaded by Insecurity

India faces a formidable security environment. To its north lies China, with which it has had a protracted border dispute and by whom it suffered a humiliating defeat in the 1962 Sino-Indian conflict. China's nuclear arsenal also has a commanding presence in the region. Moreover, China is widely believed to have provided substantial nuclear and missile program aid to India's western neighbor, Pakistan, with which India has fought three wars since independence in 1947. Pakistan has long regarded India as a threat, and since its dismemberment in the 1971 war with India (when East Pakistan became Bangladesh), its sense of vulnerability has grown more acute. Given balance of power considerations in South Asia, the surprise is not that there were nuclear tests, but that it took so long for them to occur.

Since independence, India has attempted to develop an autonomous foreign policy. This policy has resisted accepting the international order created in the aftermath of World War II. During the cold war this meant an insistence on nonalignment: a refusal to become permanently attached to any great power, and a desire to establish a regional zone free of great power competition. Indians view the current international order as protecting the prerogatives of the five declared nuclear powers (Russia, the United States, China, Britain, and France), none of which has displayed a credible commitment to disarmament. And this order seems particularly incapable of attending to the security aspirations of emerging powers like India.

Whatever their other differences, successive governments in India have kept the nuclear option open by refusing to sign the nuclear Non-Proliferation Treaty and the Comprehensive Test Ban Treaty. Indeed, India's tests would not have been technically feasible unless previous governments had laid the groundwork. But while it had long ago compromised the idealism of the early days of the nonaligned movement, none of its previous governments had been able to publicly jettison entirely the high moralism bequeathed to India by its first prime minister, Jawaharlal Nehru. The BJP has, in this respect, simply articulated more expressly the desire for a nuclear deterrent that had guided Indian policies all along but had never been quite owned up to.

There ought to be many legitimate misgivings about the fact that this decision was taken by the BJP. For example, there are factions allied with the ruling BJP whose brand of nationalism perilously strains India's minorities. But the overwhelming support for the tests and the long-range policy decisions from which they emerged make them more than an artifact of the BJP's political caprice.

The Nuclear Choice

India's road to nuclear power status began as early as 1948, with the establishment of an Atomic Energy Commission; by 1954 a Department of Atomic Energy was receiving steady funding. The objectives of the program, at least until the 1962 Sino-Indian conflict, were primarily long-term civilian needs.

The 1962 conflict with China, however, convinced many Indians that intimidation by China would always be a prospect. In 1964, the year China became a declared nuclear power, Prime Minister Lal Bahadur Shastri gave the go-ahead for a nuclear program to reduce the time needed to build nuclear weapons to six months.

India's strategic environment after the 1971 war with Pakistan led to renewed urgency on the nuclear matter. Although Pakistan was dismembered and did not pose an immediate security threat, the emerging thaw in Sino-American relations and the perceived United States tilt toward Pakistan only underscored India's sense of insecurity. President Richard Nixon's dispatch of an aircraft carrier task force to the Bay of Bengal during India's war with Pakistan over Bangladesh's independence did nothing to alleviate fears of a United States-China-Pakistan axis. That provided the context for India's first nuclear tests in 1974 under Prime Minister Indira Gandhi. In the early 1990s, Prime Minister Rajiv Gandhi is widely believed to have given India's nuclear program a further impetus.

Thus, although the BJP-led government was the first to openly declare India a nuclear weapons state, India's nuclear option has been kept open throughout the years, in part because of a palpable sense that it alone had to meet its security needs. Although India had close ties with the Soviet Union, these were not enough to overcome its sense of isolation. The end of the cold war, with Russia no longer a dominant power, the Sino-American relationship on a better footing than ever, and well-grounded suspicions of Chinese aid to Pakistan, only increased India's sense of isolation.

In recent years these strategic conundrums have converged with India's psychological anxieties. The last two decades have been trying ones for India. A spate of secessionist movements, a widespread sense of declining importance in world affairs, and a realization that many of its highest hopes remain substantially unredeemed have underscored India's insecurities and vulnerabilities. With two pillars of India's self-image since independence—its state-led mixed economy and its central role in the nonaligned movement—appearing increasingly irrelevant, India has been struggling to redefine itself. Economic reforms carried out in the early 1990s have brought a new vibrancy to certain sectors of the economy, but these have yet to be translated into enduring gains for the entire nation. Although its democracy remains the repository of immense hopes, its institutions often appear overburdened and ineffective in the face of the overwhelming tasks that confront them. The uncertainties of its emerging economic and political landscape and its sense of marginalization have contributed to an evident, if quiet, crisis of confidence.

These anxieties make the politics of the global nuclear regime appear to many Indians to be as much about cultural authority as about strategic interests. The ability of the five nuclear powers to publicly define India's concerns and capacities as they see fit is considered linked to their own technological superiority. The five are also viewed as discriminatory for not allowing India to act on the kind of strategic considerations that they have acted on themselves in continuing to possess nuclear arsenals. But there is also a perception that the furor over India's nuclear capacities rests on unstated cultural assumptions: that the subcontinent is full of unstable people with deep historical resentments, incapable of acting rationally or managing a technologically sophisticated arsenal. Both the stridency of some Western responses, and India's sense of being treated with indifference and contempt, stem from this politics of cultural representation.

India's Nuclear Potential

Type	Number Deployed	Range (km)	Payload (kg)	Country of Origin
Aircraft				
Jaguar	116	2,600	4,750	Great Britain
MiG-27	200	1,100	4,000	Russia
MiG-29	74	1,500	3,000	Russia
Su-30	8+	3,000	8,000	Russia
Mirage 2000	42	1,850	6,300	France
Land-based missiles				
Prithvi-150	Operational	150	1,000	India/USSR
Prithvi-250	Development/Tested	250	500	India/USSR
Prithvi-350	Development	350	500	India/USSR
Agni	Development/Tested	2,000	1,000+	India/US/France
Surya	Development	12,000	n/a	India
Submarine-launched ballistic missiles				
Sagarika	Development	300	500	India/Russia?

Sources: Tracking Nuclear Proliferation (Washington, D.C.: Carnegie Endowment, 1998) and www.ceip.org/programs/npp.

The View from India

Given the character of the Chinese regime and its record on Tibet and on nuclear proliferation, the refrain frequently heard in India during the nuclear tests—Why does the West trust China more than India?—was as much a question about cultural perceptions of the two countries in the West as anything else. The tests were greeted with overwhelming public support in India because they seemed to represent the fact that, despite the fragmentation of its politics, the country was still capable of carrying out a national project of some technological sophistication.

The structure of international power merely reinforces these grievances. India, despite its size and flourishing democracy, is only a marginal player in most international institutions. Indians perceive themselves as part of an international order that confines India to an inferior status. In a paradoxical sense, the failure of the five declared nuclear powers to show any credible commitment to abolishing nuclear weapons contributes to a sense of inferiority by reaffirming that the rules of the international order are applied differently to India.

It has been clear for some time that India considers China a prime source of its strategic worries. But the West has insisted that relations between India and Pakistan are the only significant variables in the strategic scenarios in South Asia. To be sure, there are elements in both India and Pakistan that are obsessed with each other. But from India's standpoint, China's emergence as the second most important power in the world looms large. To India's humiliation in 1962 has been added the perception that an emerging Sino-American relationship would forever marginalize India in Asian and global geopolitics. It is not entirely an accident that India's first nuclear tests in 1974 came after a thaw in Sino-American relations; the recent tests have been conducted against the backdrop of the perception that Washington will do little to stand up to Beijing.

India has kept the nuclear option open because of fears about its own territorial security, its strategic isolation, and its wounded cultural pride. These larger concerns have a disproportionate effect on its relations with Pakistan. The Indian state of Kashmir, for example, has been the object of a protracted dispute since both India and Pakistan became independent and will continue to generate tensions. But there are significant silver linings. India and Pakistan have not gone to war over Kashmir since 1965. Indeed, many observers argue that the existence of deployable nuclear weapons on the subcontinent may have done much to prevent outright war between the two countries since 1971.

What Next?

The transition from what has been described as a state of "existential nuclear deterrence"—wherein each side denied possessing nuclear weapons but was nevertheless cognizant of the other side's capabilities to produce them—to an overt deployment of weapons poses immense challenges.

The government's official line is that India aims to acquire a "credible minimum deterrent." But there is a good deal of uncertainty over whether India is capable of committing the resources that such an endeavor may require. Oddly enough, India's defense expenditures have fallen from an average of 3.6 percent of GDP in the 1970s and 1980s to around 3 percent of GDP in the 1990s.

While there was public support for the tests, support for massive militarization is more tepid and may not extend beyond this government. Shortly after conducting the tests, India undertook a "no first use" pledge, declared its intent to voluntarily abide by the requirements of the Comprehensive Test Ban Treaty, and put stringent controls on transferring technology to other countries.

The years of nuclear ambiguity had the disadvantage of preventing India and Pakistan from developing confidence-building measures that the possession of nuclear arsenals requires. The challenge of articulating and implementing such measures is now heightened by the two countries' ballistic missile capabilities, which will have to be the subject of any confidence-building negotiations.

On the Indian side the domestic pressures impeding such talks are twofold. On the one hand there is great reluctance in India to make Kashmir a central issue in talks between the two countries. This slows down dialogue considerably in other areas as well. And the domestic political pressures that make Kashmir a nonnegotiable issue for India are unlikely to abate soon. On the other hand, India is entering a period of political uncertainty and coalition governments. Each of the important political parties is unsure of its own stance on the nuclear issue. The BJP oscillates between belligerence and restraint; the Congress, the BJP's main rival, has not made its views clear on any of the basic issues involved. The lack of political clarity will hamper the formation of a national consensus on the issue, which may in turn complicate negotiations with other states and international organizations.

But, paradoxical as it may sound, without the nuclear tests, India would have found it politically difficult to reconsider its past opposition to the Comprehensive Test Ban Treaty. It has already signaled some flexibility in this direction. It can now claim that it is entering negotiations after attending to its technological needs, on its own terms. It is not insignificant that India's hawkish scientific establishment, which had all along insisted that India needed to conduct further tests, given the low yield of the first tests conducted in 1974, has conceded (at least in principle) that no further tests are required to retain a credible nuclear deterrent. In this respect India will emulate France and China, both of whom conducted tests just before joining the treaty.

Much will depend on the negotiations between the United States and India. Since the tests, high-level officials from both countries have had three rounds of talks. Few details have been made public, but the fact that the talks are being held is interpreted in India that some progress is occurring in narrowing the differences between the two sides. There is little chance that India will be accorded formal recognition as a nuclear power— since that would be seen as rewarding India—but it may settle for less. Principally, it will look for credible restraints on Chinese proliferation to Pakistan and the lifting of restrictions on India's access to dual-use technologies. If it achieves this much it can present the signing of the Comprehensive Test Ban Treaty as a political victory.

The Beginnings of Hope?

The strategic drama in South Asia is far from over, but both Pakistan and India need to attend to their domestic challenges and to the surer foundation on which power rests: economic well-being. In the short run the cost of economic sanctions has been considerably higher for Pakistan than for India. But if these tests can lay to rest some of the politics of self-esteem that has characterized the subcontinent, they may in the long run enhance the confidence of both countries in their dealings with the rest of the world. The presence of weapons of mass destruction ought not to be a matter of celebration under any circumstances. But somewhere in the space between complacency and alarmism may lie the beginnings of hope.

2. The (Nuclear) Testing of Pakistan

December 1998

SAMINA AHMED

On May 28 and 30, 1998, Pakistan conducted a series of nuclear tests, a tit-for-tat response to those India had carried out on May 11 and 13. The implications of the tests for Pakistan are multifaceted, with international, regional, and domestic security repercussions.

At the international level, Pakistan's decision to follow India and claim the status of a nuclear weapons power has created new challenges for the global nonproliferation regime. And international reaction to these challenges has led to myriad problems for Pakistan, including economic sanctions imposed by the United States.

Regionally, Pakistan's troubled relations with India have been further strained. Nuclear ambiguity has been replaced by overt nuclear weapons policies, which have increased the danger of a nuclear exchange between two hostile adjoining states. At the domestic level, nuclear testing has deepened internal fissures along regional and ethnic lines that will be exacerbated as the international sanctions regime begins to affect Pakistan's fragile economy. Pakistan's Muslim League government thus confronts domestic instability and impending economic collapse at a time when the country's security environment has become more uncertain.

A Nuclear Nadir

Pakistani suspicions of Indian motives are deeply ingrained. The country's humiliating defeat by India in the 1971 war that saw its eastern region reborn as Bangladesh has continued to rankle. It is this history of mutual suspicion and competition that has fueled the conventional and nuclear arms race in South Asia. And it is this legacy of hostility that contributed to the Pakistani decision to test following the Indian nuclear explosions in May.

Pakistani policymakers saw India's abandonment of its long-standing policy of nuclear ambiguity as a challenge that had to be met in kind. Issues of prestige played an important role in determining a response. Announcing the Pakistani nuclear tests, Prime Minister Nawaz Sharif declared, "Today we have settled scores with India. We have paid them back." An enhanced sense of insecurity was an additional motive. In the wake of the Indian tests, Pakistan was warned by India's governing hardline Bharatiya Janata Party (BJP) to abandon its support of Muslim militants in the disputed region of Kashmir or face the consequences in a changed strategic environment. For Pakistan's decision-makers—especially the military—only a demonstration of the country's nuclear weapons capability could offset Indian pressure in view of the disparity in conventional arms.

Since the tests, relations with India have sunk to a new low. Pakistan accuses India of destabilizing South Asia with its aggressive nuclear posture. India, for its part, claims that its decision was directly related to the security threats from and the nuclear collaboration between two neighboring hostile states—Pakistan and China.

The war of words between Pakistan and India further intensified in July and August with clashes between their militaries along the Line of Control dividing Pakistani-controlled from Indian-held Kashmir. Neither country has shown an interest in deescalating tensions. Since the Pakistani test, India's BJP government has reiterated its warning to Pakistan to end its support for Kashmiri dissidents.

International Carrots and Sticks

The fear of a nuclear confrontation between India and Pakistan has lent new urgency to international efforts to persuade both states to end their nuclear arms race. Hoping to nip the nuclear rivalry in the bud, the United States attempted to dissuade Pakistan from testing in the weeks after India's nuclear explosions. High-level United States delegations tried to convince the Sharif government that Pakistan would gain in international prestige if it refrained from testing.

As an incentive for nuclear restraint, the United States offered to repeal the 1985 Pressler amendment, which had led to a ban on United States economic assistance and military sales to Pakistan in 1990 after President George Bush failed to certify to Congress that Pakistan did not possess nuclear weapons. Since the imposition of the ban had adversely affected the conventional capabilities of Pakistan's armed forces, the United States hoped to dissuade the Pakistani military—the dominant domestic actor in the nuclear decision-making apparatus—from supporting a retaliatory Pakistani nuclear test.

With the Pakistani economy in a shambles because of mismanagement by successive governments, economic incentives were also deployed. These reportedly included the resumption of bilateral economic assistance, loans, and grants, as well as United States support for similar assistance from multilateral agencies such as the World Bank, the IMF, and the Asian Development Bank.

The incentives were accompanied by the threat of sanctions. In their discussions with Pakistani authorities, United States officials warned of the dire consequences of nuclear testing. Not only would the Pressler amendment ban stay in place, but under the 1994 Glenn amendment the United States would be forced to end government financing and insurance for investment in Pakistan and would oppose multilateral loans. Japan, Pakistan's major aid donor and one of its main trading partners, also tried to dissuade Pakistan from testing by offering incentives and threatening sanctions. On May 28 Pakistan responded to both countries' entreaties by conducting the first of its nuclear tests.

Predictably, the international community condemned Pakistan for undermining the international nonproliferation regime. Japan was among the first to impose economic sanctions, halting all but humanitarian assistance. Japanese sanctions have had a severe effect on development activities in Pakistan, which are mainly financed by external donors. But it was the United States decision to block preferential loans from international financial institutions such as the World Bank that has had the greatest impact on the Pakistani economy, which is heavily dependent on external credit for foreign debt-servicing and for the import of essential commodities.

Pakistan's Maneuverings

The Sharif government was at first unconcerned about international criticism of its overt nuclear posture and did not appear to fear the potentially adverse impact of United States and Japanese sanctions. Why such complacency? First, in assessing the international reaction to India's nuclear tests, the government had assumed that the Western industrialized countries would remain divided over the issue of sanctions, undermining United States efforts to oppose lending to Pakistan from multilateral agencies. Second, in the perceptions of Pakistani policymakers, economic sanctions would be short-lived because of Pakistan's geopolitical and strategic significance as well as Western fears of resurgent Islamic fundamentalism in an unstable, overpopulated, Muslim-majority state. Third, it was believed that sympathetic Middle Eastern Muslim states such as resource-rich Saudi Arabia would come to Pakistan's rescue, and that allies such as China would help Pakistan overcome its international isolation.

Initially it appeared that Pakistan was correct in predicting that the international community would not uniformly counter the challenges posed by the new South Asian nuclear environment. On June 5, the UN Security Council passed a resolution strongly deploring Pakistan and India's nuclear tests and calling on them to sign the Comprehensive Test Ban Treaty (CTBT) and refrain from deploying nuclear weapons delivery systems. Neither Russia nor China, however, favored a punitive response. Britain and France also refused to impose economic sanctions. Pakistani policymakers were also reassured when China, its close ally and a major source of conventional and nuclear assistance, blamed India for provoking Pakistan's decision to test. China's reaction was understandable since the BJP government had partly justified India's nuclear tests on the grounds of a perceived Chinese nuclear threat.

But Pakistan's hopes that it would retain Chinese support for its nuclear weapons program have been dashed. Since India's and Pakistan's tests, the Chinese have become far more aware of the dangers posed to regional stability by an overt nuclear arms race between two rival states in their immediate neighborhood. Although China has more forthrightly condemned the Indian nuclear tests, it has also called on Pakistan to restrain its nuclear weapons program.

In a surprising degree of confluence on the issue of South Asian nuclearization, China and Russia have jointly rejected Pakistani and Indian claims to nuclear weapons status, calling on their respective South Asian

Pakistan's Nuclear Potential

Type	Number Deployed	Range (km)	Payload (kg)	Country of Origin
Aircraft				
A-5	60	600	1,000	China
Mirage III/5	180	500	3,500	France
F-16	32	850	2,500	United States
Land-based missiles				
M-11	Storage (36+)	280	800	China
Hatf 1	18	80	500	Pakistan/France?
Hatf 1A	n/a	100	500	Pakistan/France?
Hatf 2	Development	280–300	500	Pakistan/China?
Hatf 3	Development?	600	500	Pakistan/China?
Ghauri	Development/Tested	1,500	500–750	Pakistan/North Korea

Sources: Tracking Nuclear Proliferation (Washington, D.C.: Carnegie Endowment, 1998) and www.ceip.org/programs/npp.

allies to unconditionally sign the nuclear Non-Proliferation Treaty (NPT) and the CTBT. The Chinese have also indicated that they are willing to accept United States demands for an end to the transfer of nuclear weapons–related technology and missiles to Pakistan. Should China implement these pledges, technological and financial constraints will severely hinder the expansion of Pakistan's nuclear weapons program.

Under American and Japanese pressure, the Group of Eight has also agreed to defer all but humanitarian loans from international financial institutions to Pakistan and India. The suspension of lending has created the very real threat of a Pakistani default on its external debt; foreign cash reserves are less than $500 million and Pakistan's foreign debt exceeds $38 billion, which is approximately 72 percent of the country's total GDP. According to Commerce Minister Ishaq Dar, economic sanctions will cost Pakistan $4 billion annually: $1.5 billion in concessional loans and aid, and $2.5 billion in foreign investment and remittances. Attempts to acquire bilateral assistance from Middle Eastern allies such as Saudi Arabia and the United Arab Emirates have proved futile, since lending from institutions such as the Islamic Development Bank has been made contingent on IMF approval.

Signs of Movement

The United States has made the resumption of bilateral or multilateral lending contingent on a number of nonproliferation conditions. These include demonstrated Pakistani support for negotiations on a Fissile Material Cutoff Treaty (which would ban the production of highly enriched uranium and plutonium for nuclear weapons) and a commitment to sign the CTBT. The United States has also demanded restraints on the assembly and deployment of nuclear weapons and their delivery systems; the non-transfer of nuclear weapons and missile technology; and a dialogue on normalizing relations with India.

In a recent rethinking of its exclusive focus on sanctions, the United States has considered the use of incentives to halt the South Asian nuclear arms race. In late October, President Clinton signed legislation that allows the president to lift sanctions on Pakistan and India for one year.

This combined approach of sanctions and incentives has begun to pay off. In a major departure from previous policy, Pakistan has indicated that it is willing to unilaterally sign the CTBT in return for the lifting of economic sanctions. The government has also agreed to participate in the negotiations for a Fissile Material Cutoff Treaty and has pledged its willingness to open a dialogue on normalizing relations with India. In return, the United States has announced that it will not block IMF lending to Pakistan.

The resumption of IMF lending will ease the pressure on the Pakistani economy, averting an immediate debt default. However, Pakistani accession to the CTBT will face considerable domestic opposition, especially from Islamist parties. Should the Pakistan government sign the CTBT, it will face an internal backlash at a time when a resurgent opposition is attempting to overthrow Prime Minister Sharif, who has already lost the backing of his allied parties in at least two of Pakistan's four provinces.

Domestic Fallout

The decision to test and the manner in which it was taken have driven a wedge between the governing Muslim League and one of its allies, the Baluchistan National Party (BNP), the ruling party in Baluchistan. The decision to opt for a retaliatory test was made by a policymaking apparatus dominated by Punjabis, Pakistan's ethnolinguistic majority. Punjabis control Pakistan's powerful civil-military bureaucracy. Prime Minister Sharif and his Muslim League are thus seen as the representatives of the Punjab.

The nuclear test site was located in Baluchistan, which forms 44 percent of Pakistan's territory but comprises only 4 percent of its population—a majority Baluch and minority Pakhtoon population. Chief Minister Sardar Mengal, an ally of Sharif, was incensed at the decision to hold the test on Baluchi territory without first telling the provincial leadership. Tensions between the BNP leadership and the central government escalated as the BNP and its student wing, the Baluch Student's Organization, denounced the nuclear tests, pointing out that the Sharif government has ignored Baluchistan's pressing developmental needs. In July, the BNP government was dismissed after it lost a no-confidence vote. According to Chief Minister Mengal, the assembly was manipulated by the central government in response to his government and party's opposition to the nuclear tests.

The testing of Pakistan's nuclear weapons capability has also been opposed by the Awami National Party (ANP), a predominantly Pakhtoon party that has considerable support in the North-West Frontier Province (NWFP). The ANP leadership believes that Pakistan's nuclear policy has promoted tensions between Pakistan and India that have endangered regional security. Also a former ally of the ruling Muslim League, the ANP has only recently parted ways with the central government over perceived incursions on provincial autonomy. Should the ANP succeed in replacing the Muslim League provincial government in the NWFP, the Sharif government will confront yet another ethnoregional challenge to its political authority, including the direction of its nuclear policy.

Ethnic and regional opposition to centralized decision making and control, especially toward the central government's appropriation of the resources of the provinces, is also likely to grow should the international economic sanctions regime remain in force long enough to create serious problems for Pakistan's faltering economy. It is the economic implications of nuclear testing that have the most serious consequences for Pakistan's security and that have received the most attention in the internal debate on Pakistan's nuclear policy.

The United States sanctions imposed after the tests saw the Karachi stock exchange crash; it has lost $5 billion of its value since the May tests and has yet to recover. The value of the rupee continues to fall, adversely affecting industrial productivity. The government's attempts to expand its domestic resource base by measures such as additional direct taxes (including a 10 percent income tax surcharge) and an increase in fuel prices have contributed to inflation and rising social discontent.

Hawks, Doves, and Nuclear Policy

Although influential segments of Pakistani public opinion have internalized official Indocentric justifications for the decision to test, the domestic euphoria that immediately followed the nuclear tests has dissipated. There is growing internal criticism of the government's decision to opt for overt nuclearization. Domestic opposition has been exacerbated by shortsighted government policies, such as the imposition of a state of emergency that included the suspension of fundamental rights at midnight on May 28, the day Pakistan conducted the first of its nuclear tests.

Another divide—that between nuclear hawks and doves—has also widened since the nuclear tests. Among the nuclear hawks, it was the military high command that was responsible for the decision to test and that continues to strongly support the retention and expansion of Pakistan's nuclear weapons capability. Elected governments will find it difficult, if not impossible, to oppose the military's nuclear preferences even if a change in nuclear ambitions is needed to avert an economic breakdown and social unrest. The military is thus unlikely to cede its authority over nuclear policy to civilian politicians, and it will continue to resist foreign restraints on Pakistan's nuclear weapons policy.

Yet Pakistan's decision-makers realize that economic sanctions have increased internal tensions and have created domestic constituencies supportive of tangible steps toward nuclear nonproliferation. This means that the main goal for Pakistan's establishment is to ease and ultimately reverse the economic sanctions regime but not compromise the nuclear weapons program.

Pakistani planners are also aware that Pakistan would be the loser in a no-holds-barred nuclear arms race with India. Should war break out again, asymmetries in conventional and nuclear capability would work to Pakistan's disadvantage. Pakistan's nuclear weapons establishment wants to retain the country's nuclear weapons capability while restraining India's.

To meet these policy objectives, the government has adopted a multipronged strategy. To prove that a nuclear-capable Pakistan is a responsible member of the international community and to meet United States demands for a regional dialogue for peace, Pakistan has reiterated its desire to resolve tensions with India so as to minimize the chances of nuclear conflict. Although there have been meetings between Pakistani and Indian policymakers—including the first and only face-to-face meeting between Prime Minister Sharif and Indian Prime Minister Atal Bihari Vajpayee in July—no progress has been made in reducing these tensions. Pakistan's insistence on a resolution of the Kashmir dispute as an essential precondition for normalized relations with India effectively retards progress toward that goal.

Pakistan uses the state of heightened tensions with India to justify its need for a countervailing nuclear capability. The government has continued to appeal to the international community, especially the United States, to intercede before the Kashmir dispute leads to an outbreak of conventional conflict that, Pakistan claims, could acquire a nuclear dimension. Although the United States and other foreign actors have not shown any interest in playing a mediatory role, they are more favorably inclined toward Pakistani calls for nuclear restraint between the two South Asian rivals.

Pakistan's support for the "stabilization" of the nuclear arms race in South Asia is clearly a bid to acquire de facto recognition of its nuclear weapons capability as well as international acceptance of an unverifiable freeze. At the same time, Pakistani proposals for other steps toward nuclear restraint, such as nonweaponization and nondeployment of Indian and Pakistani nuclear weapons and missile systems, would also work to Pakistan's advantage in view of India's more developed nuclear infrastructure.

This is the strategy that Pakistan is pursuing in its negotiations with the United States on the nuclear issue, which includes the Pakistani decision to sign the CTBT while rejecting the NPT. According to Pakistani officials, the quid pro quo for these concessions should include the removal of economic sanctions, including an easing of United States restrictions on multilateral lending to Pakistan (which, at present, still cover all multilateral agencies except the IMF). In Pakistani perceptions, the advantages of signing the CTBT far outweigh the domestic costs. Signing the treaty would divert international attention from Pakistan to India; economic sanctions would be eased; Pakistan's nuclear weapons status would not be threatened; and the treaty's entry into force is uncertain.

Pakistan's success in obtaining international acceptance of its nuclear weapons status is largely dependent on the United States. Should the United States decide that Pakistani accession to the CTBT is sufficient reason to remove sanctions on all multilateral lending, then Pakistan's nuclear weapons program will continue to progress beyond its present non-weaponized status. However, should the United States insist on further progress toward nonproliferation before relaxing or removing bilateral and multilateral sanctions, then continued pressure on Pakistan's economy might force its policymakers to reconsider their nuclear ambitions.

Until economic sanctions are eased, Pakistan will remain on the edge of financial bankruptcy. If bilateral and multilateral sanctions are left in place, funding in the pipeline from sources such as the World Bank will end by 1999. Even if Pakistan avoids default by acquiring an adequate stopgap package from the multilateral agencies such as the IMF and the Islamic Development Bank, its present foreign exchange reserves are already insufficient even to purchase commodities such as fuel that are essential to keep its domestic economy afloat.

Appeals to national unity by invoking the Indian threat are unlikely to divert domestic attention from the harsh economic climate as well as the crisis of governance within. Facing a rejuvenated opposition and accused of failing to protect the country's internal and foreign interests, the Sharif government might just find itself a victim of the problems that have emerged because of its decision to test Pakistan's nuclear capability.

3. Toward Nuclear Rollback in South Asia

December 1998

TOBY F. DALTON

India's and Pakistan's nuclear tests in May 1998 shocked the world and forced international policymakers to reassess the viability of their efforts to constrain these two bitter neighbors. In the wake of these provocative tests and amid the frequent battles over the contested territory of Kashmir, could the international community convince India and Pakistan not to deploy nuclear weapons and end their dangerous confrontation?

The international community was unable to forge a coordinated response. Although the United States immediately imposed comprehensive economic sanctions on India and Pakistan, many American allies merely condemned the actions. Most nonproliferation analysts viewed the nuclear tests and the lack of a cohesive Western response as a failure by the United States to keep the conflict between India and Pakistan at a manageable level and their respective nuclear weapons programs "in the basement." The meager success of United States policy since the May tests, however, indicates a larger problem. Sanctions have not forced India and Pakistan to join the nonproliferation regime, and United States–led negotiations toward this end, which began immediately after the tests, have achieved little.

A new agenda is required to stabilize the situation in the short term and increase bilateral cooperation in the long term. This agenda should include measures adapted from lessons already learned in the past two decades from successful nonproliferation efforts, including the bilateral process that led Argentina and Brazil to end their military nuclear programs and South Africa's unilateral decision to destroy its arsenal of nuclear weapons. A policy of bilateral confidence building through dialogue and cooperation based on these lessons could ameliorate, if not end, the nuclear weapon scourge in South Asia.

Building the Bomb

The conflict between India and Pakistan did not escalate into the realm of nuclear weapons overnight. Since their independence in 1947, India and Pakistan have fought three wars: two, in 1947 and 1965, over the contested territory of Jammu and Kashmir, and the third, in 1971, over the territory that is now the nation of Bangladesh (formerly East Pakistan). India began to consider the nuclear option in the mid-1950s. It received its first nuclear assistance (a Canadian-supplied Cirus research reactor and fuel) under the Eisenhower-era program to disseminate nuclear technology for "peaceful" uses that was dubbed "Atoms for Peace." By 1964, just before China's first nuclear test explosion, India had the necessary ingredients for an atomic bomb: nuclear fuel from Cirus and a facility to reprocess this fuel into weapons-grade plutonium.

India acquired several nuclear power and research reactors through the Atoms for Peace program without arousing suspicion that it had anything more than civilian intentions. In May 1974, however, India destroyed the spirit of peaceful cooperation when it conducted what it called a "peaceful nuclear explosion." This test (former Indian nuclear weapons scientist Raja Ramanna admitted in October 1997 that it was indeed a weapons test) was India's first knock on the door of the elite nuclear weapons club. The nuclear Non-Proliferation Treaty (NPT) recognized only the United States, Russia, the United Kingdom, France, and China as nuclear weapons states when it was concluded in 1970. Both India and Pakistan have refused to sign the treaty because they perceive it as unfairly limiting their ability to protect their national interests; India, especially, has long argued that the treaty is founded on a double standard that allows the nuclear powers to remain nuclear while prohibiting other nations from developing nuclear weapons.

Shortly after its defeat in the 1971 war with India, Pakistan began work on a nuclear weapons program of its own. India's 1974 test gave added impetus to this program and in 1975 Pakistan assigned Dr. Abdul Qadeer Khan, a German-trained uranium specialist, to build a facility to produce highly enriched uranium. By 1986 Pakistan had produced enough weapons-grade uranium for an atomic bomb, and had tested the nonnuclear components of a bomb design it purportedly received from China in the early 1980s. By 1995 United States intelligence officials estimated that Pakistan had enough material for about 10 weapons.

On May 11, 1998, India tested several nuclear explosive devices at its test site in Pokaran; two days later it conducted additional tests. (Most Western analysts doubt India's claim that it exploded a total of five devices; the exact number is unknown.) Pakistan, which thus far had not openly tested its nuclear capability, followed suit, carrying out several tests of its own (it claims a total of six) on May 28 and 30. Both nations have now declared themselves "nuclear weapon powers." Conservative estimates suggest that India has enough plutonium to construct 75 weapons, while Pakistan likely has enough highly enriched uranium for 25 weapons.

Western officials do not believe that either nation has actively deployed nuclear weapons, but both have acquired several means of delivery. India possesses two missile systems capable of delivering nuclear weapons: the Prithvi, with a range of 150 to 250 kilometers, and the Agni, with a range of 1,500 to 2,000 kilometers, giving it the capability to hit any target in Pakistan. It also has several nuclear-capable fighter aircraft, including the French Mirage 2000 and Soviet-era MiG-27 and MiG-29. Pakistan also has both missile and aircraft delivery options: the Chinese M-11 missile, with a range of nearly 300 kilometers; the 600-kilometer Hatf-III missile; the recently tested Ghauri missile, with a range of about 1,500 kilometers (which could hit Mumbai and possibly Calcutta); and French Mirage and United States F-16 fighter aircraft.

Outside the Regime

The nuclear tests this May were undoubtedly a significant challenge to the viability of the interlocking network of treaties, agreements, and forums that make up the international nuclear nonproliferation regime. India and Pakistan are not members of this regime, having decided that forswearing nuclear weapons is not in their national security interests. International nonproliferation experts worried that these tests might encourage other potential proliferants to break out of the regime, creating a chain of proliferation that could flow into the Middle East. Some even said that Pakistan might decide to share its so-called Islamic Bomb with other Muslim nuclear weapon aspirants, including Iran.

Nevertheless, all indications suggest that the nonproliferation regime, although weakened, remains an effective barrier. Even the newest element of the regime—the global norm against nuclear explosive tests established by the 1996 Comprehensive Test Ban Treaty (CTBT)—appears to have survived the South Asia crisis. Indeed, the NPT itself gained some strength when Brazil, one of the last holdouts, acceded to the treaty in September 1998.

The greater consequence of the Indian and Pakistani nuclear tests is the increased chance that what has been a protracted conventional conflict now may become nuclear. This has been a concern since at least 1993, when United States Director of Central Intelligence James Woolsey noted in Senate testimony that "the arms race between India and Pakistan poses perhaps the most probable prospect for future use of weapons of mass destruction, including nuclear weapons."

"A nuclear exchange on the subcontinent would be devastating," Woolsey continued. Dense population centers exist close to the border on both sides. Should a nuclear exchange take place, Islamabad, with about 4 million residents, and New Delhi, with approximately 9 million, would surely be targeted.

To reduce the chances of a nuclear exchange between India and Pakistan and to try to bring them into the nonproliferation regime, the United States has encouraged India and Pakistan to sign the CTBT and contribute to negotiations for a Fissile Material Cutoff Treaty (FMCT), which would ban the production of bomb-grade material. United States Deputy Secretary of State Strobe Talbott has pushed this agenda in several rounds of official talks with Jaswant Singh, a defense adviser to Indian Prime Minister Atal Bihari Vajpayee, and with various Pakistani officials close to Prime Minister Nawaz Sharif.

Most of the United States effort has centered on the CTBT, and it appears to be slowly paying off. In a September 23 address to the United Nations General Assembly, Prime Minister Sharif said that Pakistan is willing to sign the CTBT within the next year, but only if India also signs and if all current sanctions on Pakistan are lifted. India has made similar gestures, including a pledge not to test in the foreseeable future. Defense adviser Singh suggested in the September–October 1998 issue of *Foreign Affairs* that "since India already subscribes to the substance of the test ban treaty, all that remains is its actual signature." And Prime Minister Vajpayee told the UN on September 24 that India is engaged in talks on signing the CTBT that he expects to conclude successfully by September 1999. He noted a day earlier, en route to the UN, however, that "there are questions that are unresolved."

India's and Pakistan's hesitancy to sign the CTBT indicates an underlying resistance to joining any element of the nonproliferation regime. This resistance dates to the NPT negotiations in the late 1960s, and is based in large part on perceived security needs: neither country believes that it can accept formal treaty limitations on its ability to construct nuclear weapons for self-defense. But part of this resistance also stems from domestic politics: it would be difficult for any government in either nation to sell its constituents on joining the nonproliferation regime after having criticized it for 30 years as legitimizing "nuclear apartheid." India in particular believes that joining the regime would hinder its progress toward great power status and permanent membership on the UN Security Council. In light of this resistance, a new agenda focused on improving bilateral nuclear relations between India and Pakistan may enjoy greater chances for success.

Lessons on Nonproliferation

India and Pakistan present a unique challenge to international security thinkers: at no time in history have two nuclear adversaries shared a common border, let alone fought periodic battles. With the potential for conflict so high, the international community should engage India and Pakistan on new initiatives based on lessons drawn from two nonproliferation success stories over the past two decades. The first was the decision by Argentina and Brazil to shelve plans for nuclear weapons programs, and the second South Africa's decision to destroy its arsenal of six nuclear weapons. All three nations are now contributing members of the nonproliferation regime, yet only 15 years ago all stood in defiance of the regime and harbored clandestine nuclear programs.

The story of Argentina's and Brazil's denuclearization more nearly resembles the situation in South Asia. A border dispute and low-level nuclear rivalry had troubled their relations for a number of years. The two countries began their nuclear programs in the 1950s, with a focus on acquiring civilian nuclear power capabilities; the nuclear rivalry emerged immediately as each nation sought greater capabilities than the other. Significantly, both refused to join the Treaty of Tlatelolco (which established a nuclear-weapon-free zone in Latin America in 1968) and the NPT, and objected to International Atomic Energy Agency (IAEA) inspections of their nuclear facilities. In the 1970s, the Argentine and Brazilian militaries began to explore the option of a nuclear weapons capability, and built facilities to manufacture the necessary fissile material; Brazil even excavated a shaft that could have been used for an underground nuclear explosive test.

In a significant turnaround, Argentina and Brazil resolved their territorial dispute in 1979, and in the early 1980s, with the return to civilian rule, both countries began to abandon their military nuclear programs. In November 1985 a process of confidence building began with the formation of a Joint Committee on Nuclear Policy to discuss nuclear issues at the foreign minister level. The process continued with reciprocal head-of-state visits to former secret nuclear facilities, scientific exchanges, and constant discussion in the Joint Committee. These confidence-building measures produced an agreement in 1990 on a Common Nuclear Policy, and in 1991 the Brazilian-Argentine Agency for Accounting and Control of Nuclear Materials was formed to conduct joint inspections of nuclear facilities. The successful completion of this nuclear rapprochement cleared the path for Argentina and Brazil to join the NPT in 1995 and 1998, respectively.

South Africa, like Argentina and Brazil, is also a proliferation success story, but for a singularly different reason: South Africa actually destroyed an existing nuclear weapons stockpile. In the late 1970s, South Africa had decided to construct a deterrent force of six nuclear weapons because of its international isolation (due to its apartheid policies) and fear of Soviet expansion into southern Africa (50,000 Soviet-allied Cuban troops had been introduced into neighboring Angola beginning in 1975). The cessation of the cold war in 1989 resolved South Africa's external security fears, and the scrapping of its apartheid policies ended its international isolation, giving President F. W. de Klerk reason to question the utility of its nuclear deterrent and ultimately to decree the destruction of its nuclear weapons. South Africa joined the NPT in 1991, and was a strong participant in the 1995 NPT review conference that resulted in indefinite extension of the treaty.

A New Agenda for South Asia

While pushing for participation in the CTBT and negotiations on FMCT, the international community also needs to encourage a parallel agenda devoted to strengthening India and Pakistan's bilateral relationship and based on measures common to the Latin American and African successes. Carrying out these measures will fall primarily on India and Pakistan, but the international community needs to strongly support the measures politically

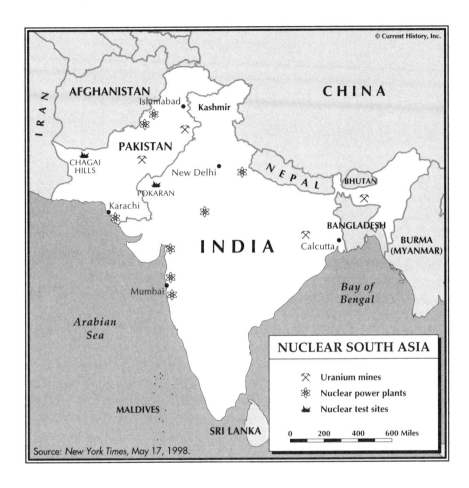

© Current History, Inc.

AFGHANISTAN

Islamabad   Kashmir

CHINA

IRAN

PAKISTAN

CHAGAI
HILLS

New Delhi

NEPAL

BHUTAN

POKARAN

Karachi

INDIA   Calcutta

BANGLADESH

BURMA
(MYANMAR)

Mumbai

Arabian
Sea

Bay of
Bengal

NUCLEAR SOUTH ASIA

⚒ Uranium mines
❀ Nuclear power plants
👑 Nuclear test sites

MALDIVES

SRI LANKA   0   200   400   600 Miles

Source: *New York Times*, May 17, 1998.

and financially to garner sincere participation from both nations. This new agenda consists of six elements.

1. Facilitate Technical Cooperation

Technical cooperation catalyzed political cooperation between Argentina and Brazil. This cooperation began as scientific exchanges between civilian nuclear facilities, joint work on the nuclear fuel cycle, and research projects on nuclear safety and safeguards technologies. This civilian cooperation eventually led to cooperation at facilities that worked on secret military projects. As John Redick, an expert on the nuclear programs in Argentina and Brazil, points out, technical cooperation and good relations between scientists and officials became the foundation for the Brazilian-Argentine Agency for Accounting and Control of Nuclear Materials.

Similar exchanges could take place between India and Pakistan, beginning with visits to civilian nuclear reactors that are already subject to IAEA inspections. In time, this cooperation could expand to other areas, including research reactors and uranium enrichment and plutonium reprocessing sites. A political dialogue could develop through exchanges between officials of India's Department of Atomic Energy and Atomic Energy Commission and Pakistan's Atomic Energy Commission. Reciprocal high-level visits at military nuclear facilities, like those that eventually took place at secret facilities in Argentina and Brazil, would also build further trust.

2. Create a Joint Committee on Nuclear Policy

Argentina and Brazil formed a committee to discuss general nuclear issues and nuclear policy. This committee included members from the nuclear scientific community, atomic energy agencies, and ministries of energy and foreign affairs. The key to the success of this committee was, surprisingly, its lack of a clear aim. It discussed any and all nuclear issues without the burden of a set agenda. While the committee did ultimately assist in the establishment of a bilateral inspections regime, it arrived at this decision independent of its original mission.

India and Pakistan should establish a similar joint committee. This committee would be responsible for running the program of technical cooperation described earlier. In addition, it could serve as a forum for discussion of nuclear policy, civilian nuclear energy issues such as waste, and other areas in which cooperation could benefit both nations. In time it could work to develop an inspection regime similar to the Brazilian-Argentine Agency for Accounting and Control of Nuclear Materials. Issues such as Kashmir should not, however, politicize this committee.

3. Debunk Nuclear Theology

Pronuclear statements by leaders in Argentina, Brazil, and (in the form of hints and ambiguous threats) South Africa increased public support for the idea of acquiring nuclear weapons. Politicians in India and Pakistan undertook a similar effort before the May tests. Many of their statements invoked a feeling of victimization by the declared nuclear weapons powers, especially in India. Changing this public opinion will be crucial to rollback efforts. Politicians and intellectuals must begin to address popular fears and misconceptions, and encourage newspaper editors to reinforce an antinuclear message. To some degree this process has already begun in both India and Pakistan. According to Dr. W. P. S. Sidhu, an Indian security expert, public opinion polls in both countries show that support for nuclear weapons fell from about 97 percent immediately after the tests to about 65 percent in early October. While this decrease is significant, it shows that a concerted effort is still needed to sway the majority.

4. Create International Incentives

Although Argentina and Brazil arrived at their decision to denuclearize on a bilateral basis and South Africa did so unilaterally, positive incentives from the international community influenced their choices. South Africa hoped to end the ban on nuclear assistance and regain its seat at the IAEA, and Argentina and Brazil wanted to increase trade in high-tech goods. Western nations should offer similar incentives to India and Pakistan, including advanced nuclear assistance in exchange for IAEA safeguards. The United States could relax the current sanctions regime once India and Pakistan make sufficient progress toward this goal. Other positive incentives could include high-tech assistance in the growing computer and electronics fields in both countries (including joint ventures that would retain intellectual capital), cooperation on improving agricultural output, or combating the "Year 2000" computer problem.

5. Resolve National Security Issues

The resolution of national security threats is critical to nuclear rollback. Argentina and Brazil signed a 1979 treaty to manage their energy and water disputes in the Rio de la Plata region, and South Africa destroyed its nuclear weapons once the Soviet threat had disappeared. For India and Pakistan, resolving the Kashmir dispute is the key to improving their bilateral relationship on all issues. It is unlikely that international intervention will result in a short-term solution to the Kashmir problem, but the international community and the UN in particular should seek a long-term solution by first proposing that both sides draw down their military forces near the border under the guidance of the UN Military Observers Group in India and Pakistan (UNMOGIP).

Since 1949 UNMOGIP observers have patrolled the border and reported infractions. Currently 43 observers are deployed in Kashmir, and their mandate could be expanded, with Indian and Pakistani cooperation, to include establishing weapon and troop limitation zones, similar to the Conventional Forces in Europe treaty, which places verifiable limits on troops and armaments in strategic regions. India and Pakistan could explore further confidence-building measures in this context, including military observer exchanges, use of existing hot lines, and prenotification of military exercises. Further meetings between Prime Ministers Sharif and Vajpayee, as well as the resumption of high-level dialogue on Kashmir, are critical to this effort. (Indian Foreign Secretary Krishnan Raghunath and Pakistani Foreign Secretary Shamshad Ahmed held preliminary discussions on Kashmir and the nuclear issue in Islamabad from October 16 to 18, 1998; they are to meet again in February 1999.) India and Pakistan could also expand existing bilateral treaties to cover additional Kashmir-related issues. For example, the 1985 no-attack agreement—in which each country pledged not to attack the other's nuclear infrastructure, and to exchange lists of nuclear facilities—could incorporate a new agreement to place military observers at key military bases in the region.

For India, resolving national security concerns with China, as South Africa did with its neighbors, will also be critical to any decision to roll back its nuclear program. Although India and China have not fought since a 1962 border conflict, Indian Defense Minister George Fernandes proclaimed on May 3, 1998, that China is India's "potential threat number one." Until India no longer feels threatened by China's nuclear weapons, it is unlikely to willingly give up its nuclear capability. Improvement of relations between India and China could proceed within the framework of existing border treaties. Further talks between the two countries on, for example, military cutbacks near the border and nonsupply of nuclear technology to third countries (especially preventing further Chinese aid to Pakistan) would help to address bilateral security concerns.

6. Prevent Deployment of Nuclear Weapons

The deployment of nuclear weapons would destabilize the situation in South Asia to the point that a nuclear exchange might be unavoidable. If one nation were to discover that the other had covertly deployed weapons near its border, it would be forced to deploy its own weapons, and the tit-for-tat pattern established with the May nuclear tests could result in full deployment—and possibly even a preemptive strike by one side. Deployment on ballistic missiles would allow one country to launch a quick attack against the other with very little warning. Flight times, should these missiles be deployed close to the border, would be less than 20 minutes, meaning the target of any attack would have little time to decide on a response.

The lack of trust on both sides makes preventing the deployment of nuclear weapons a difficult objective. India and Pakistan could, however, amend their 1985 no-attack treaty to include nondeployment provisions. Verification of nondeployment is challenging but not impossible, and the international community could provide satellite surveillance and independent observers, perhaps under the auspices of UNMOGIP, to monitor key air and military bases where missiles or nuclear-armed aircraft might be deployed.

Back from the Brink?

It will take time for the initiatives that have been proposed to take root. Argentina and Brazil took 10 years to progress from minimum cooperation to a multilateral inspection regime, and India and Pakistan will almost certainly take even longer. For this agenda to succeed, the major powers—the United States, Russia, Japan, and the European Union—must provide encouragement and incentives for India and Pakistan. China must play an especially active role given its proximity to both nations, history of conflict with India, and controversial nuclear cooperation with Pakistan.

It is equally important that this process of bilateral cooperation have general aims rather than an explicit goal or predetermined outcome. In Argentina and Brazil, a technical cooperation arrangement turned into an inspection regime with the assistance of the IAEA. Changes in South Africa's leadership concurrent with the end of the cold war led to its decision to review the utility of nuclear weapons and conclude that these weapons hindered economic and political progress—and did little to bolster national security.

If India and Pakistan pursue better relations based on this agenda, they may eventually form their own bilateral inspection regime similar to the Brazilian-Argentine Agency for Accounting and Control of Nuclear Materials. More favorable outcomes are also possible—the lessons of Argentina,

Brazil, and South Africa demonstrate that nuclear rollback is achievable. If this dialogue is successful, and the Kashmir dispute can be resolved, India and Pakistan could, in the long term, end their nuclear rivalry entirely by destroying their nuclear weapon stockpiles, weapons-grade plutonium and uranium, and bomb production facilities, in a transparent process open to international verification. Then, India and Pakistan may decide to finally join the nonproliferation regime as non-nuclear-weapon states.

PART II

Ethnic Conflict and Violence

4. Afghanistan's Civil War

January 1995

GILLES DORRONSORO

After Soviet troops were withdrawn from Afghanistan in February 1989, the mujahideen (Islamic guerrillas), who had waged a nearly decade-long war of liberation, turned their guns on the Soviet-installed regime of President Najibullah. But it was not until the fall of the communists in Moscow in August 1991 and the end of Soviet aid that they were able to deal a decisive blow to the regime in Kabul. The combined forces of mujahideen Commander Ahmad Shah Massoud and Abdul Rashid Doestam, an Uzbek militia leader who had defected from Najibullah's camp, took the capital in April 1992.

Fighting immediately began among the victorious parties in a country that had been at war since 1979. This new war's frequently shifting alliances give the impression of irrationality and chaos, but everything that has happened since 1992 has been the result of a rigorous political logic. The Afghan civil war is not "primitive" or "tribal," but strongly political. Ethnic identification and tensions play a part, but the country's warring parties invoke and feed these to mobilize supporters.

The interim government under President Burhanuddin Rabbani, sworn in 1992, has been under attack in Kabul by the government's erstwhile partners: the forces of Prime Minister Gulbuddin Hekmatyar since 1992 and, since January 1994, by General Doestam. The challenge facing the numerous groups involved in the conflict is the establishment of a new political balance and the development of a workable political system in Afghanistan. The many battles waged around the capital are explained by the parties' need to control the symbolic and actual heart of this process.

Four Parties for a Strong New State

Well aware of its strong position in the country, Massoud's Jamiat-i-Islami (Islamic Society) is willing to become the backbone of a new governing coalition. The principal group in the north, it also boasts strong support in the west and the south in Kandahar province. It has a presence in or dominates Kabul, Herat, the provincial capital Kandahar, and most of the other leading cities except Jalalabad, near the Pakistani border, and Mazar-i-Sharif.

The Jamiat-i-Islami is an Islamic party composed mainly of Sunni Muslim Tajiks (the second-largest ethnic group in the country), and besides Massoud numbers among its members President Rabbani and mujahideen commander Ismael Kahn. Its leadership favors the rapid construction of a centralized state. Either to forward their ideological project or out of simple administrative necessity, party leaders have begun fostering embryonic regional states in Herat and in the zone controlled by Massoud in the northeast.

The Hezb-i-Islami (Islamic Party), led by Prime Minister Hekmatyar, is a Sunni group with a radical vision of an Islamic state. Its recruits come from the intelligentsia, and are mainly Pashtun, the largest and most influential ethnic group in the country. When the other parties were putting the struggle against the Soviets first, the Hezb-i-Islami chose to focus instead on eliminating its rivals, thus poisoning relations with most of them. Furthermore, the group hoped to take control of Kabul by itself and impose its idea of an Islamic state.

Hezb-i-Islami's hand has weakened considerably over the past two years. It has been driven from positions it held in the west and north, thus paying for its war strategy and its opposition to the Jamiat-i-Islami. Today its forces have regrouped to the south of Kabul and on the road leading to Jalalabad (and to Pakistan). Finally, for a party whose cadres are mainly urban, the Hezb-i-Islami has suffered a significant defeat: it does not control one important city.

The Harkat-i-Inqilab-i-Islami (Islamic Revolutionary Movement) is also mainly made up of Pashtuns. Its leadership is controlled by the Sunni *ulema,* or religious scholars. Mohammad Nabi, Harkat leader, wants to build a state based on sharia (Islamic law); he openly opposes talk of self-determination among Afghanistan's ethnic and religious minorities.

The last of the parties supporting a strong new state, the Ettehad (Alliance), led by Abdul Rasul Sayaf, is generously financed by the conservative Wahhabite networks in Saudi Arabia. Pashtuns west of Kabul and in Kunduz province in the northeast supply the bulk of recruits for this fundamentalist group. Wahhabite support obligates the Ettehad to oppose the Shia (and therefore, indirectly, Shiite Iran) and to impose an Islamic regime that is outwardly conservative on morals. Anti-Shiite feeling in Afghanistan has long been expressed and reinforced by racist behavior toward the Hazara ethnic group, a Shiite people who have traditionally opposed the Pashtun. And a conservative morality is natural to the social base of the party, clerical as well as Pashtun. Ettehad has been behind symbolic measures such as the withdrawal of female television show hosts.

Three Parties against a Strong State

Much of the tension that has arisen since the fall of Najibullah arises from the refusal of two parties, the Hezb-i-Wahdat and the Jumbesh, to accept a stabilized political situation. For their different reasons, both groups fear the creation of a strong centralized state.

The Hezb-i-Wahdat (Unity Movement) is essentially a regrouping of the Shiite Hazara, an ethnic group originally from central Afghanistan that has traditionally been despised, especially by Pashtuns. The movement espouses an ideology based on the beliefs of Iran's Ayatollah Ruhollah Khomeini. From the beginning of the conflict in Afghanistan, the Hazara have been, in practice, autonomous from the state and the Sunni parties.

The Hezb views a rebuilt centralized state, which would surely fall into the hands of the Sunnis, as a threat to Hazara independence. Furthermore, no other party is currently willing to recognize cultural or judicial autonomy for the Hazara minority. So the Hezb-i-Wahdat feels blocked. It hesitates between involvement in government in exchange for certain guarantees (a federal system, for example) and going into opposition to prevent the formation of a state in order to maintain its own independence.

Rashid Doestam's Jumbesh (Front) was formed in 1922 by former communist cadres and militiamen from the north. The group controls large stretches of northern Afghanistan and employs a "Turkish" (Uzbek and Turkmen) nationalist rhetoric, although its supporters also include a sizable number of ethnic Tajiks. Because its members fought the mujahideen almost until the end, as well as because of its former secularism, the

Jumbesh is not recognized as legitimate by the groups that resisted the Soviet invasion. In the long run it cannot hope to remain a political force in a pacified Afghanistan.

With no possibility of playing a part in peaceful politics, the Jumbesh's only chance for survival lies in divisions between the mujahideen. It plays on these to weaken the strongest party at any given moment and so prevent the formation of a dominant coalition.

Maulvi Yunis Khalis, a former theology teacher, founded the relatively small but well-armed Hezb-i-Islami of Yunis Khalis, a breakaway faction of Gulbuddin Hekmatyar's Hezb-i-Islami. The majority of the group's militants are Pashtuns from eastern Afghanistan, which is, in the absence of a strong central government, currently undergoing a "retribalization" (also taking place in other Pashtun areas, but on a lesser scale). With the fragmentation of tribes in the region, a multitude of political affinities based on clan ties have developed. Strictly political factors such as party membership and ideology have lost importance; the conflicts arising in these zones are thus seldom dependent on the situation in the country as a whole. The political authorities in these regions—the tribal leaders—have no great desire to influence the future of the state, preferring instead to stay at a distance to preserve their tribal autonomy, which has historically been threatened by a central government.

Because of its lack of cohesion, Khalis's Hezb-i-Islami does not have a strong national strategy. Its absence from the battlefields of Kabul is in this sense systematic. The group's most important commanders act independently, following regional interests. The group seems satisfied controlling its region, counting on the tribal system to protect the eastern Pashtuns from a centralized state.

The Transforming Alliances

There are presently two alliances in Afghanistan: one centered around the Jamiat-i-Islami, supporting Rabbani as president of the republic, and the other around Hekmatyar's Hezb-i-Islami, which regroups the enemies of the government. Two oppositions structure the political maneuvering between the two groups: first, the impossibility of Hezb-i-Islami and the Jamiat-i-Islami ever forming a real alliance, which has been demonstrated by their continued clashes since the end of the 1970s; and second, the antagonism between the Hezb-i-Wahdat and the Ettehad, rooted in ethno-religious differences (Shia-Hazara against Sunni-Pashtun). Over the past two years the Jamiat-i-Islami, which controls most of Kabul, has tried to create a coalition capable of restoring the state, while the Hezb-i-Islami directs its rockets against its foe, determined to wreck any attempt at political stabilization.

The alliances went through several transformations before arriving at this point. Najibullah's ouster in 1992 apparently marked a shift toward an ethnic logic. At first, what was effectively a coalition of Jumbesh, Jamiat-i-Islami (chiefly speaking, Commander Massoud), and Hezb-i-Wahdat shared power in the capital. All three wanted to swiftly accept a UN plan for a peaceful transition of power and finish with Hekmatyar, who threatened to take the city. To Massoud, control of Kabul meant the possibility of placing the Jamiat-i-Islami at the heart of any future settlement. Najibullah's ouster permitted Doestam to take control in the northern provinces and enter the new political game while attempting to make people forget Jumbesh's past. The Hezb-i-Wahdat seized the opportunity to build up support in Kabul, where there is an important Hazara community. The Hezb-i-Wahdat's military presence in Kabul, Hazaras hope, would allow them to influence the country's future.

In fact, the Hezb-i-Wahdat and the Jumbesh believed that Massoud would become a convert to "ethnic realism" and restrain his influence in Afghanistan's northeastern quarter, which would legitimate the division of the country on a politico-ethnic basis. However, the Jamiat-i-Islami viewed its alliance with the other two parties as a tactic to gain control of the capital and oust the Hezb-i-Islami; it never renounced its goal of a united Islamic state. Thus a new, anti-Pashtun coalition based on ethnic solidarity burst onto the scene, causing another dramatic shift in alliances.

The second phase began in fall 1992, when Massoud launched an operation to disarm the Hezb-i-Wahdat in Kabul. The pretext was that the Hezb had engaged in organized extortion from the non-Hazara population; in reality, Massoud wanted to break with the Hazara party because the alliance with it had prevented the Jamiat-i-Islami from including Pashtun parties in the government coalition. The disarmament effort was not a military success, but with the Hezb-i-Wahdat out of the coalition the Harkat-i-Inqilab-i-Islami took the step of becoming a member of the interim government. The Ettehad followed suit, abandoning its alliance with the Hezb-i-Islami.

The third, most recent phase started when the Jumbesh rallied the opposition against the government last January, some months after adopting a neutral stance in the clashes between the Hezb-i-Islami and the Jamiat-i-Islami around Kabul. The Jumbesh's decision to oppose the government was probably forced by the Hezb-i-Wahdat's rapprochement with the Jamiat-i-Islami in fall 1993. It seemed plausible that Hezb-i-Islami forces around Kabul might at last be marginalized, which would remove any justification for the Jumbesh's presence in the capital. The Jumbesh feared that the Jamiat-i-Islami's dominance, combined with stabilization of the political situation, would quickly marginalize it. Finally, in September, the Hezb-i-Wahdat abandoned its neutrality and joined the groups opposing the government coalition.

The War's Regionalization

After the Soviet Union withdrew, the Afghan crisis essentially became regional, making the policies of the neighboring powers—Iran, Pakistan, and Uzbekistan—especially important. Each of these three countries is linked to one of the parties in Afghanistan: Pakistan with the Hezb-i-Islami, Iran with the Hezb-i-Wahdat, and Uzbekistan with the Jumbesh. Relations are a matter of reciprocal manipulation: each tries to command the other to further its own interests. The three neighboring powers all oppose the rebuilding of the Afghan state by the coalition led by the Jamiat-i-Islami, but they cannot agree on a common course. The divisions among the three states correspond to those between their client parties; one can see the flaw in the assumption that eliminating certain actors in the now-regionalized conflict in Afghanistan will automatically ensure stabilization.

In Pakistan, the policy toward Afghanistan that had been defined by General Zia ul-Haq in the 1970s and 1980s continues to hold sway, despite Prime Minister Benazir Bhutto's attempts during her first government (1988-1990) to take Afghan policy out of the army's hands. Pakistan's basic objective is to weaken the Afghan state, which since 1947 has favored an alliance with India. Pakistan's military and political support for the Hezb-i-Islami is thus partially attributable to the Hezb's lack of nationalist rhetoric (the party even went so far as to advocate confederation between Pakistan and Afghanistan). This consistent backing of one party has in practice contributed to destabilization in Afghanistan—which, incidentally, undermines Pakistan's pretensions to play an important role in postcommunist Central Asia, since Afghanistan is a crucial passageway to that region.

Pakistani influence in Afghanistan has greatly diminished since Kabul's fall to the mujahideen. The northern coalition was formed in reaction to Pakistani influence, and Pakistan's allies (principally Hezb-i-Islami) found themselves left out of the government coalition. And the return of Afghan parties that had operated out of Pakistan during the war has further sapped Pakistan's bargaining power at the parties' negotiating table. Since the mujahideen victory, anti-Pakistan sentiments have been expressed more openly by Afghan leaders, and a nationalist reaction to Pakistani intervention has developed—predictably, in the north, less so in Kandahar province in the south.

Iran also wants to play a major role in the regional balance of power. But it has adopted a defensive posture toward the former Soviet Union and Afghanistan, while taking a more overtly offensive line toward the Middle East.

With Afghanistan, Shiite, Persian-speaking Iran could have tried to develop ties on the basis of shared language (the Hazara and Tajiks speak Persian) or shared religion (since the Hazara are Shiites). However, only solidarity with the Shia has been encouraged; the Sunni Islamist parties in Afghanistan have kept their distance. During much of the Soviet occupation, Tehran was preoccupied with its war with Iran, and so gave mainly verbal support to Afghanistan's mujahideen. As a result, Iran's relations with the parties that fought the Soviets remain cool to this day.

Since the Soviet withdrawal, Iran's policy toward Afghanistan has been to avoid the establishment in Kabul of a Saudi-backed Islamic regime, which would mean the isolation of Afghanistan's Shiites, who constitute the only card Iran now holds in the country. The formation of the Hezb-i-Wahdat in 1990 was largely an Iranian initiative, aimed at bringing together all Shiites in Afghanistan, or at least the Hazaras. But the Hezb-i-Wahdat's departure from the government alliance has indirectly weakened Iran's grip on the party; the group's Hazara nationalist logic, unconstrained by membership in the government, has often run contrary to Iranian diplomatic initiatives.

The Afghan crisis has fewer implications for Uzbekistan than it does for Pakistan or Iran. Uzbekistan's main worry is the Afghan refugees on Uzbek soil, but these number only a few thousand and in any case are under strict control. The Uzbek government's key external objective is to guarantee all international frontiers to prevent the destabilization of Central Asia. The border with Afghanistan is particularly important; President Islam Karimov's secular regime fears an Islamic contagion emanating from Afghanistan (or, indirectly, from Tajikistan, where an Islamic -based insurgency rages).

Uzbekistan has backed the Jumbesh in Afghanistan in the quest for a reliable ally to guard its southern border—not because of ethnic solidarity with Uzbeks in Afghanistan. In fact, the revival of Uzbek nationalism that the Jumbesh is sponsoring is not necessarily in Uzbekistan's interests, since Tashkent is eager to preserve the existing border with Afghanistan. However, the Afghan Islamist parties' backing of the Islamist insurgents in Tajikistan, and the absence of a working central government in Afghanistan force Uzbekistan to support the Jumbesh. Uzbekistan's backing has its limits, but this does not prevent Jumbesh jets from landing at the Termez base in southern Uzbekistan.

So long as the Jumbesh controls an important piece of the border, it is assured of Uzbekistan's backing. The risk for the Jumbesh is that it will remain confined to a small part of Afghanistan; for Uzbekistan, the danger is being shut out of future political developments in Kabul.

In the Hands of the Generals

The radical transformation of the two coalitions in Afghanistan is unlikely in the coming months. The Jamiat-i-Islami may hope for a relatively stable alliance with the Harkat-i-Inqilab and the Ettehad since the relationship is based on alliances between local commanders in different provinces and compatible ideological projects. The Jamiat-Harkat-Ettehad axis, representing an alliance between Pashtuns and Tajiks, is the key to the government coalition's stability. If the alliance breaks up, the Jamiat-i-Islami will lose much of its influence in the south. For the time being, the outlook is favorable since the government coalition controls more territory than its enemies.

The second alliance, built around the Hezb-i-Islami, is not based on a political project. Between the Jumbesh, the Hezb-i-Wahdat, and the Hezb-i-Islami, there are no common interests other than the tactical one of preventing the government coalition from restoring the state.

The logic of the alliances has been mainly political up to now. Despite the impression the first, northern-based coalition might have given, no ethnic opposition is expressing itself in the logics of the current alliances. The opposition is instead organized thus: the more fragmented and tribal south against a north organizing itself on the model of regional ministates.

Finally, the UN, discredited after the failure of its 1992 transition plan, is encouraging a new agreement. But the military situation is still open, making a negotiated outcome improbable—especially since it is difficult to see on what terms the still powerful regional powers would sign an agreement. Military evolutions remain the determining force in a country that has lived in war for 15 years.

5. The Kashmir Conflict

April 1996

ROBERT G. WIRSING

The conflict between India and Pakistan over possession of the state of Jammu and Kashmir will soon reach its fiftieth anniversary. During this half-century Kashmir has figured in three major international wars—two between India and Pakistan in 1947-1949 and 1965, and one between India and China in 1962. It has been the subject of protracted boundary negotiations between India and Pakistan, and between India and China, and a constant source of low-level violence within Kashmir and on its borders. It is also one of the UN's oldest peacekeeping missions, and has been the subject of extensive, though unsuccessful, multilateral diplomacy. Kashmir has been an extremely contentious issue in the domestic politics of India and Pakistan, and it has been a thorny problem for both countries in their relations with the rest of the world. Moreover, the popular uprising that erupted in the state in 1989 presents India with perhaps the most difficult challenge yet to its democratic and secular political order.

On the surface the Kashmir conflict does not appear to warrant extensive world attention. A place of legendary beauty, Kashmir lies in the northernmost corner of the South Asian subcontinent. While it is geographically large (approximately 85,000 square miles), its population, especially when measured against that of the rest of the subcontinent, is tiny. That part of Kashmir controlled by India (roughly 45 percent, with Pakistan controlling about 35 percent and China 20 percent) had an estimated 1991 population of 8 million—about 0.7 percent of the total population of India, Pakistan, and Bangladesh (the territory of the former British Indian Empire).[1] But in the

---

1. The state of Jammu and Kashmir is an amalgam of peoples of diverse ethnolinguistic and religious background who were combined into a single princely state by the British in the nineteenth century. Indian-controlled Kashmir today consists of three main divisions: The

last seven years the Kashmir conflict has taken on a far more menacing character than these figures might imply.

A Colonial Legacy

The conflict between India and Pakistan over Kashmir began in 1947. It came in the wake of the British government's reluctant decision to transfer power over its soon-to-be independent Indian colony to two separate states—one, India, predominantly Hindu, the other, Pakistan, predominantly Muslim. The British partitioned the territory mainly on the basis of the principle of communal majority—contiguous Muslim-majority areas were assigned to Pakistan, and contiguous non-Muslim (Hindu and Sikh) majority areas were assigned to India. This partitioning did not apply to the vast areas occupied by the 565 so-called princely states, such as Kashmir, that had enjoyed semiautonomous status under the British during the colonial era. These princely entities, although technically recovering independence with Britain's "lapse of paramountcy" on August 15, 1947, were in fact pressured by Britain's last viceroy in India, Lord Louis Mountbatten, to accede by that date to India or Pakistan.

As the process of integrating the princely states unfolded, there were only three major holdouts: Hyderabad, Junagadh, and Kashmir. Two, Hyderabad and Junagadh, were forcibly integrated into the Indian Union within months of independence by the new Congress Party-led government of Prime Minister Jawaharlal Nehru. In the case of Kashmir, however, its ruler's attempt to hold out for independence precipitated a violent struggle between India and Pakistan over accession. An invasion of Kashmir by Pakistan-backed Pathan tribesmen in October 1947 prompted the frightened ruler of the state, Maharaja Sir Hari Singh, to accede to India. By a quirk of history, Singh was a Hindu in a largely Muslim state; though he was officially entitled to make the decision on accession on behalf of his subjects, his failure to do so on the basis of their religious identity disappointed the Pakistanis, whose leader, Muhammad Ali Jinnah, promptly charged India with masterminding a conspiracy to deprive Pakistan of its "natural" territorial inheritance.

Kashmir Valley, Jammu, and Ladakh. The Kashmir Valley is overwhelmingly Muslim, Jammu is mainly Hindu, and Ladakh is mainly Buddhist. The Pakistan-controlled sector is divided into two parts, Azad (Free) Kashmir and the Northern Areas. The Chinese control the Aksai Chin region in northeastern Ladakh.

The Kashmir conflict has since impeded the establishment of friendly relations between India and Pakistan. During the 1970s and 1980s, and especially in the latter decade when Pakistan's attention was diverted from Kashmir by major difficulties on its northwestern border arising from Soviet intervention in Afghanistan, the Kashmir conflict was put on the region's back burner. The "temporary" territorial arrangement achieved by the earlier wars had seemingly hardened into a permanent, if grudging, acceptance of the status quo on all sides. Events in the 1990s, including a major uprising against Indian rule by the Kashmiri Muslims, have upset this complacent view and serve as a reminder that the Kashmir conflict not only remains very much alive but is, in fact, in greater need than ever of settlement.

Escalating Military Tensions

The Kashmir conflict has not been among the twentieth century's most destructive regional conflicts. The wars India and Pakistan have fought over it were short-lived, not especially bloody, and ended in cease-fires with neither side able to claim victory. In contrast, most reports of the Kashmiri Muslim uprising, now in its seventh year, place the death toll at over 20,000. Of course, when measured against Bosnia, Rwanda, Sudan, and many other similar contemporary cases, even that figure doesn't seem terribly frightful. But unlike most of these other cases, the Kashmir conflict militarily engages three of the most populous and heavily armed states on the planet. The three, China, India, and Pakistan, ranked first, third, and twelfth respectively in military expenditure in 1990; and first, second, and seventh in the number of troops among all developing countries in 1991. Between 1988 and 1992, India ranked first and Pakistan seventh among major arms importers in the developing world; and between 1950 and 1985, India ranked first among indigenous arms producers in the developing world, accounting for 31 percent of the total.[2] China, India, and Pakistan are also among the world's eight known nuclear-weapons or nuclear-weapons threshold states.

India and China have not fought each other since 1962. The recent measures they have taken to avoid military clashes along their long international

---

2. Remy Herrera, *Statistics on Military Expenditure in Developing Countries: Concepts, Methodological Problems and Sources* (Paris: Organization for Economic Cooperation and Development, 1994), appendices 2, 6, 7.1, and 8.1.

border—including plans to delimit the Line of Actual Control (LAC) that divides their troops in the Aksai Chin region of Ladakh in northeastern Kashmir—are clearly steps in the right direction.

Unfortunately, India and Pakistan have been extremely reluctant to move in the same direction. For 12 years they have engaged in open combat in the Karakoram Mountains over possession of the Siachen Glacier. This 1,000-square-mile area of cathedral peaks and icy wilderness, dubbed by journalists "the world's loftiest battleground," lies at the northern end of the 500-mile-long Line of Control (LOC) that divides the Indian from the Pakistani-controlled sector of Kashmir. Apart from costing thousands of lives and billions of dollars, the Kashmir conflict has inflicted significant damage on the Siachen Glacier's pristine mountain environment.

More worrisome than the fighting over Siachen, which at least has the virtue of taking place in an extremely remote area, has been the breakdown of the cease-fire on the LOC, the 1972 successor to the cease-fire line agreed on by Pakistan and India at the conclusion of their first war in 1949. The disengagement of forces envisioned in the original cease-fire has long since been abandoned, replaced in recent years by crossborder mortar, sniper, and heavy artillery firing, the constancy of which makes a complete mockery of the LOC's function. The evidence is overwhelming that armed conflict—and not just minor skirmishing—is now a routine feature of India-Pakistan relations in the disputed area of Kashmir.

With generally fewer than 40 officers, the small UN peacekeeping detachment in Kashmir (the UN Military Observer Group in India and Pakistan, or UNMOGIP) cannot even begin to investigate the thousands of violations of the LOC perpetrated by both sides, much less monitor the military movements and installations of the two armies in its vicinity. Regular Indian army troops deployed in Kashmir probably number more than 200,000, and their activities can no longer be scrutinized by the peacekeepers since India unilaterally barred UNMOGIP from carrying out its mandated functions on the Indian side of the LOC in 1972. In practical terms, UN peacekeeping in Kashmir exists in name only.

One other sign of the LOC's dwindling ability to act as a pacifying instrument in Kashmir is the now routine passage of Kashmiri militants across the LOC. Labeled "antinational elements" by the Indians and widely regarded in India as no more than terrorists, the militants have long found refuge, arms, and other forms of support on the Pakistani side of the LOC. While Indian news reports last November that "1995 has seen the highest number of trained militants coming into the [Kashmir] Valley from across the border,

and even conservative estimates put the figure at 1,000 a month" are probably overstated, there has undoubtedly been a large influx.

The ranks of Kashmir's homegrown militants are being augmented,
moreover, by fighters from Afghanistan, Pakistan, and other Muslim countries rallying to the cry of jihad in Kashmir. Citing intelligence estimates,
India's premier newsmagazine, *India Today*, reported in September 1995 that
at least 1,600 foreign Islamic militants had crossed the border into Kashmir
during the summer of 1995 to fight on the side of the Kashmiri Muslim
insurgents. Foreign collaboration on this scale does not pose a major military threat to Indian forces, but it does promise to help sustain the insurgency.

While the nuclear alarm has perhaps been rung for South Asia with more
frequency (and with fewer ascertained facts) than the situation actually war-
rants, it is still important to note that escalating hostilities in Kashmir are
taking place in a region containing two nuclear, or at least nuclear-weapons
capable, powers. The extent to which these two powers came close to war
during military exercises by India in late 1986 and early 1987, and then again
during an especially tense period in 1990, is a matter of considerable controversy.[3] What is clear, however, is that South Asia's military dangers are
proliferating and growing deeper.

Democracy's Disintegration and the Communal Divide

Whether dwelling on the Indian side of the LOC or in Azad (Free) Kashmir,
the Pakistani-controlled portion of the state, Kashmiris can point to few
elections since 1947 that can be called free and fair. On both sides wholesale
rigging has been the standard from the beginning. Neither India nor Pakistan has considered the denial of political rights or the imposition of corrupt governance on Kashmiris too great a price to pay for national security.

This dismal political record has recently been augmented, especially in
Indian-controlled Kashmir, by a no less dismal record of human rights
abuses that include torture, assassination, custodial deaths, and prolonged
detention without trial or charges. The Indian security forces have been
prominently implicated in these abuses, but they are clearly not the only

---

3. See for example Kanti P. Bajpai et al., *Brasstacks and Beyond: Perception and Management
of Crisis in South Asia* (New Delhi: Manohar, 1995); and Michael Krepon and Mishi Faruqee,
eds., *Conflict Prevention and Confidence-Building Measures in South Asia: The 1990 Crisis*
(Washington, D.C.: The Henry L. Stimson Center, Occasional Paper no. 17, April 1994).

participants in this conflict with unclean hands. The circumstances of insurgency and counterinsurgency are such, moreover, that these abuses are unlikely to be terminated until the conflict is resolved.

The continued abuse of human rights will also fundamentally damage the political systems in which such incidents occur. Political scientists are already issuing warnings about the "crisis of governance" and the political "deinstitutionalization" let loose in South Asia in recent decades, and they routinely point out the potential for the complete destruction of political democracy in the region. The Kashmir conflict is, without doubt, exacerbating these trends.

An even more frightening political impact is the conflict's polarizing effect on the subcontinent's Muslim and Hindu religious communities.

Because the Kashmir conflict pits, at the international level, mainly Muslim Pakistan against mainly Hindu India, and, at the domestic level, mainly Muslim Kashmiris against mainly Hindu security forces, it encourages a popular understanding cast overwhelmingly in religious and communal terms. In greatest immediate danger here, of course, is India's huge Muslim minority of about 110 million (12 percent of India's population). This group has long been hostage to the Kashmir conflict; today it seems under greater suspicion than ever of "divided loyalties" and potential for "fifth column" activity in the event of renewed war with Pakistan. The persistent appeal of Islamic militancy in Pakistan, and the recent electoral rise of Hindu nationalism in India, only underscore the Kashmir conflict's capacity to incite South Asians to greater political extremism.

The Kashmir Linchpin

The South Asian Association of Regional Cooperation (SAARC) formally commits India and Pakistan, along with the region's five other states (Bangladesh, Sri Lanka, Nepal, Bhutan, and the Maldives), to the promotion of regional economic, technical, and cultural cooperation. Since its founding in 1985, it has registered a number of significant agreements. One of the most recent—and possibly the most important—was the November 1995 signing, by all seven countries, of the South Asian Preferential Trading Arrangement (SAPTA), which calls for an immediate reduction in tariff barriers and the eventual creation of a free trade zone. But when measured against most other regional organizations of its kind, SAARC's record of achievement is far from luminous.

Clearly one of the major reasons for SAARC's lackluster performance is the fierce rivalry between India and Pakistan over Kashmir. That rivalry infects every aspect of their relationship, including their willingness to allow their athletes to participate in international sports matches. It has also led them to engage relentlessly in acts of sabotage, espionage, diplomatic one-upmanship, and saber rattling.

Indian and Pakistani objectives outside South Asia are also hostage to the Kashmir conflict. Indian aspirations to gain permanent membership on the UN Security Council, for example, or for inclusion as full member of the Association of Southeast Asian Nations (ASEAN), partly depend on New Delhi's ability to persuade the world that it can keep its house in order—and, of equal importance, that it can do so without violating international human rights norms. By the same token, Pakistan's global agenda, which includes the desire to be recognized as a willing and able contributor to UN peacekeeping missions around the world, is hardly supported by its neighbor's constant accusation that it routinely sponsors acts of terrorism in Kashmir.

The Price of Nonsettlement

Launching talks on Kashmir will not produce an immediate or massive "peace dividend" for Indians and Pakistanis. Converting defense expenditures into social and economic investments is neither a simple nor a certain affair. Even if talks between India and Pakistan resulted in a settlement of some kind, that alone—in the unruly strategic environment in which they are located—would not eliminate the requirement for strong militaries.

There is no question, however, that the Kashmir conflict requires both sides, especially India, to maintain extremely large numbers of security forces in Kashmir for border defense and internal policing. Nor is there any question that maintaining these forces at combat readiness is extremely costly. Of greater importance is that Kashmir inspires an across-the-board enmity between India and Pakistan that results in a far more intense arms rivalry than would otherwise be the case.

Pakistan, which is the smaller and economically weaker of the pair, has been especially hard hit by the strained relations. Sustaining anything resembling arms parity with India has forced it to spend roughly twice the percentage of its gross national product on defense that India does. This has meant in recent years that the Pakistani treasury, once central revenue receipts for defense expenditures and debt servicing have been set aside, has had little left for social and economic development.

A few statistics should give some idea of just how much both countries pay in lost education and health alone. Nearly 50 years after winning independence, 65 percent of adult Pakistanis and 52 percent of adult Indians remain illiterate; 40 percent of Pakistani children under the age of 5 and 63 percent of Indian children in the same age group are malnourished. These are startling figures, even for low-income countries, and add a powerful moral dimension to the material reasons for these two societies to get under way with serious talks on the Kashmir conflict.

What Military Conflict Wouldn't Solve

India's overwhelming military power would seem to assure the ultimate success of its armed forces in Kashmir; they have certainly never been seriously challenged there. A recent study notes that as of January 1995, Indian security forces had suffered 400 regular army plus 500 paramilitary troops killed.[4] These figures, spread over the first six years of the uprising (1989–1994), yield an annual average of about 150 killed. From that perspective, the Kashmir conflict is clearly a low- intensity conflict. Fighting has tended to be "hit and run," with no reports of prolonged ground combat and with the resistance forces relying thus far entirely on light weapons.

Throughout much of Kashmir, especially in rural areas, Indian forces have already prevailed over the resistance, at least in a strictly military sense. But they cannot control the region fully unless they can seal the border against outside assistance—which, as a technical project, has so far been deemed impossible.

In the meantime, it is clear that the Indian government, despite its apparently strong wish to do so, cannot declare the uprising over and then set elections for the state assembly. Elections would no doubt be welcomed by many, perhaps even most Kashmiris. It would certainly be welcomed by the 150,000-200,000 Hindu Kashmiris (called *pandits*) who were driven from their ancestral homes in the Kashmir Valley in the earlier days of the uprising in what has justifiably been described as "ethnic cleansing." But there are enough determined Muslim opponents of elections to make a

4. Paula R. Newberg, *Double Betrayal: Repression and Insurgency in Kashmir* (Washington, D.C.: Carnegie Endowment for International Peace, 1995), p. 27.

mockery of New Delhi's plans. The government may, of course, stage elections in Kashmir, or at least in parts of it, under extraordinary precautions and with limited participation by Kashmiri Muslims. But it is hard to see what this would accomplish. It would not bring peace, or anything resembling genuine self-rule, back to the Kashmir Valley. For that, a political solution is needed.

Finding a Solution

Talks between India and the Kashmiri rebels need to acknowledge, at a minimum, the legitimacy of Kashmiri Muslim claims to greater cultural and political autonomy than they now possess. In deciding how much autonomy should be allowed, three prior agreements struck between Indian and Kashmiri leaders can be used as models. The first, the Instrument of Accession, was agreed to by the governments of Prime Minister Nehru and Maharaja Hari Singh in 1947. It provided for the provisional accession of Kashmir to India. In securing it India acquired formal but temporary control over Kashmir's foreign affairs, defense, and communications. The question of Kashmir's ultimate status was to be decided in an internationally supervised plebiscite. The provisional nature of accession implied that Kashmir retained strong autonomy. This model, since it includes the provision of plebiscite and possible accession to Pakistan, is extremely unlikely to be chosen by India.

The second accord, the Delhi Agreement, was reached between Nehru and Kashmiri leader Sheikh Abdullah in 1952. It reaffirmed and reinforced the unique status and special rights granted to Kashmir in Article 370 of the 1950 Indian constitution. In particular, New Delhi conceded in this agreement that the question of Kashmir's ultimate status was to be decided by the Kashmir constituent assembly. Accession to India was thus implicitly subject to legislative review. The agreement implied fairly strong autonomy for Kashmir. New Delhi can be counted on to strongly resist anything resembling this model.

The third, the Kashmir Accord, was struck between Prime Minister Indira Gandhi and Sheikh Abdullah in 1975. This agreement made accession to India final. Article 370 was reaffirmed, but in a much weakened form. The formal installation of central parliamentary oversight powers in Kashmir was agreed. The Kashmir Accord implied weak autonomy for Kashmir. New Delhi's most likely preference is a variation on this accord—in other words, something more cosmetic and symbolic than substantive. It will get a very cold reception from Kashmiris.

Only the 1952 Delhi Agreement comes anywhere near the kind of compromise that might conceivably be achieved today. Too much has transpired in the more than two decades since the 1975 Kashmir Accord was signed for any of its agreements to be reinstated intact. They are useful starting points, however, and none should be dismissed outright.

Talks between India and Pakistan should be aimed strictly at breaking the current deadlock. This is necessary to induce both sides to pull back from their military brinkmanship and to restore a genuine cease-fire. No grand settlement of the Kashmir conflict is likely at the moment and none should be attempted.

But progress of any kind is unlikely unless both sides are prepared to relinquish—publicly and formally—the most extravagant, unrealistic, and bellicose portions of their claims to Kashmir. For India this means dropping its claim to the Pakistani-held sector of Kashmir (Azad Kashmir and the Northern Areas). For Pakistan it means jettisoning its insistence on a plebiscite limited to a bifold choice between accession to India or to Pakistan. The Indian government long ago made plain its willingness to rest content with the conversion of the LOC into a permanent international boundary. For its part the Pakistani government has occasionally hinted that it is willing to entertain a trifold plebiscitary plan, one that would grant the Kashmiris the opportunity to choose what they seem to want anyway—a Kashmir independent of both India and Pakistan.

Over the course of what might well be prolonged and difficult negotiations, the complexities of the Kashmir conflict are likely to keep each side from getting all, or even most, of what it wants. But if India and Pakistan cannot take these two steps, neither of which entails any real material costs, then it is likely that, saddled with unending conflict, they will get even less of what they want.

6. An Opportunity for Peace in Kashmir?

December 1997

SUMIT GANGULY

After a four-year standoff, India and Pakistan agreed in June 1997 to resume bilateral talks with a view toward improving long-strained relations. In a significant concession, India agreed to place the Kashmir dispute on the negotiating table.[1] Despite India's seeming willingness to address a perennial Pakistani concern, any hopes of quick movement on this highly contentious question were soon dashed. In the wake of the talks, the Indian foreign secretary, Salman Haider, made it clear that while India was prepared to discuss Kashmir, the discussions would have to focus on the Pakistani-controlled portions of the disputed territory. The Pakistani press greeted Haider's surprise announcement and negotiating stance with understandable dismay. The government's reaction was more muted: though expressing disappointment, the Pakistani political leadership said that the talks would nevertheless continue.

In late July Indian Prime Minister Inder Gujral, in his first official visit to Jammu and Kashmir, offered to hold talks with Kashmir-based insurgents and cautioned Indian forces about human rights violations. The prime minister also reiterated his government's commitment to continue talks with Pakistan. In September high-level bilateral talks were held, despite a backdrop of escalating violence along the Indian-Pakistani border in Kashmir.

---

1. Kashmir's status has been disputed since the partition of the subcontinent in 1947. The Indian state of Jammu and Kashmir is composed of three districts: the Kashmir Valley, which is predominantly Muslim; Jammu, which is largely Hindu; and Ladakh, which is mostly Buddhist. The Pakistani portion of Kashmir is composed of the northern territories of Gilgit and Hunza and the nominally independent Azad Kashmir ("Free Kashmir").

Regardless of the diplomatic minuet that the two sides will no doubt engage in, the prospects for a quick resolution of the Kashmir dispute are close to nil. Domestic politics in both countries and a legacy of mutual mistrust will hamper movement toward a resolution. Yet a propitious moment may at last have arrived for taking incremental steps toward a final Kashmir settlement. With a degree of imaginative diplomacy, and despite their decades-old formal positions, India and Pakistan may finally be able to bottle the genie that has tormented their relations since they gained independence from Britain in 1947.

Is this optimism unfounded? A number of past attempts to settle the dispute through peaceful means have been unsuccessful. The two Indo-Pakistani wars that were fought over Kashmir (in 1947–1948 and 1965) also failed to achieve a lasting solution. The past is strewn with the detritus of wars and failed negotiations. Despite this dismal history, a plausible argument can be made that an opportunity now exists for a meaningful and viable resolution of the Kashmir dispute. Structural conditions at the international level and more immediate factors at the regional and local levels could finally provide enough impetus to reach a settlement.

At the international level, none of the great powers are prepared to expend significant resources to help resolve the Kashmir dispute. The United States, which had a pronounced pro-Pakistani bias during much of the cold war, has adopted a dispassionate position on the question, and Russia does not have any compelling interest in helping resolve the issue. More to the point, India's relationship with Russia lacks the same closeness that characterized the Indo-Soviet nexus. As a consequence, India lacks the support of a veto-wielding power to protect it from possible international censure on the Kashmir issue in the United Nations Security Council.

At the regional level, in spite of concerted support for the Kashmiri insurgency since 1989, Pakistan has been unable to loosen India's grip on the territory. Though the uprising has cost more than 25,000 lives, it now appears to be on the wane. India's strategy of repression followed by national and local elections has largely undermined the driving forces behind the insurgency. An elected government is now in place in Jammu and Kashmir. Some guerrilla groups, most notably the Hizb-ul-Mujahideen, the Harkat-ul-Ansar, and the Laskar-i-Tulba, remain utterly unreconciled to Indian rule. Nevertheless, today they do not command the degree of support that they did at an earlier stage of the insurgency.

The Roots of Conflict

What animates this seemingly intractable conflict that has been so costly and bloody? The origins of the dispute are closely linked to the subcontinent's British colonial heritage. As the British Labour government of Prime Minister Clement Attlee, bowing to the rise of Indian and Pakistani nationalist sentiment, prepared to depart from South Asia after World War II, Lord Mountbatten, the last viceroy, made a critical pronouncement. He declared that the 562-odd "princely states," which were nominally independent but recognized the "paramountcy" of the British crown, had to join one of the two emergent states of India or Pakistan. The option of independence was effectively ruled out. The state of Jammu and Kashmir posed a particular problem because it shared borders with both India and Pakistan, and had a predominantly Muslim population but a Hindu monarch, the Maharaja Hari Singh.

Pakistan's claim to Kashmir was irredentist.[2] Its nationalist leadership in general, and the architect of Pakistan, Mohammed Ali Jinnah, in particular, had espoused the "two-nation" theory. Jinnah had argued that the Hindus and Muslims of the subcontinent constituted two distinct, primordial "nations." According to this principle, he had propagated the idea that the Muslims of South Asia deserved a separate homeland.

In keeping with this belief, Jinnah believed that Kashmir should be merged with Pakistan based on its demographic composition and geographic contiguity. India's political leadership was, however, equally interested in Kashmir's accession to India. Prime Minister Jawaharlal Nehru and many others in the nationalist Congress Party desired Kashmir's merger into India to demonstrate that a Muslim-majority state could thrive under the aegis of a secular polity.

To the dismay of both Indians and Pakistanis, Maharaja Hari Singh harbored visions of independence and proved unwilling to accede to either state. As the maharaja vacillated on the question of accession, the Pakistani authorities aided a tribal rebellion that had broken out in the western reaches of Kashmir. As the rebels approached the capital city of Srinagar, Singh appealed to India for assistance. India's Nehru agreed to help Singh on two conditions: Kashmir had to accede to India and the accession had to receive the imprimatur of Sheikh Mohammed Abdullah, the leader of

2. On this point see Sumit Ganguly, *The Origins of War in South Asia: The Indo-Pakistani Conflicts since 1947*, 2d ed. (Boulder, Colo.: Westview, 1994).

the Kashmir National Conference, the largest secular and popular political party in Kashmir. Only after these two conditions were met did Nehru send troops to Kashmir. The introduction of these forces stopped the Pakistani-assisted tribal advance but not before the invaders had occupied a significant portion of the state. On January 1, 1948, on the advice of Lord Mountbatten, Prime Minister Nehru referred the case to the UN Security Council. A series of UN resolutions designed to end the conflict were passed but to little avail. Eventually, on January 1, 1949, the two sides agreed to a UN-sponsored cease-fire. Over the next 15 years the Security Council generated a plethora of proposals for a negotiated settlement to the dispute, but none proved acceptable to the two parties.

Resorting to War, Again

A congeries of international and domestic factors prompted the Pakistani military dictatorship of General Ayub Khan to try to wrest Kashmir from India in the early 1960s. At the international level, the UN had steadily lost interest in the conflict. A series of bilateral negotiations held in 1963 under Anglo-American pressure ended in stalemate. And the Indian defense modernization program in the aftermath of the 1962 Sino-Indian border war provoked Pakistani fears that over the longer haul India's expanded military capabilities would effectively foreclose any possibility of seizing Kashmir by force.

An incident in the Kashmir Valley was the catalyst that led Pakistani decision makers to forge a strategy to attack, occupy, and seize the territory. In December 1963 anti-Indian demonstrations were held in Srinagar. The demonstrations stemmed from the theft of the *moe-e-moqaddas* (a hair of the Prophet Mohammed) from the Hazratbal mosque. The Pakistani leadership incorrectly construed the anti-Indian tone of the demonstrations as a manifestation of widespread pro-Pakistani sentiment. Their attack proved to be a complete failure. Local Kashmiris turned the Pakistani infiltrators in to the authorities and the Indian army promptly moved to seal the border. Full-scale war erupted on September 1, 1965, but a Security Council resolution brought the fighting to a close later that month. American unwillingness to mediate enabled the Soviet Union to enter the breach. Soviet President Leonid Brezhnev negotiated a postwar settlement enjoining the two parties to return to the status quo ante. The Pakistani leadership nevertheless remained committed to its claim on Kashmir.

In 1971, India and Pakistan again went to war. On this occasion, how-ever, Kashmir was not the focal point of the dispute. Internal developments within Pakistan and the violent repression of Bengali demands for auton-omy in East Pakistan had culminated in the emergence of a secessionist movement in East Pakistan. Pakistan's continued repression resulted in the mass exodus of refugees into India. Faced with this extraordinary burden and little tangible support from the international community, Indian lead-ers decided that it would be cheaper to resort to war than absorb the refugees into India. India emerged as the clear-cut victor in this war. In the aftermath of the conflict, Indian Prime Minister Indira Gandhi and Pak-istani President Zulfiqar Ali Bhutto reached a settlement in the town of Simla. Under the terms of the Simla Accord, the UN Cease-Fire Line in Kashmir was converted into the Line of Actual Control (LOC). Both sides agreed not to use force to settle the Kashmir dispute.

The breakup of Pakistan in 1971 dealt a fatal blow to Jinnah's "two-na-tion" principle. The linguistic solidarity of the Bengalis of East Pakistan had proved more powerful than the bonds of Islam. With Indian assis-tance, the new state of Bangladesh was created. Consequently, the irreden-tist basis of Pakistan's claim to Kashmir suffered a critical setback, although its rhetoric and commitment remained intact.

A New Level of Conflict Emerges

In the 1980s, the secular features of the Indian state eroded. The exigencies of electoral politics led Prime Minister Indira Gandhi and her son and suc-cessor, Rajiv Gandhi, to pander to the Hindu majority. India's continued commitment to Kashmir's status in the Indian union stemmed more from the imperatives of statecraft than from adherence to a normative principle.

The abrupt rise of a violent, secessionist, ethnoreligious movement in Kashmir in 1989 can be traced to the related processes of political mobiliza-tion and institutional decay in India. India's investments in literacy, higher education, and mass media in Kashmir had led to a dramatic transforma-tion of the political consciousness of the electorate. For example, the over-all literacy rate in Jammu and Kashmir grew from 17 percent in 1961 to 36 percent in 1981. Overall college enrollment expanded from 2,779 people in 1950–1951 to 34,000 in 1992–1993. Finally, in 1965 a mere 46 newspapers were published in the state; by 1984 the number had climbed to 203.

This growth in educational standards and media exposure contributed to heightened political awareness and led to increased demands for political participation by a new generation of Kashmiris. Earlier generations, though discontented with various aspects of misrule, mounted only sporadic challenges. They lacked the political consciousness and the requisite organizational skills to launch a full-scale movement designed to undermine the established political order. Furthermore, as political consciousness and, concomitantly, an increased drive for participation, grew in Kashmir, the central government in New Delhi initially attempted to address these aspirations. Specifically, following the release of the former chief minister of Kashmir, Sheikh Mohammed Abdullah, in 1974 after a long period of incarceration, he and Indira Gandhi reached an agreement under which he would be returned to the chief ministership. In exchange, Abdullah agreed to work within the framework of the Indian constitution and uphold India's territorial integrity.

In 1977 Sheikh Abdullah and the National Conference won an overwhelming victory in the Kashmir state assembly elections. According to all observers, this election was free from the political chicanery that had long characterized electoral politics in Kashmir. The sheikh's return to office was cut short by his death in 1982; his hand-picked successor, son Farooq, a physician with little or no political experience, took over. Despite his inexperience, as the inheritor of the sheikh's mantle Farooq managed easily to win a wide mandate in the state assembly elections of 1983. This election, too, was largely free of charges of coercion and voter intimidation.

Prime Minister Indira Gandhi's decision to dismiss Farooq's regime on specious grounds in 1984 proved to be a catalytic event for political developments in Kashmir. The dismissal was a crass attempt to obtain a toehold for the national Congress Party in Kashmir. Within two years Rajiv Gandhi, Indira's son and political successor, brought Farooq back as chief minister. Farooq's dismissal and subsequent alliance with Rajiv and the Congress dramatically undermined his standing in Kashmir. The Congress–National Conference alliance jointly contested the state assembly elections of 1987. Widespread electoral malfeasance characterized this election, effectively denying the expression of popular discontent through institutional channels. Younger Kashmiris, embittered by the undermining of democratic institutions, came to the ineluctable conclusion that the government in New Delhi was unprepared to extend the same rights to Kashmiri Muslims that other Indians enjoyed in most parts of the country.

With no other avenue for the articulation of their grievances, significant numbers of disaffected young Kashmiris organized a violent ethnoreligious movement.

Sensing an opportunity to undermine India's hold on Kashmir, Pakistan's political and military leadership decided to fuel the existing discontent through propaganda and material support. It is clear that Pakistan's involvement in Kashmir was opportunistic and not the source of the insurgency. Nevertheless, Pakistani training, weaponry, and sanctuaries provided considerable succor to the insurgents.

The Indian state's initial response to the insurgency, pursued by the New Delhi–appointed governor, Jagmohan Malhotra, was ham-fisted and counterproductive. Far from curbing the insurgency, it inflamed passions further and resulted in extensive human rights violations as poorly trained and ill-equipped soldiers panicked or used inordinate force (there have also been allegations of torture). In May 1991 Jagmohan was replaced by Girish Saxena, the former head of the Research and Analysis Wing, India's counterintelligence service. Saxena, with considerable experience in counterinsurgency operations, pursued a more calibrated strategy that sowed discord among the insurgents.

Saxena was replaced in 1993 by General Krishna Rao, a former chief of the Indian army, but the government's tactics remained similar. By early 1996, despite a number of tragic incidents, including the destruction of a fourteenth-century shrine in May 1995, the Indian counterinsurgency strategy was yielding the desired results. The constant harrying of the rebels had left them in disarray. Long-standing tensions among some of the principal insurgent groups, most notably the Jammu and Kashmir Liberation Front and the Hizb-ul-Mujahideen, had come out in the open, certain insurgent groups had been co-opted, and a degree of war weariness was settling into the local population. Sensing an opportunity to restore a modicum of legitimacy to its writ in Kashmir, the government in New Delhi decided to hold elections in conjunction with India's eleventh general election in May 1996. This electoral effort proved to be stillborn. In an attempt to ensure a significant turnout, the security forces goaded voters to show up at the polls. Most observers called into question the results.

The newly elected Indian national coalition government of Prime Minister H. D. Deve Gowda was quick to realize the folly of the earlier electoral effort. In September 1996, assembly elections were held in Kashmir. These elections, apart from minor incidents of fraud, were indubitably fair. The various insurgent groups did attempt to disrupt the voting but to little avail. The only other discordant note was struck by the All Party Hurriyat Conference (APHC), an agglomeration of Kashmiri political parties and activists opposed to Indian control of Kashmir, which boycotted the elections.

Settling the Dispute

The tortured history of the Kashmir dispute virtually precludes a prompt settlement. Despite the current atmosphere of bonhomie in New Delhi and Islamabad, significant impediments to a resolution remain. In India, the coalition government of Prime Minister Gujral depends on the Congress's parliamentary support. It is unclear whether a future regime, especially one dominated by the jingoistic Bharatiya Janata Party, will continue the policies that the present regime has initiated. In Pakistan, segments of the military still harbor a sense of implacable hostility toward India. These factions would prefer to pin India down indefinitely in Kashmir rather than settle the dispute and improve relations. These impediments notwithstanding, the relative isolation of both states in the international system, the marked weakening of the insurgency, and the renewed willingness of the present political establishments in both states to start negotiations augur well for the future.

What are the contours of a potential settlement? No resolution can entirely accommodate the divergent positions of the three key protagonists, namely the Kashmiri insurgents and the Indian and Pakistani governments. All sides will have to make concessions if this dispute is to be settled without further violence.

Contrary to popular assertions, there is no unified Kashmiri opinion about the terms of a possible settlement. The insurgents are deeply divided, the APHC's seeming unity is tenuous, and the inhabitants of Jammu and Ladakh have little in common with the inhabitants of the Kashmir Valley. Nevertheless, since most of the disaffected population does live in the valley, some effort has to be made to assuage its discontent and sense of alienation. To this end, any government in India will have to restore popular faith in a variety of local political institutions and processes. Strategies for achieving this might include aggressively recruiting Kashmiri Muslims for positions in the state bureaucracy, restoring the local judiciary's independence, reining in the paramilitary forces, and punishing those members of the security forces involved in human rights violations. Also, the regime in Kashmir needs to carefully and adroitly seek to bring the APHC into the political fold. In the interest of bringing a degree of normalcy to political and civic life in Kashmir, the National Conference should seriously entertain some power-sharing arrangement with the APHC.

At the national level, New Delhi must move toward restoring Kashmir's compromised autonomy. Finally, at the bilateral level, India should reiterate its offer to Pakistan to accept the LOC in Kashmir as an international border and permanently renounce its claim to the Pakistani-controlled portions of the territory. Pakistan, in turn, must abandon its quixotic quest to wrest Kashmir from India and instead focus on addressing its myriad domestic problems. As the two nations enter their sixth decade of independence, it is time indeed to close a tragic chapter that has bedeviled their relations from the very outset.

7. Sri Lanka's Civil War

December 1999

MANIK DE SILVA

Nineteen eighty-three is generally regarded as the year Sri Lanka's ethnic conflict began. It has since escalated into a full-blown civil war, claiming the lives of over 58,000 people and not showing any signs of ending. But the roots of the problem between the majority Sinhalese and minority Tamils, who have lived together for centuries in a 25,000-square-mile island home, go back many years before July 1983, when thousands of Tamils first in Colombo and then in many other parts of the country were brutally attacked by Sinhalese.

One watershed date would certainly be 1956. This was the year when Prime Minister Solomon Bandaranaike, a polished Oxford-educated orator, swept into power on the nationalist slogan "Sinhala Only" in an attempt to replace English as the official language of Ceylon, as Sri Lanka was then known. Bandaranaike touched a receptive chord in the Sinhalese psyche and scored a landslide victory over the United National Party (UNP), which he had quit a few years earlier to found the Sri Lanka Freedom Party (SLFP).

Essentially a liberal, Bandaranaike, who promised to impose "Sinhala Only" within 24 hours of taking office, did not intend to discriminate against the country's Tamil minority. His efforts at being fair to the Tamil and other minorities after making Sinhalese the country's only official language were thwarted by chauvinist forces within his own party and an opposition determined to exploit the same sentiments that had been such a potent source of votes. Colvin de Silva, a leader of the Trotskyist Equal Society Party, which advocated both Sinhalese and Tamil as the official languages of the country—to its electoral detriment—made the remarkably accurate prophecy, "One language, two nations. Two languages, one nation." The Tamil separatist movement in great measure owed its genesis to the "Sinhala Only" campaign.

Tracing the Divide

Although it is generally accepted that Tamils felt discriminated against after "Sinhala Only" was imposed, the demand for a separate Tamil state, although never stridently or convincingly made, existed before 1956. In 1945 the All Ceylon Tamil Congress (ACTC) of G. G. Ponnambalam, then the dominant party of the Tamils, presented to a British commission on Ceylon's independence a scheme of "balanced representation" in the legislature between the Sinhalese and Tamils. This was rejected by the commission, which said that "any attempt by artificial means to convert a majority into a minority is not only inequitable but doomed to failure."

In 1949 (after independence the previous year), S. J. V. Chelvanayakam broke away from the ACTC to form what was called in Tamil the Ilankai Thamil Arasu Kadchi, which literally translated means the Lanka Tamil State Party but was called (some say dishonestly) the Federal Party (FP) in English and so presented in Sinhalese areas. Chelvanayakam and the FP played dominant roles on behalf of the Tamils in the years between 1956 and 1970, when two serious attempts to settle the differences between the two communities on the basis of regional autonomy for predominantly Tamil areas were shot down by opportunistic Sinhalese politicians playing on chauvinist elements within their community.

A perception among many Sinhalese that the Tamils enjoyed a privileged position, especially with regard to English education and employment before independence (profiting from Britain's strategy of "divide and rule"), exacerbated ill feelings between the two communities. The Sinhalese also had an instinctive fear of being engulfed by the very large number of ethnic Tamils living in southern India, which is separated from the predominantly Tamil north Sri Lanka by the narrow Palk Strait. These fears fueled the many riots that Tamils living among the majority Sinhalese outside the north and east faced in 1958, 1977, 1981, and 1983. Since a large number of Tamils—over 50 percent of both Sri Lankan and Indian Tamils—live in the seven provinces outside the north and east, they became vulnerable to attacks generally triggered by Sinhalese criminal elements intent on profiting by looting.

That the Sinhalese themselves bear no intrinsic hatred for the Tamils, and that many of them at considerable risk to themselves protected Tamil families during communal rioting, is confirmed by S. Thondaman, the leader of the country's Indian Tamil community, who has held cabinet office under the governments of both the UNP and SLFP, which draw most of their support from the Sinhalese. Thondaman argued in parliament after the 1983 riots that "there are many people who claim that these disturbances are a further manifestation of the Sinhala uprising against the Tamils. But I do not share the view. The vast majority of the Sinhala people condemn these atrocities on these innocent Tamil people and have shown sympathy and understanding. . . . To say that this is a Sinhala uprising against the Tamils is absurd."

"The Boys" Who Became Tigers

But the 1983 riots did lead to an uprising—by Jaffna Tamil youth led by a group of young men disillusioned with the Tamil community's existing political leadership. They believed that there was no nonviolent way to achieve what they perceived to be justice for Tamils. This group of militants would develop within a few years into the Liberation Tigers of Tamil Eelam.

The LTTE has deservedly acquired the reputation of becoming one of the world's most effective guerrilla forces or, as the Sri Lanka government and the vast majority of the Sinhalese people would have it, terrorist outfit. Originally a guerrilla group considered by the army unable to engage in a conventional war, the Tigers have repeatedly demonstrated their military capability by overrunning several major military installations in Sri Lanka's north.

The Tigers are led by the 45-year-old Velupillai Prabhakaran. The group had its genesis in the young Tamil men in the Jaffna peninsula, affectionately referred to in the early days as "the boys." They increasingly pushed the traditional Tamil political leadership, which was then dominated by the Tamil United Liberation Front (TULF) (a grouping of the Federal Party, the ACTC, and the Ceylon Workers Congress of Thondaman), to adopt a more militant stance on Tamil demands that culminated in the Vadukoddai Resolution of May 14, 1976 for a separate state of Tamil Eelam "consisting of the Northern and Eastern Provinces of Sri Lanka."

SRI LANKA'S MAJOR ETHNIC GROUPS

At the time of independence from Britain in 1948, Sri Lanka's demographic composition was 69 percent Sinhalese; other large groups included Sri Lanka Tamils, who made up 11 percent of the population; Indian Tamils 12 percent; and Muslims 6 percent. The Sri Lanka Tamils were the indigenous Tamils largely concentrated in the north of the country and less so in the east, while the Indian Tamils were mostly people brought to the country from India by the British rulers to work on the tea and rubber plantations and their descendants. A substantial number of the Indian Tamils were repatriated back to India under the terms of two treaties entered into by Prime Minister Sirima Bandaranaike of Sri Lanka with Prime Ministers Lal Bahadur Shastri and Indira Gandhi of India.

Following this repatriation after 1960 and the grant of Sri Lanka citizenship to those who opted to stay, the demographic composition changed with the proportion of both the Sinhalese and the Sri Lanka Tamils increasing. The Sinhalese increased to 74 percent, the Sri Lanka Tamils to 13 percent, and the Muslims to 7 percent. The proportion of the Indian Tamils decreased to 6 percent.

From 1972 various youth groups of Tamils, including Prabhakaran's Tamil New Tigers, had become active and had together with the TULF engaged in a prolonged and continuous campaign of disobedience that included murder, bombings, and arson. Although the TULF always distanced itself from the violence of "the boys," the youth movements played a major part in its electoral successes in the north and east. The TULF swept the Tamil areas in the general elections of 1977 and claimed a mandate, on the basis of its manifesto, to establish a separate state of Tamil Eelam in the Northern and Eastern provinces. By then the Tamil New Tigers had become the LTTE and had made its presence felt when Prabhakaran personally assassinated Alfred Duraiappah, the Sri Lanka Freedom Party mayor of Jaffna, signaling the militants' growing disenchantment with establishment Tamils.

It was not long before the increasing violence, including the routine murder of policemen and police informers whose bodies were hung on lamp-posts as examples to others, forced President Junius Jayewardene's government to send Brigadier Tissa Weeratunge to Jaffna with orders to "eliminate the menace of terrorism." Despite "Bull" Weeratunge's best efforts, the militancy grew and by the early 1980s the various youth groups, including the LTTE, were strong enough to take over police stations, seize weapons, and rob banks. By the time the anti-Tamil riots of July 1983 erupted, following an LTTE ambush near Jaffna University that killed 13 soldiers, the Tigers had the capability to detonate landmines under military convoys and an armory that included grenades and automatic weapons.

The 1983 riots blackened Sri Lanka's image internationally largely because the security forces and police, angered by the killing of their fellow officers in the Tamil-dominated north, ignored or sometimes encouraged attacks on Tamils in the Sinhalese majority areas of the south. These events attracted global attention to the separatist drive as thousands of Tamil refugees fled to the neighboring state of Tamil Nadu in south India. With public opinion in Tamil Nadu and in the West favoring the Tamil cause, and with India actively arming and training the rebels, the LTTE was able to grow considerably in strength, brutally eliminating rival militant groups and increasingly challenging the military. Even the TULF that had once nurtured "the boys" was not spared, with many of its leaders assassinated both in the north as well as in Colombo.

Prabhakaran, who had indoctrinated young Tamils on the need for a separate state, has been able to inspire fanatical devotion to his cause. A core of suicide cadres, including the young woman who killed Prime Minister Rajiv Gandhi in India in 1991, has been developed, giving the Tigers a frightening terrorist capability. The trademark cyanide capsule that LTTE members wear around their neck to bite if captured—so that they will tell no tales even under torture—has often been used. Though banned as a terrorist organization in some countries such as India (where Prabhakaran is wanted for Rajiv Gandhi's assassination), the United States, and Canada, the LTTE has been able to establish an effective international presence in Western Europe and North America. Its fundraising abilities (including extortion), especially among nearly a million expatriate Tamils living and working in the West, are immense. In addition to arms captured from the Sri Lanka army, military hardware including sophisticated weapons are regularly procured and landed in the war zone under its control. Sri Lanka now spends between 5 and 6 percent of GDP on the war with the Tigers, and the security forces have been expanded from 10,000 in 1983 to 120,000 today.

An awesome ability to carry out terrorist strikes anywhere within Sri Lanka remains a potent weapon in the LTTE armory. Although the security forces continue to enjoy a monopoly on air power in the war, the Tigers in recent years have acquired an antiaircraft capability and have shot down several government aircraft, requiring the air force to fly circuitous sea routes to reach airfields in government-controlled northern and eastern areas.

The India Factor

The civil war in Sri Lanka continues, despite the enormous resources deployed to militarily subdue the LTTE, because of the active role India played in fostering the early insurgency. India came into the equation in the post-1983 period, justifying its role in arming and training the rebels by pointing to "subregional sentiments" in Tamil Nadu favoring the "struggle" of fellow Tamils in Sri Lanka. The influx of Sri Lankan Tamil refugees into Tamil Nadu strengthened its hand. The Indian national press and the international media routinely exposed the help given the Tamil rebels by various Indian governmental agencies.

J. N. Dixit, who served as India's high commissioner in Colombo through the 1980s, has explained India's involvement by noting that President Jayewardene government's "serious apprehensions" of the rise in Tamil militancy in Sri Lanka were used by the United States and Pakistan to create a "politico-strategic pressure point against India." Dixit argues that with large-scale sympathy for the plight of Sri Lanka's Tamils in Tamil Nadu, which was governed by an ethnic Tamil political party, Prime Minister Indira Gandhi had to take note of subregional sentiments.

"There was a perception," Dixit wrote in 1998, "that if India did not support the Tamil cause in Sri Lanka, and if the government of India tried to question the political and emotional feelings of the Sri Lanka[n] Tamils, there would be a resurgence of Tamil separatism in India. India, who could therefore not remain unconcerned about Sri Lankan developments during Mrs. Ghandi's second tenure, chose the option of supporting the Sri Lankan Tamils."

Apart from its role of arming and training the militants and providing them with staging and basing facilities in Tamil Nadu, India played a major part in helping the LTTE survive the fiercest military thrust launched against it, the Sri Lanka army's Operation Liberation of 1987. That effort was on the verge of success when India signaled that unless the operation was abandoned, it would militarily intervene; Indian fighter plane–escorted aircraft entered Sri Lankan air space to drop token food packages over the northern Jaffna peninsula where people, New Delhi claimed, were being starved by the Colombo government. President Jayewardene called off the operation, paving the way for India to offer its "good offices" for a settlement of Sri Lanka's ethnic problem. It was an offer that Jayewardene could not refuse despite widespread Sinhalese opposition.

Indian Prime Minister Rajiv Gandhi came to Colombo in July 1987 to sign the Indo–Lanka accord, under which it was agreed that Sri Lanka would grant regional autonomy to its provinces, similar to what had been obtained in the Indian states. In return, the LTTE was required to lay down its arms and enter the political mainstream. India was to underwrite the agreement and send a peacekeeping force to the northeast to ensure that all parties conformed to the terms of the agreement. But the Tamil claim of the Northern and Eastern provinces as their traditional homeland was a sticking point, since non-Tamils constituted the majority in the Eastern province, which is populated by Sinhalese, Tamils, and Muslims in approximately equal proportions. It was, however, agreed that the Northern and Eastern provinces would be temporarily merged, and within a year the people of the east would determine by referendum whether they wished to remain linked to the north. This referendum has never been held.

The Liberation Tigers flatly turned down the accord when it was first shown in New Delhi. It took a great deal of persuasion, including a personal meeting between Prabhakaran and Rajiv Gandhi, financial sweeteners, and a guarantee that the LTTE would be given the dominant role in the administration of the merged Northeast, before Prabhakaran reluctantly agreed.

Although India naïvely believed that the Tigers were sincere when they consented to the agreement, Prabhakaran voiced his suspicions in the first public speech he made after signing the accord. "I do not think that as a result of this agreement there will be a permanent solution to the problems of the Tamils. The time is not far off before the monster of Sinhalese racism will devour us. . . . I have unrelenting faith in the proposition that only a separate state of Tamil Eelam can offer a permanent solution to the problem of the people of Tamil Eelam."

The Indian peacekeeping force arrived in northeast Sri Lanka on July 30, 1987 and supervised what was an obviously token surrender of arms by the Liberation Tigers. Meanwhile, a vicious insurrection opposing the Indian intervention flared in the predominantly Sinhalese areas of south Sri

Lanka, forcing President Jayewardene to deploy the army, which was confined to its barracks in the northeast, to the south. This rebellion, led by the People's Liberation Front, took the country to the brink of anarchy but was eventually quelled in 1989 under the presidency of Ranasinghe Premadasa, who had succeeded Jayewardene the previous year.

The Indian peacekeeping force saturated the northeast with troops; the first Indian-supervised election in November 1988 to the temporarily merged Northeastern Provincial Council, which had been created under the terms of the accord, was won by the Eelam People's Revolutionary Liberation Front. The Liberation Tigers boycotted this election; the Indians backed the front.

The Indian peacekeeping force quickly found itself at war with the LTTE and was soon charged with the same human rights violations once leveled against the Sri Lankan army. The Indians helped Tamil militant groups opposed to the Liberation Tigers to form what was called the Tamil National Army in preparation for their eventual withdrawal, while the war against the LTTE intensified. Meanwhile, President Premadasa, who had strongly opposed the Indian intervention, began making common cause with the LTTE to secure the Indian withdrawal. When the peacekeeping force was "de-inducted" (that is, withdrawn) in March 1990, the LTTE moved in to take control of the northeast. The Northeastern Provincial Council was dissolved by Colombo, its chief minister going into exile with the Indians. The Tigers then turned to the Tamil National Army and its allies, killing thousands of members and supporters and seizing their arms while the survivors fled to India in large numbers.

No Settlement in Sight

Having burnt its fingers badly both militarily and diplomatically, India is unlikely to intervene again in Sri Lanka's internal affairs. Fences between Colombo and New Delhi have been mended, and India, which has proscribed the LTTE as a terrorist organization, currently cooperates with Sri Lanka on security matters. No Tamil militants can now find safe haven on Indian territory. Nevertheless, the LTTE maintains informal supply lines in India, and, despite naval patrolling, there is regular boat traffic between the south Indian and north Sri Lankan coasts, facilitated by fishermen from both countries. Despite the fallout from Rajiv Gandhi's assassination, the Tigers are not altogether without friends in India.

Although the Tigers have been outlawed in the United States and Canada, where large numbers of Tamils live, the LTTE retains its fundraising capabilities in these countries as well as in Western Europe. It also maintains an international secretariat in London; Britain remains reluctant to accede to Colombo's request to close it down because there is no hard evidence that it is used for purposes of terrorism.

The major obstacle to any settlement of the conflict is the Liberation Tigers' demand for a separate state. Although the guerrillas have repeatedly indicated they are open to negotiation on this question, past experience has made Colombo wary. But given the war weariness of the Sri Lankan people, conditions are conducive for peacemaking, although formidable obstacles exist. On one side is the seeming intractability of the LTTE's demand for a state, and on the other, growing Sinhalese fears that the devolution package proposed as a basis of settlement will only aggravate an already unhappy situation (under the plan a "union of regions" would be granted substantial powers currently held by the central government).

A strong body of opinion in Sri Lanka holds that peace will be possible only following the military subjugation of the LTTE. Having abandoned the peace platform on which it was elected in 1994, President Chandrika Kumaratunga's government has tried to weaken the Tigers through several major military offensives, with heavy casualties on both sides. The government hopes it can isolate the Tigers by winning acceptance of other Tamil groups to its devolution proposals for regional autonomy. Many of these Tamil groups can survive Tiger attacks only because of government-provided security and are unable to travel freely in those areas where the LTTE is active. Most recently, the TULF's Neelan Tiruchelvam, who played a major role in drafting the government's devolution proposals, was assassinated in Colombo by a suicide killer.

The prospects of an early end to the war seem remote. The LTTE favors third-party mediation, but Colombo has rejected this approach (although Foreign Minister Lakshman Kadirgamar officially has said there is no objection to a "facilitator"). Direct negotiations with the LTTE are inevitable if the war is to end. It is also necessary that the two main political forces in the south, the ruling People's Alliance and the opposition United National Party, present a common front to the Tigers. But with a presidential election scheduled for early 2000, and with a parliamentary election to follow, nothing in this direction can happen in the short term.

Despite the periodic communal rioting they have faced, large numbers of Tamils continue to live, work, and buy property in predominantly Sinhalese areas of the country, an implicit acknowledgment that 1983 is now only a bad memory. And many Tamils have fled territory contested by the government and the LTTE to live in predominantly Sinhalese areas where they feel safer and living conditions are infinitely superior. Even if there is to be a separate Tamil state in the future, large numbers of Tamils living among the Sinhalese will not want to return to it.

8. Making Peace in Sri Lanka

April 2001

MIRIAM YOUNG

The conflict in Sri Lanka has been raging with varying degrees of intensity since 1983. Termed the "No Mercy War" by the International Committee of the Red Cross, it has caused at least 65,000 deaths, displaced up to 1 million people, resulted in severe human rights abuses, and slowed Sri Lanka's once-promising development. The war has received little attention outside the region, but in April 2000, as the conflict intensified on the battlefield, it took on an international dimension involving Norway, the United States, and India.

Politicizing the Ethnic Divide

An island nation off the southeastern tip of India, Sri Lanka gained independence from Britain in 1948. Its population is made up of Sinhalese (74 percent), Tamils (18.1 percent), and Muslims (7.1 percent). The Sinhalese are mainly Buddhist, the Tamils Hindu; members of both groups make up the small population of Christians. Although religion plays a role in the conflict, most Sri Lankans view its origins more in ethnic than religious terms.

Sri Lanka's troubles are rooted primarily in the practices of its former colonial power and in unaddressed political and economic grievances following independence. The country has had three colonial masters, beginning with the Portuguese in the 1500s, followed by the Dutch in the eighteenth century, and finally the British. Although the Portuguese and Dutch colonized the coastal areas and imposed their religion on portions of the population, it was the British who, in 1815, succeeded in conquering the entire island, taking control of the former Kandyan kingdom in the central highlands. The British established a political and administrative structure throughout the island.

Unlike India, Sri Lanka did not wage a violent struggle for independence from Great Britain. But the members of the Sinhalese majority in particular resented the long years under colonialism that had deprived them of their language and culture, and had diminished the role of Buddhism in their society. Anti-Western sentiment drove the development of a Sinhalese Buddhist nationalist ideology. The goal of the movement was to restore Sinhalese society to its original "glorious" state, with an emphasis on traditional Buddhist values of morality and piety. Sinhalese villagers would return to their agricultural livelihoods, and the Buddhist monk would regain his status as head of the community. However, what began as anti-Western sentiment and a search for identity began to take on an anti-Tamil tone as well.

The Descent into War

The British practiced their "divide-and-rule" tactic in Sri Lanka as they had in many of their colonies. British missionaries, finding it difficult to counter the influence of Buddhist monks, focused their attention on the Tamils in the north of the country. Tamils consequently benefited from missionary education and were favored for positions in the colonial administration. Successive postindependence Sinhalese governments tried to reverse this perceived injustice, instituting policies that increasingly put Tamils at a disadvantage for both government positions and jobs in the professions.

The most polarizing moves were the institution of the "Sinhala-only" language act in 1956, regulations for university admissions that effectively required Tamil students to receive higher marks to qualify, and, in 1972, a new constitution creating the Republic of Sri Lanka that gave the "foremost place" to Buddhism. Tamil political parties protested these moves and demanded constitutional guarantees for equal rights, but to no avail. The unwillingness of successive governments to address these grievances escalated a political conflict to a violent and multidimensional one. Communal violence that began in the late 1950s but had its worst outbreak in 1983 killed thousands of Tamils and left many more homeless.

Feeling increasingly marginalized, some Tamils gave up trying to secure their rights within the Sri Lankan state and organized armed groups to fight the government. Calls for greater autonomy turned into a call for secession. The Liberation Tigers of Tamil Eelam (LTTE), which emerged as the region's most militarily efficient and ruthless guerrilla group, is locked in battle with the government's forces. The LTTE's stated goal is the creation of Tamil Eelam, a separate Tamil state that would comprise the north and east of the island. Despite being vastly outnumbered by government troops, the LTTE has combined guerrilla tactics and conventional warfare to engage the government in a drawn-out war that most observers believe cannot be won on the battlefield.

Although the government of Sri Lanka is a party to the Geneva Conventions, and the LTTE has expressed its commitment to respect them, both sides are guilty of torture, illegal detention, disappearances, and extrajudicial execution. Few prisoners are taken, and the numbers of dead are difficult to assess since access to the conflict areas by independent journalists is not permitted and the government imposes censorship on war reporting. Information in LTTE zones is under their complete control.

Provision of food and medicine to both the displaced and resident civilians in LTTE-controlled regions is a volatile issue. The government imposes heavy restrictions on all such items and aid agencies walk a tight line between voicing their protest and risking denial of permission to work at all. The country also suffers from a brain drain as thousands of educated Tamils (and many Sinhalese) have left Sri Lanka to seek better lives.

Several obstacles have prevented a peaceful settlement of the conflict: the intense rivalry between the two main Sinhalese political parties—the People's Alliance (PA) and the United National Party (UNP); the fierce opposition of the Buddhist clergy to any accommodation of Tamil grievances, which it views as threatening to Sinhalese Buddhism; government reluctance to accept outside, third-party assistance; and the apparent unwillingness of the LTTE to entertain any settlement short of a separate state. Following the December 1999 presidential elections (which returned Chandrika Kumaratunga for a second five-year term), it seemed that the UNP would support the ruling PA's proposals for constitutional changes that, by devolving power to the provinces, would help address Tamil grievances. The UNP dropped its support, however, when the reforms were introduced into parliament in August 2000, and the PA then withdrew the proposals.

Peace Prospects

The Sri Lanka government has traditionally opposed any form of third-party involvement in negotiating a settlement of the conflict, while the LTTE has consistently asked for international mediation. A hopeful sign appeared early in 2000 when Norway confirmed that it had begun talks with both sides. Since then, Norway's specially appointed envoy, Erik Solheim, has traveled repeatedly to the capital city of Colombo to meet with the government and other political parties, and to London to meet with the LTTE's main negotiator, Anton Balasingham.

But events took an unexpected turn at the end of April, when the LTTE captured an army base (called Elephant Pass) at the foot of the northern peninsula of Jaffna. The LTTE appeared set to take back the peninsula—the heart of the traditional Tamil homeland—that it had lost to the army in 1995. Faced with a humiliating defeat, the government embarked on a massive arms-buying campaign. The LTTE turned to international fundraising efforts and apparently stepped up their recruitment of children (to be trained for their guerrilla cadres). Both sides rejected offers of a cease-fire, and Norway's peace initiative was overshadowed as the focus returned to the battlefield.

Several developments over the last few months now seem to offer a glimmer of hope. Norway's Solheim has continued to shuttle between Colombo and London, holding talks with the government and the LTTE's political representative.[1] To prepare the ground for negotiations, Solheim has pushed for the government's agreement to lift its economic embargo on food and medicine to the north; in return the LTTE would desist from its practice of sending suicide bombers to attack civilian targets in the south. The talks would also take place in the framework of maintaining the territorial integrity of the country, something the international community has made absolutely clear is not negotiable.

The sincerity of the two antagonists about holding peace talks is open to debate, but several factors have encouraged both sides. The government's defense budget is crippling the economy. Development projects have been put on hold as defense expenditures have increased drastically. At a recent meeting in Paris, Sri Lanka's donor governments made it clear

---

1. Norway is one of several countries that have offered over the years to facilitate talks between the Sri Lanka government and the LTTE. It is the only country that has been accepted by both sides, perhaps due to its perceived neutrality and its record in aiding the start of the Middle East peace talks.

that resolving the ethnic conflict was key to further development of the country. The LTTE is under the shadow of recently passed legislation against terrorism in the United Kingdom. In February the British government named the LTTE, along with 20 other groups, to its official terrorist list. While the exact implications of such a ban are unclear at this time, it seems at least likely that the LTTE will be unable to maintain its political representation in London and that it will suffer further damage to its public image.

The LTTE seized the diplomatic initiative in December 2000 when it announced a month-long unilateral cease-fire, which it has renewed twice since. Although under pressure from the Western diplomatic community to reciprocate, the government has maintained that peace talks can begin even while the war continues. Unfortunately, the increased military power has led some elements of the government and the extreme Sinhalese factions of society to believe the war can be won militarily.

Attracting America's Interest

Until the recent escalation of the conflict, Sri Lanka's war has played mostly to the side of the world stage, with little interest from the international community. The war has appeared to hold no strategic value for the United States other than as a potential gateway to trade on the subcontinent, despite occasional claims of United States military interest in the eastern port of Trincomalee.

Successive Colombo governments have succeeded in portraying a country mainly unaffected by the war, except for a "terrorist" problem in the north and east. From the late 1970s the socialist-oriented policies of earlier governments were abandoned to embrace a market economy, and to conform to International Monetary Fund and World Bank structural adjustment policies. These factors have earned Colombo United States support, and however flawed its democracy might be in practice, the Sri Lanka government generally enjoys an automatic "benefit of the doubt" when it comes to war conduct and human rights abuses.

The Clinton administration generally restricted its role in the conflict to expressing support for a negotiated political settlement that protects the rights of minorities and guarantees equal rights for all Sri Lankans. It strongly supported the current government's proposed constitutional changes known as the devolution, or peace package, even after its usefulness was questioned because of process concerns and a progressive weakening of the document. In 1999 the United States State Department expressed its willingness to serve as a facilitator for talks if requested by the Sri Lanka government, an indication of increasing potential involvement, although the same offer has been made by other governments.

Washington has been willing to criticize the Sri Lankan government on certain human rights issues, but it usually stops short of voicing its displeasure publicly, as illustrated by its unwillingness to sponsor a resolution at the United Nations Commission on Human Rights in Geneva. United States officials have attempted to make use of the recent Leahy Amendment (which prohibits training of any foreign military personnel known to have committed human rights abuses) to screen Sri Lankan military officers for American training.

Previously the United States had been fairly receptive to the concerns expressed both by the Sri Lanka government and the LTTE, but this changed in 1997 when the LTTE was formally designated by the United States government as a terrorist organization. This label has had the unfortunate consequence of removing channels of communication between the United States and the LTTE and has reduced its potential ability to influence the LTTE. The United States has admitted that the terrorist designation has had no effect on the behavior of the LTTE, and no alternative initiatives apparently have been tried.

American officials have downplayed media reports about increasing United States military assistance to Sri Lanka, yet some major United States weapons purchases by the Sri Lanka government and increased joint training exercises with the Sri Lankan forces would seem to support this claim. The United States has carried out military cooperation activities with Sri Lanka, including the training of Sri Lankan security forces by the Green Berets and Navy SEALS in areas such as long-range patrolling, tactical reconnaissance, and rapid-reaction air and sea attacks. The United States must also approve the sale of United States–made military equipment used in foreign-built weaponry. Sri Lankan purchases of Kfir jets from Israel— secured after Sri Lanka suddenly reestablished severed diplomatic ties with Israel—required United States approval because of the American-made engines in the jets.

Given the growing United States relationship with India, and its secondary interest in Sri Lanka, Washington has had no problem deferring to

India as the regional power.[2] The escalation on the battlefield and Sri Lanka's turn to India for diplomatic help shifted the attention away from Norway's peace initiative to power politics, and set up a Norway-India-United States triangle.

The United States and Peace in Sri Lanka

Norway has demonstrated a serious commitment to acting as a facilitator in ending the Sri Lanka conflict. This is not an appropriate role for Washington. However, the United States can and should play a constructive role in long-term efforts to bring about a resolution. The United States can use its influence to increase pressure on Sri Lanka on issues of governance and human rights. Human rights and democracy activists have noted the steady erosion of democratic norms and practices over the course of the war, increasing levels of violence in society, the lack of prosecutions for serious human rights abuses, crackdowns on freedom of expression, and fraudulent election practices. American criticism of the draconian security measures during a visit last year by Undersecretary of State Thomas Pickering surely had a role in the subsequent easing of censorship on foreign media and lifting of the ban on public gatherings.

The United States must also continue to raise the issues of impunity, torture, freedom of expression, and provision of food and medical care to the displaced Tamils. It can, for example, encourage the Sri Lanka government to host a visit from UN High Commissioner Mary Robinson as well as the UN special rapporteur on freedom of expression.

Unless consistent pressure is placed on both the LTTE and the government, neither is likely to make efforts to change. Although the parties cannot be forced to the negotiating table, points of leverage must be considered. One such lever is aid, an option donor countries previously

2. The crisis in Jaffna brought India back onto the scene for the first time since the late 1980s, when it attempted unsuccessfully to make peace in Sri Lanka with the Indo-Lanka accords. Events in Sri Lanka, particularly the outcome of the conflict, will have an impact on India's complex domestic scene. Although the LTTE has the sympathy of many of India's Tamils in the state of Tamil Nadu, the group's leader, Velupillai Prabhakaran, stands accused of the assassination of Indian Prime Minister Rajiv Gandhi in 1991. India faces many of its own separatist movements and would view a newly formed state to its south as a threat to its territorial integrity.

have been unwilling to use but which they now appear to be reconsidering, given that the Sri Lanka government is presently channeling a far higher proportion of its resources into the war. At the same time, it would be helpful for the United States to find a way to open communication with the LTTE, as it has done this with other guerrilla groups.

For any negotiations to succeed, process and the negotiators' degree of preparedness are important factors. Do the parties have the necessary abilities for talks to have a chance of success? Neither the government nor the LTTE has exhibited such skills in the past, and neither seems to have sufficiently prepared for talks. The United States and other governments should not overlook this in a sudden hurry to begin negotiations. They must urge both sides to prepare carefully by learning negotiation techniques and by encouraging a slow, step-by-step process to the talks.

Civil society organizations in Sri Lanka opposed to the government's military solution are working to create a momentum for peace as well as to counter the increasing level of violence within society as a result of the war. Surveys of the population indicate that a significant percentage of Sinhalese do not believe the war can be won on the battlefield. Increasingly they favor resolving the conflict through peaceful negotiations; several impressive demonstrations for peace have brought together thousands of Sri Lankans from all ethnic groups. The space for such groups to work has narrowed, however, and extreme elements of Sinhalese society are drowning out their voices. The United States should encourage these civil society groups and assist them in being heard.

United States military assistance has no place in a war that requires a political rather than a military solution. Whether or not the level of such assistance is significant, it sends a message that does not encourage efforts in Sri Lanka to resolve deep-seated conflict and ensure the protection of minority rights.

Sri Lanka's troubles will be solved only through a political settlement that guarantees the fundamental freedom and human dignity of all Sri Lanka's citizens, regardless of ethnic or religious identity. The United States must make stronger efforts to move the government in that direction while discouraging the military option.

9. Why Peace Won't Come to Kashmir

April 2001

ALEXANDER EVANS

The Kashmir problem is at once both simple—and complex.[1] In the nineteenth century the state of Jammu and Kashmir emerged as a quiltwork of different regions and peoples. It was mainly established by conquest as its Hindu prince gobbled up different territories near his capital city of Jammu. These gains included the famous Kashmir Valley, which was purchased from the British in 1846. The Kashmir Valley has long been the romantic destination of choice in South Asia. A fertile valley 85 miles long and 25 miles deep, it sits amid some of the most dramatic mountains imaginable. Approximately 3.5 million people live there today, over 95 percent of whom are Muslim. Since the 1930s the valley's inhabitants have agitated against rule by outsiders—rulers who have neither spoken their language nor granted them the right to run their own affairs. Until 1947 this antagonism was mainly directed against the Hindu maharaja, who imposed heavy taxes and did as much as he could to forestall the rise of democracy in his state.

Since 1947 much of this disaffection has been transferred to India, which today controls the eastern part of the old princely state, effectively composed of three regions. There is the Kashmir Valley, font of much florid British and Mughal poetry. There is the barren, arid, and vast region called Ladakh. Sparsely populated, its inhabitants are mostly Buddhist and look toward Tibet and India. Even the significant Shia Muslim minority in

1. Useful accounts of contemporary Kashmir include Victoria Schofield, *Kashmir in Conflict: India, Pakistan and the Unfinished War* (London: I. B. Tauris, 2000); Sumantra Bose, *The Challenge in Kashmir: Democracy, Self-Determination, and a Just Peace* (New Delhi: Sage, 1997); and Robert Wirsing, *India, Pakistan, and the Kashmir Dispute* (London: Macmillan, 1998).

Ladakh tends away from Pakistan, perhaps driven by commercial and sectarian logic: in Indian hands, they reside on a major trade route between the Kashmir Valley and Ladakh. And Shia-Sunni tensions in Sunni-majority Pakistan are well known.

The third part of Indian Kashmir is the Jammu region. Once majority Muslim, this low-lying area of hills saw massive population transfers in communal violence in 1947 and 1948 that accompanied the independence of India and the birth of Pakistan. Hindus and Sikhs fled the Pakistani-controlled zone for Indian Kashmir, and Muslims were driven in the opposite direction. The Dogra Hindus compose a majority of Jammu province. They formed the core of the old princely state, and even today took to India as their home. The remaining Muslim minority in Jammu province has more mixed views.

Pakistan controls two other regions of the former princely state: Azad ("Free") Kashmir, a crescent-shaped slice of western Kashmir, and the vast, mountainous northern territories. The inhabitants of these regions are almost entirely Muslim, and they are mostly comfortable under Pakistani rule. But in Pakistani Azad Kashmir, there is also an independence movement, concentrated mainly in the southern Mirpur district.

The division of Kashmir came about in October 1947. Following partition of India and Pakistan, the maharaja could choose to join India or Pakistan. By the time he opted for India a war was already raging in his state between supporters of pro-Indian and pro-Pakistani factions. After a year of fighting that effectively set the division of Kashmir that exists today, the UN stepped in. But UN resolutions promising a plebiscite, and two more wars (in 1965 and 1971) between India and Pakistan over Kashmir, have failed to deliver a solution. Both countries lay claim to the entire state of Jammu and Kashmir.

In 1988 an insurgency began in the Kashmir Valley. Led by young nationalists from the Jammu Kashmir Liberation Force (JKLF), it was supported by hundreds of thousands of Kashmiris, who flooded onto the streets in early 1990 to demand a plebiscite on the future of Kashmir. India responded with force; it called the insurgency a proxy war by Pakistan and sent security forces into the state. The militancy (as it is called by supporters and opponents alike in Kashmir) gathered strength after 1990 and has become mainly driven by armed groups seeking union with Pakistan. Pakistan in turn supported the militants. A JKLF cease-fire in 1994, however, helped turn the militancy more Islamist, as groups like the Lashkar-e-Toiba and Harkat-ul-Ansar joined, bringing hardened fighters from the Afghan war. These fighters form the militant core today, and continue to wage guerrilla war on Indian forces.

In response to the insurgency, the Indian government reintroduced direct rule in Kashmir in 1990, with India ruling through a series of appointed governors who exercised executive authority. Indian security forces moved in, and the Kashmiri civil administration collapsed, with the educational system disrupted, taxes and services unpaid, and the courts in disarray.

Various explanations for the origins of the violence have been given, but generally it can be said to have been a combination of internal causes (disaffection with Indian rule, administration, and policies) and external factors (support from Pakistan and changes to the international system in 1989).[2] In India it is generally viewed as a proxy war, initiated and supported by Pakistan.[3] Pakistan sees it as an indigenous uprising for self-determination.[4] Inevitably, it is more complicated. But as one militant put it, "When Pakistan alone tried to create militancy, it failed. When Kashmiris alone tried to do it, they also failed. But in a combination it worked in 1988."

Each year the insurgency has continued, fresh graves have been dug in Kashmir. Families across the valley bury their sons while Indian families receive news that their sons too have fallen in the fighting. But India loves Kashmir too much to let it go, and despite their casualties militants believe that only force will persuade India to leave. Since the insurgency began at least 35,000 people have been killed. Most, inevitably, are civilians. Another recent estimate suggests that the conflict has created 100,000 orphans. It is certainly the case that each and every family in the Kashmir Valley has been touched by the state of siege that has endured there. And while Kashmiris are generally tired of the violence, there seem to be few alternatives. India pinned many of its hopes to resolve the militancy and restore Kashmiri support with local assembly elections in September 1996, which despite a poor turnout produced a Kashmiri state government led by Farooq Abdullah.

Promising jobs and autonomy, Abdullah's arrival led to a brief spurt of optimism, and some dampening of militancy, between 1996 and 1998. But

---

2. See Sumit Ganguly, *The Crisis in Kashmir: Portents of War, Hopes of Peace* (New York: Cambridge University Press, 1997); and Schofield, *Kashmir in Conflict*.

3. A sophisticated version of this is Manoj Joshi, *The Lost Rebellion: Kashmir in the Nineties* (New Delhi: Penguin Books India, 1999).

4. See Tahir Amin, *Mass Resistance in Kashmir: Origins, Evolution, Options* (Islamabad: Institute of Policy Studies, 1995).

all too soon this façade of normality crumbled. Economic development is out of the picture since the government depends on subsidies from New Delhi just to pay official salaries. And Abdullah's proposals for autonomy, presented to the Indian government in 2000, were unceremoniously rejected. As a result—and aided by continuing Kashmiri resentment—the militancy has picked up once more.

The War for Public Opinion

The militancy represents only one aspect of the Kashmir crisis: the simplistic frames through which Kashmir is presented to the public in India and Pakistan make public opinion a force to be reckoned with. Information is a battleground in Kashmir. Some of the propaganda images tell a story in themselves. In the office of Khem Sharma, assistant director of information for Jammu and Kashmir, hangs a photo of a Kashmiri woman entirely covered from head to toe in a black *burqa*, a traditional conservative Muslim style of dress. She holds up a cardboard slogan: "I love my India, I hate Pakistan." This is relatively sophisticated, but exaggeration and disinformation persist on all sides. Nasim Zera, a Pakistani analyst, claims that 700,000 Indian troops occupy the Kashmir Valley (while difficult to verify, the actual number is less than 350,000).

In India, public opinion, as articulated by a more independent and private-sector broadcast media, is now a major factor in the country's foreign policy. This was evident during the mountain war fought between India and Pakistan near the Kashmiri town of Kargil in 1999, which ignited a strong burst of patriotic fervor. It was also a feature of the parliamentary elections the same year, in which an emotionally charged campaign was conducted on Indian television. Many of the numerous private cable-television companies that have sprung up since economic liberalization was initiated in India in the 1990s carried heroic images of Indian soldiers at the war front. On the cable channel Music Asia, the "Song for Kargil" music video was interspersed with footage of artillery shelling and Indian soldiers marching up mountains. Public opinion demanded a "strong" response from the Indian government to the Kargil intrusion by Pakistani forces, which explains why Indian forces pressed on against military common sense to retake mountain positions with heavy losses (official Indian figures state that 500 soldiers were killed in the offensive).

This potent combination of a competitive, private-sector broadcast media and a greater role for instant snapshots of public opinion reduces the Indian government's room to maneuver on Kashmir-related issues. Major concessions on Kashmir, even if there were a faction within government willing to offer them (which there is not), would be very difficult in the face of wide public opposition.

In Pakistan, public opinion on Kashmir is also important, but for different reasons. In the early 1990s, Pakistani Television (PVT) was at the forefront of a strong public-awareness campaign on Kashmir. State run, it was intended both to bolster support for the Kashmir cause and also, to more cynical analysts, provide a useful issue around which to mobilize a fractious nation. This campaign, aided and abetted by other forms of mass communication (for example, Kashmir Liberation Cells—state-sponsored propaganda centers—set up around the country) has been successful. Even with a military government in power, Kashmir remains too delicate a public issue for any Pakistani administration to deviate easily from the formal and long-standing policy toward Kashmir (although, as we will see, there have been some slight moves in that direction). But changing the emphasis of a policy is one thing; making major concessions of substance another.

In short, both India and Pakistan have active publics that make substantive concessions on Kashmir fraught with political danger. A brave administration in either country, well established, might be able to take the initiative. But the ease with which it could then be outflanked on the Kashmir issue and accused not of just weakness but of abandoning long-held national positions on Kashmir makes the cost-benefit analysis favor inertia. And this inertia partly explains the intractability of the Kashmir issue.

Peace Moves?

On February 22, 2001 India extended the cease-fire in Kashmir it originally announced in November 2000 for another three months. In announcing the move, Indian Prime Minister Atul Behari Vajpayee confounded skeptics who felt there was insufficient progress on the ground. Despite two previous extensions of the cease-fire, militant violence continued to wrack Kashmir. As it happens, 100 more people died in the 75 days following the initial Indian cease-fire than were killed in the same previous period.

Meanwhile, Pakistan's main initiative, to pull back some of its troops from the Line of Control that separates Indian and Pakistani Kashmir, continues. Since early December the line has fallen silent, in sharp contrast to the daily exchanges of small-arms fire and artillery that used to echo across the mountains. The only explosions that disturb the Jhelum Valley, leading up to the front line, are those set by work crews taking the opportunity to reconstruct the road. In the shadow of Indian and Pakistani bunkers Kashmiri farmers are trying to till their fields once more. For a brief moment no shells threaten them.

These developments during the winter of 2000 follow an earlier cease-fire by a leading Kashmiri militant group, the Hizbul Mujahadeen (HM). On July 24, 2000 HM's valley commander, Majid Dar, called a halt to operations against India. With him were the majority of his unit commanders in the valley. While all the other Kashmiri militant groups fought on, killing nearly 100 people over the next 24 hours, his surprise move left analysts wondering what might be happening behind the scenes. The cease-fire, however, swiftly crumbled when fighting broke out again on August 8.

Dar had failed to get political support from the separatist Kashmiri alliance, the All Parties Hurriyat Conference (APHC), which was angered that it had not been consulted. And Dar's own leader in Pakistan, militant chief Syed Salahuddin, was soon calling for the immediate direct involvement of Pakistan in any talks. This upset the Indians, who had been edging away from what at first was a novel position. Instead of suggesting talks on the basis of the Indian constitution—the maximum offer that has been made in the past—Prime Minister Vajpayee chose to offer a process in the name of *insanyat* (humanity). Sufficiently ambiguous, the banner of *insanyat* offered a way around the formal politics of the Kashmir issue. But even *insanyat* was too large a step for Indian hard-liners, and Vajpayee found himself backtracking within a few days. Once he made it clear that talks could only be within the Indian constitution, this window of opportunity was closed.

The winter 2000 process has been different. First, Kashmiri separatist politicians are at the center of the process—some being wooed by Delhi, others suspicious of Delhi's motives. The APHC, given a greater role by Pakistan, has been willing to give the Indian cease-fire the benefit of the doubt. But it is doubt in general that surrounds a process that, while it might deliver direct Indo-Pakistani talks, dances around some of the key differences that mark the Kashmir dispute.

The peace moves are being triggered not only by India and Pakistan but also the United States. All three countries have widely varying policy objectives on Kashmir.

Pakistan is economically weak and short of friends. Unwilling to compromise on Taliban-related issues, Pakistan's military leader, General Pervez Musharraf, is keen to make progress on the Kashmir issue. To this end there has been some movement from Islamabad.

Pakistan has signaled a subtle shift in its Kashmir policy, moving away from a position that it has held for over 50 years. This original position offered only two theoretical alternatives: the full accession of Kashmir to India or to Pakistan. Instead of calling for a solution in full accordance with 1948 United Nations resolutions (which call for demilitarization of the whole state, followed by an impartial plebiscite with only two choices: union with India or with Pakistan), Pakistan's military leaders are now stressing self-determination. This could be more flexible. Could it pave the way for the repartition of Kashmir, or even independence? Conservative Pakistanis say no, but the tone of the new position is more accommodating.

On February 12 the Pakistani interior minister, retired Lieutenant-General Moinuddin Haider, announced that the government had decided to ban fundraising by militant groups for jihad. It thus appears that the Pakistani government may be readying itself for confrontation with Islamist militant groups. It has also written to many of the madrassahs (Muslim religious schools) that provide militant recruits, asking for information about their activities. It is one thing to collect information on the groups, and on the madrassahs that feed recruits to them. But to crack down on them presents the military regime with a tremendous challenge.

As the militant groups themselves admit, Pakistan can probably cut off their access to Indian Kashmir. But this would be a major undertaking; as Brian Cloughley, a Western defense analyst puts it, the Pakistani army along the Line of Control would have to be willing to shoot members of the more Islamist militant groups. No matter how intact military discipline, he thinks that such orders might be disobeyed. The real problem is whether action can be taken to curb the activities of radical militant groups in Indian Kashmir when Pakistan itself is most vulnerable to their activities. As the government searches for investors and domestic political stability, it cannot afford the uncertainties these actions could bring.

India, however, is in a very strong position, and knows it. Although India formally lays claim to the entire state of Jammu and Kashmir, it does not really expect—or want—to rule the nearly all Muslim northern territories and Pakistani Kashmir. What it would like is recognition by the West—and Pakistan—of its current hold over Jammu, Kashmir, and

Ladakh. It has little to offer in return, but it does not need to. An end to militant violence would be a bonus, since it costs India financially to maintain such a major counter-insurgency in Kashmir. But India is willing to bear the cost, and can afford to.

The Indians are certainly delaying the issue of travel documents for a delegation of APHC leaders who have been invited to Pakistan. This may reflect serious divisions inside the Indian cabinet, with Home and Defense Ministers L. K. Advani and George Fernandes arguing that the cease-fire process is delivering little. Neither wants early talks with Pakistan, especially when militant violence continues. There are also divisions between those dealing with Kashmir. Officials in the prime minister's office, led by national security adviser Brajesh Mishra, support the process. But their counterparts in the Ministry of Home Affairs are said to be critical, perhaps in part because their responsibilities for Kashmir have been diluted. The latest, somewhat provocative comment from the home minister is an assertion that the cease-fire is merely a cessation of active operations. While strictly true, statements like this make it much harder for the APHC, militants, or Pakistan to respond favorably.

As the status quo power, India is seeking to legitimize the situation on the ground; Pakistan seeks to overturn it. The question of legal title to Kashmir, or what different segments of the Kashmiri population themselves want, is important but is subsumed to this compelling reality. Moves toward peace are likely to founder here—India can afford to wait, whereas Pakistan cannot.

Behind the scenes, the United States is pushing for direct Indo-Pakistani talks. It wants less tension in the region, and a corresponding reduction in the risk of war. While a solution to the Kashmir problem would be an added bonus, few American officials doubt the scale of that challenge. A new administration could make major mistakes in South Asia if it took too active a stance on Kashmir. Pakistan might welcome the interest, but not pressure, while India remains suspicious of American involvement in the first place.

Why Peace Won't Come

What is the answer to the Kashmir problem? It is clear that Valley Kashmiris just want to be left alone to run their own affairs. But whether they seek independence, union with Pakistan, or perhaps even autonomy within

India remains an open question. Local elections in Indian Kashmir offer limited choices. As one local journalist wryly noted, you can be anything you like so long as you're Indian. Muzaffarabad, the capital of Pakistani Kashmir, is not much different. While less publicized, the military government has been arresting Kashmiri proindependence activists once more.

But a walk up some of the narrow streets in Muzaffarabad's bazaar, with its splendid array of small shops, selling everything from carpets and candles to posters to prayer mats, offers a different perspective. In a few, collection boxes for different militant groups sit, waiting for spare change. While items for sale include luridly printed jihad folders for schoolchildren, it seems that some Kashmiris living on the Pakistani side of the line have views of their own, with a number of bazaar shopkeepers expressing their preference for independence. The militant groups, on the other hand, all seek the union of Kashmir with Pakistan.

Most international specialists on Kashmir tend to agree. An assortment of views are held about what different segments of Kashmiri society might want, if they could truly choose. But a solution to the problem of Kashmir remains in the hands of three distinct players: the Kashmiris, and the governments of India and Pakistan. No viable and lasting solution can emerge unless all three achieve some degree of satisfaction from the final agreement. And no talks can take place if possible concessions cross the increasingly visible line of public opinion in South Asia.

For now, peace process or not, the future of Kashmir looks much the same as the past. The Indian security forces will be around for a while. The militancy is not likely to go away quickly. And most of the world will still think of sweaters, or perhaps mountains, when it hears the word Kashmir.

10. Rebuilding Afghanistan

March 2002

MARINA OTTAWAY *and* ANATOL LIEVEN

Afghanistan after the Taliban may easily turn into a quagmire for the international community, and the wrong kind of international strategies may easily worsen both its problems and America's. In particular, to begin with a grossly overambitious program of reconstruction risks acute disillusionment, international withdrawal, and a plunge into a new cycle of civil war and religious fanaticism.

Ambitious plans to turn this war-hardened, economically ravaged, deeply divided country into a modern democratic state are being proposed and have even been incorporated into the December 5, 2001 Bonn agreement among Afghan leaders. But nobody is proposing the full-fledged, long-term military occupation that would be required even to attempt such a transformation—one reason being that past occupations, whether British or Soviet, have ended in utter disaster. At most, the international community is speaking of a relatively lightly armed presence in Kabul and certain other centers.

The chances of successfully imposing effective modern democratic state structures on Afghanistan thus are negligible. Even with a massive Western military presence on the ground, the West has already run into serious problems in transforming tiny Bosnia. Afghanistan is a country 12 times the size of Bosnia with 26 million people; an extremely difficult terrain; an ethnically, tribally, and religiously segmented society; and a fearsome array of battle-hardened warlords who have no good reason to give up their power.

But the world cannot afford to turn its back on Afghanistan in frustration, as it has done in the past, lest the country again become a haven for terrorists and an international threat. Afghanistan needs a modest reconstruction program that does not require full-fledged military occupation and is tailored to the reality of the country.

A Century of Troubled State Building

The Afghan state is a recent, partly colonial creation that has never commanded the full loyalty of its own citizens. Even today, many—perhaps most—Afghans give their primary allegiance to local leaders, ethnic groups, and tribes.

Afghanistan was only created at the end of the nineteenth century. All of its borders were determined by the British Empire, and reflected not an internal historical or ethnic logic, but an imperial one. Its northern border marked the furthest extent to which Britain was prepared to see the Russian empire advance. Its southern and eastern borders were the furthest limit to which the British Indian Empire felt it necessary and safe to extend itself. Within these borders an Afghan state with modern trappings was created by a confluence of British geopolitical interest and the ruthless government of King Abdur Rahman, the so-called Iron Amir, who reigned from 1880 to 1901. The king was a highly competent ruler who, by quite fiendish methods and with massive subsidies of money and weapons from the British, created the basis—albeit limited—for a centralized Afghan state.

Abdur Rahman's reign marked the start of the Afghan state-building process. In Europe, this process began in the early Middle Ages, stretched over several centuries with numerous catastrophic setbacks, and was attended by immense cruelty, resistance, and devastation. It therefore is hardly surprising that the very short Afghan state-building process met fierce resistance, had limited success, and ultimately collapsed—especially given the intensely warlike, independent, and anarchic traditions of many Afghan peoples, including the largest ethnos, the Pashtuns.

Abdur Rahman laid the foundations not only for the centralizing and modernizing Afghan state, but also for the alienation from that state of the religious, tribal, and ethnic groups that dominate Afghan society. This alienation helped bring about the failure of the Afghan constitutional monarchy in the 1960s and early 1970s and tore the country apart in the following decades.

Had the modern Afghan state succeeded in developing Afghanistan and bringing visible benefits to the mass of the population, hostility to the state would gradually have faded. But, as with state building in so much of the world, it failed to do so, and its one area of partial success helped seal its own fate. The modern education system, although limited to a small fraction of the population (and of course an even smaller proportion of women), created a mass of educated graduates and junior bureaucrats and military officers for whom no well-paying jobs could be found either in the impoverished private sector or state service. Their bitter frustration produced the communist revolution of 1978, which essentially was an attempt to relaunch the state's modernizing program in an ultraradical guise by returning to Abdur Rahman's savage methods.

The communists' program, like that of Abdur Rahman, depended critically on subsidies and weapons from an outside protector, in this case the Soviet Union. And as in the Iron Amir's time, this foreign support helped spark fierce resistance from a variety of religious, ethnic, and tribal groups. The resistance eventually triumphed, and between 1978 and 1992 it overthrew the communist regime and eventually the Afghan state itself, first in the mountains, then across most of the country, and finally in Kabul and the other main cities. Tragically, but not surprisingly, the resistance proved completely incapable of replacing this state with any unified authority of its own, except—after a period of violent chaos—in the pathological and temporary form of the Taliban.

The difficulty of creating an Afghan state based on anything but sheer coercion has been immensely complicated by the region's ethnic makeup. The original "state-forming" ethnic group, the Pashtuns, make up less than half the total population, with the rest divided among a wide range of different nationalities. Tajiks, Uzbeks, and Hazaras (Shias of Mongolian descent) are the largest groups and are mentioned most often, but several smaller ones play key roles in their own areas.

Equally important, the Pashtuns' own role in the history of the modern Afghan state has been profoundly ambiguous. Afghanistan is a Pashtun creation, achieved through a Pashtun dynasty, and to this day the Pashtuns constitute the core of the country. But Pashtun tribal society is highly segmented and thus radically unfit to serve as the basis for the formation of a unitary state. Pashtun and other tribal revolts against the state's modernizing policies, often led by local religious figures, plagued all Afghan rulers. They played a central part in the rebellion against communist rule, and in the general reaction against Western modernity and modern state institutions that followed.

The Choices

In the past several decades, the international community has relied on three approaches to deal with countries that descend into chaos. It has supported strongmen capable of reimposing order by force; it has given up in despair, leaving the country to sort out its problems as best it can; and, most recently, it has embarked on ambitious projects to reconstruct the country in the image of a modern secular, multiethnic, and democratic state. None of these approaches should be used in Afghanistan, but something can be learned from each of them.

A compromise approach needs to be based on an awareness both of Afghanistan's past and its present conditions, not on an image of the modern state the West would like it to become. The international community must recognize that in the northern half of the country, the coherence of the Northern Alliance is unlikely to last for long without its raison d'être of resistance to the Taliban, whereas in the Pashtun areas confusion reigns. In short, it will be extremely difficult to create any unifying political structures.

Heavily armed tribal groups will not surrender their arms or their local power unless they are forced to do so by a national government with a powerful army of its own or by an overwhelming outside force. Because the international community is not prepared to produce an occupying force on the same scale as that deployed in Bosnia and Kosovo—thus, many times larger in absolute terms—the democratic-reconstruction model cannot be implemented. Indeed, it would almost certainly fail even if such a force were deployed. The strategy therefore needs to be less invasive.

The now-discredited strongman model is historically the favored method to stabilize a country in crisis; it was freely employed, for instance, by the United States during the cold war and by France as part of its neo-colonial strategy in Africa. It is not ethically appealing, but it is cheap, can be effective for a time, and requires little effort on the part of international actors, who delegate the job of imposing order to local leaders. There is no conceivable strongman or strong organization for Afghanistan as a whole. There are, however, strongmen controlling different regions. They will remain part of the political scene, and the international community has no choice but to work with them as it has worked with other such leaders in the past.

Today's orthodox approach to restoring states is much more democratic, but also much more invasive and costly, yet not particularly successful. For the past 10 years, the explicit goal of the international community has been to transform countries in crisis into democratic states with a free market economy based on the argument that only such states benefit their citizens and safeguard the international need for stability in the long run. This Western-dominated sociopolitical engineering approach is becoming ever more complex and costly as experience reveals new areas where intervention is needed.

The components of the democratic-reconstruction model can be summarized as follows: the parties involved in the conflict must reach agreement on a new permanent political system. Elections must be held as soon as possible. The new state must be multiethnic, secular, and democratic—regardless of whether this has any basis in local tradition, or whether it is what the inhabitants of the country want. While the accord is being implemented, peace and order are guaranteed by an international force, as well as by the presence of a large number of UN administrators. The international financial institutions take on the restructuring of the country's economy. International nongovernmental organizations (NGOs) are funded to work in their specialized areas, ranging from humanitarian aid to election organizing.

Elements of the democratic-reconstruction model are already beginning to show up in the discussions of what to do in Afghanistan. The agreement reached by the Afghan factions in Bonn provides for the formation in six months of a broadly based interim government giving representation to all ethnic groups and to women, followed by elections two years later. Virtually all international organizations and NGOs demand strong action to promote women's rights. The World Bank's Afghanistan "Approach Paper" calls for helping the country to build a strong central bank and ministry of finance and for capacity building in all economic institutions. Other organizations target the strengthening of civil society. And this is only the beginning.

Not only is most of this impossible in Afghanistan today, but much of it fits only the wishes of a small minority of Westernized urban Afghans, many of whom have spent the past generation living in the West and are out of touch with their own society. They also, consciously or unconsciously, have a vested interest in Western strategies that would guarantee maximum employment and status for themselves. The model would need to be imposed on reluctant tribal leaders and warlords, on religious authorities, and probably on most ordinary Afghans, and would thus require a strong foreign military and civilian presence, projecting to the world the image of a Muslim country under foreign occupation. As in Somalia, the outcome would almost certainly be conflict between the international force and powerful local groups.

This conflict would most likely lead sooner or later to a swing in exactly the opposite direction, toward withdrawal and neglect, as happened in Somalia and in Afghanistan a decade ago. The reason was the same in both cases: the countries concerned did not appear sufficiently important to justify the effort to create order. The consequences of neglect were serious. Afghanistan became a haven for Al Qaeda. Somalia spawned not only harmless homegrown and clan-based Islamist groups but also al-Itihaad al-Islamiya, an organization aligned with Al Qaeda whose operatives were involved in the 1998 attacks on the United States embassies in Kenya and Tanzania.

In Somalia, however, neglect also had some positive consequences, and this lesson must be heeded in designing a strategy for Afghanistan. With no center to be held, and no pot of foreign aid to be fought over, fighting in Somalia was greatly reduced and mechanisms were developed to compensate for the absence of the state. This did not necessarily mean reverting to a completely primitive life within villages and clans. A new class of international traders emerged, for example, who are capable of financing complex transactions, making international payments, and developing markets.

The Somali experience has historical precedents. The "ordered anarchy" of medieval France, Germany, or Italy—characterized by multiple overlapping armed authorities—did not preclude the establishment of great and stable long-range trade routes and commercial and financial networks, major economic growth, and tremendous achievements in human culture. In the long run, these also laid the foundations for the growth of a modern judicial order, which in turn was an essential basis for the economic revolution and the modern state. The international community must initially accept some version of ordered anarchy in Afghanistan and work to attenuate its worst shortcomings.

The Right Choice

The international community's immediate aim for the Afghan government should therefore not be the impossible fantasy of a democratic government technocratically administering the country, but rather the formation of a loose national mediation committee functioning not just for the initial six months but indefinitely. This committee should seek not to create the entire apparatus of a modern state, but rather the minimal conditions for medieval civilization: the avoidance of major armed conflict, the security of main trade routes, and the safety and neutrality of the capital. These conditions should be secured not by an Afghan national army—another empty fantasy, given the present situation—but by an international force created by the United Nations and backed by the ultimate sanction of American airpower. An agreement on how to create such minimal conditions would be a greater accomplishment for the *loya jirga* called for by the Bonn agreement than would approval of a Western-style democratic constitution that could never be implemented.

Most Western aid therefore should not be directed through the Afghan government—even assuming that the appearance of a broadly based national government could be sustained—but should be provided directly to Afghanistan's regions. Aid should, moreover, be used in a quite clearheaded and tough way as an instrument of peacekeeping—as a way to give local warlords and armies an incentive not to go to war with each other. It would be a bribe of sorts, and might appear to perpetuate the power of warlords. But as Somalia and other African examples illustrate, greater risks would be involved in making the central government the chief channel for international aid, since this would make control of the government and the city of Kabul a vital goal for the country's various armed forces. Aid itself would become a source of future conflict.

Aid should also be provided directly at the local level, of course, to villages and local organizations. But the international community should have no illusion that it is possible to completely bypass warlords and tribal leaders in this fashion. In the end, as the experiences of aid agencies in many countries show, armed groups and powerful individuals always influence how aid is used in their areas.

The international strategy toward Afghanistan should therefore be based on these key principles:

- Discard the assessments of what help Afghanistan needs to become a modern democratic state and replace them with a sober evaluation of the minimal tasks a central administration needs to perform to allow a measure of normal life, economic activity, and, above all, trade.

- Work directly with regional leaders whose power is well established. Assign liaison officials to work with these leaders, monitor their behavior (especially their treatment of local ethnic minorities and their relations with other regions and ethnic groups), and make sure that they provide no shelter to terrorist groups.
- Instruct these liaison officials to work with international and domestic NGOs to ensure not only that they can work unhindered, but also that they do not become dangerously entangled in local politics.
- Create a corps of international civil servants to act as these liaison officials and otherwise assist Afghanistan. These officials should be paid generously in return for devoting a substantial term of service to this difficult and dangerous task and for investing in learning local languages, history, and customs; everything possible should be done to establish their position and prestige. A certain historical precedent here is provided by the British Empire's Indian Political Service, which managed—but, wisely, never tried to administer—the Pashtun tribal areas and handled relations with the Afghan monarchy.
- Give serious consideration to the standards that need to be met by local leaders in exchange for aid. Resist the temptation to impose unrealistic standards. Pick only a few battles to fight at one time. For example, make aid initially contingent on education for girls, but not on a comprehensive reform of legal or social codes governing the position of women in the family or major participation of women in administration. Incremental change is more likely to be sustainable.
- Accept that, even with checks and conditions, there will be corruption, and aid will help warlords consolidate their power and their client networks. Experience shows that corruption is inevitable whenever a country receives large amounts of aid, even if it is channeled through formal government institutions. Use aid quite consciously as a political tool to maintain peace.
- Establish certain basic national institutions in Kabul, but leave the question of a real national administration for Afghanistan for the distant future. Instead, treat the central government as a form of national mediation committee. Avoid making Kabul and the central government prizes worth fighting over.
- Create a substantial United Nations–mandated international force to ensure the security and neutrality of the city of Kabul as a place where representatives from different areas can meet and negotiate, and where

basic national institutions can be created. Be prepared to maintain this force for a period of several years, at least.

- Do not pursue democratic measures, such as organizing elections, that would increase competition at the center among different warlords or ethnoreligious groups: in present circumstances such elections could not possibly lead to stable democratic institutions.

What Is Needed

The United States and the international community do not need Afghanistan to become a modern democratic state—even a united one—to protect their key interests. They require a cessation of serious armed conflict and sufficient access to all parts of the country to ensure that it will not again become a haven for international terrorist groups and a source of destabilization for its neighbors. Beyond this, America's interests and capabilities are highly limited.

If Afghanistan could be turned by fiat into a Scandinavian welfare state, well run and capable of delivering services to its population, its people surely would benefit greatly. But the international community cannot deliver such a state. At best, experience shows it can deliver institutions that conform to the appearance of the modern state, but that function inefficiently and corruptly and that generate new conflicts over control.

What the people of Afghanistan need most urgently, and the international community can help them obtain, is the cessation of war and the possibility of pursuing basic economic activities free from brutal oppression, ethnic harassment, and armed conflict. They need to be able to cultivate their fields, sell their products, go to market, send their children to school, receive basic medical care, and move freely around the country. In the long run, much more would be desirable, but the first step should simply be to reestablish a degree of normal life, even if it is not life in a modern state. Just to achieve this much will require many years of careful, concentrated effort by dedicated international workers on the ground. More ambitious state-building plans must be left for another generation, and to the Afghans themselves.

11. A Blueprint for Afghanistan

April 2002

BARNETT R. RUBIN

For years, those concerned with the suffering and ordeals of the people of Afghanistan found it difficult to gain a hearing in the precincts of "high politics," where security dominated. Afghanistan was defined largely as a "humanitarian emergency" to be treated with charity. Leaders of some neighboring states, especially those from Central Asia, argued repeatedly that the failure to rebuild Afghanistan and provide its people with security and livelihoods threatened the region. Since 1998, an increase in what may, in retrospect, be called relatively small acts of terror traced to the Al Qaeda organization placed Afghanistan on the global security agenda. But the means chosen to address that threat—sanctions against the Taliban combined with humanitarian exceptions, with no reference to the country's reconstruction—showed that those setting the international security agenda had not drawn the connection between the terrorist threats to their own security and the threats to human security faced daily by the people of Afghanistan.

The Afghan people have for more than 20 years faced violence, lawlessness, torture, killing, rape, expulsions, displacement, looting, and every other element of the litany of suffering that characterizes today's transnational wars. Groups aided by foreign powers have, one after another, destroyed the irrigation systems, mined the pastures, leveled the cities, cratered the roads, blasted the schools, and arrested, tortured, killed, and expelled the educated. Statistics are few, but a 1988 study by demographer Marek Sliwinski estimated that "excess mortality," in his phrase, amounted to nearly one-tenth of Afghanistan's population between 1979 and 1987.

Some results of this destruction are summarized in the table on page 115. It shows that whatever measure of human welfare or security one chooses—life expectancy, the mortality of women and children, health, literacy, access to clean water, nutrition—Afghanistan ranks near the bottom of the human family. But this table shows something else as well. The figures in it are all rough estimates compiled by international organizations. Afghanistan is no longer even listed in the tables of the *World Development Report* published yearly by the United Nations Development Program because it has no national institutions capable of compiling such data.

In a widely reprinted 1981 lecture, Professor Amartya Sen compared the records of China and India in food security, particularly in the prevention of famine, and he demonstrated a fundamental result: access to information is a chief guarantor of human security. Sen showed that the restrictions placed on freedom of expression by the Chinese government allowed famine to rage unchecked during the Great Leap Forward in the late 1950s, whereas India's freer system more easily halted such disasters.

Afghanistan also faces a challenge of information, but an even more fundamental one than China: it has no institutions capable even of generating information about the society that could be used to govern it. Over the past two decades Afghanistan has been *ruled,* in whole or in part, at times badly and at times atrociously, but it has not been *governed.* Above all, the crisis of human security in Afghanistan is due to the destruction of institutions of legitimate governance. It is as much an institutional emergency as a humanitarian one. Accountable institutions of governance that use information to design policies to build the human capital of their citizens and support their citizens' economic and social efforts, and that allow others to monitor them through the free exchange of information, are the keys to human security.

The insecurity due to the absence of such institutions and the effect on the population accounts for many threats that Afghanistan has posed. The rise and fall of one warlord or armed group after another are largely the result of the ease with which a leader can raise an army in such an impoverished, ungoverned society. One meal a day can recruit a soldier. No authorities impede arms trafficking, and no one with power has had enough stake in the international order to pay it heed.

The expansion of the cultivation and trafficking of opium poppy constituted a survival strategy for the peasantry in this high-risk environment. Opium cultivation supplied not only income and employment, but cash for food security. Before 1978 Afghanistan was self-sufficient in food production, but it now produces less than two-thirds of its food needs. Futures

Measures of Human Security in Afghanistan

Indicators	Afghanistan	South Asia	Developing Countries	Industrial Countries
Human Development Index Rank (out of 174)	169	N/A	N/A	N/A
Percentage population with access to:				
Health care (1985–93)[a]	29	65	79	100
Safe water (1990–95)[b]	12*	77	69	100
Daily calorie supply per capita (1992)[b]	1,523	2,356	2,546	3,108
Infant mortality per 1,000 live births (1993)[b]	165	85	70	N/A
Under five mortality per 1,000 live births (1993)[c]	257	122	101	N/A
Maternal mortality per 100,000 live births (1993)	1,700[d] or 640[e]	469	351	10
Life expectancy at birth in years (1993)[a]	44	60	62	76
Adult literacy rate (%, 1993)[a,b]	28**	48	68	98

*(rural 5%, urban 39%)   **(men 45%, women 14%)

Note: All comparative data from other regions are from source (a) below. One indicator of humanitarian emergency in Afghanistan is the collapse of institutions able to produce such statistics. Hence, unlike such presumably better-governed countries such as Sierra Leone and Burundi, Afghanistan has not been listed in the standard source for such data, UNDP's Human Development Report, since 1996.

Sources:
a United Nations Development Program (UNDP), Human Development Report 1996.
b UNDP, Human Development Report 1997.
c UNICEF, State of the World's Children Report 1996.
d UNICEF/World Health Organization study, 1996.
e UNDP, 1997.

contracts for poppy have constituted the only source of rural credit, and only the cash derived from these futures contracts enabled many rural families to buy food and other necessities through the winter. The ban on opium cultivation by the Taliban during their last year in power met one Western demand, but donors withdrew even the previously meager support for crop substitution, even though pilot programs had shown some success. Cultivators and laborers suffered, while the regime continued to profit from unhindered trafficking at inflated prices of stocks remaining from two years of previous bumper opium crops.

The Fruits of Anarchy

The lack of border control, legitimate economic activity, and normal legal relations with neighbors, combined with disparities in trade policy between the free port of Dubai and the protectionist regimes elsewhere in the region, made Afghanistan a center of contraband in all kinds of goods. This smuggling economy provided livelihoods to a sector of the population while undermining institutions in Afghanistan's neighbors.

The lack of any transparency or accountability in monetary policy since the mid-1980s has both resulted from and intensified the crisis of institutions. Governments or factions posing as governments received containers of newly printed currency, which they transferred to militia leaders or other clients to buy their loyalty, bypassing the inconvenience of taxation or nurturing productive economic activity. Several different currencies remain in circulation, none of them backed by significant reserves of a functioning bank. The resultant hyperinflation has driven wealth out of the country and contributed to the already bleak prospects for investment. It virtually wiped out the value of salaries paid to government workers, including teachers, undermining the last vestiges of administration and public service, except where international organizations paid incentives to keep people on the job. Since the inauguration of the Interim Administration of Afghanistan on December 22, 2001, government employees have received salaries monthly, thanks to foreign donors, although they have barely met the deadlines.

This is the context in which Afghanistan became a haven for international terrorism. The origins of the problem date to the creation of armed Islamic groups to fight the Soviet troops and the government they had installed. Islamist radicals, mainly from the Arab world, were recruited to join the ranks of the mujahideen. But the Afghans did not want these fighters to stay after the Soviet troops left in 1989. If the people of Afghanistan had been able to rebuild their country and establish institutions of governance, they would have expelled the terrorists, as they are doing today. But in the atmosphere of anarchy and lawlessness, the armed militants were useful to some Afghan groups and their foreign supporters.

The money that could be mobilized by Osama bin Laden and his networks also played a role. As the Taliban, in particular, became increasingly alienated from the official international aid community, with their various strictures and demands concerning the status of women and other matters, they increasingly turned to this alternative unofficial international community. The financial and military support they received helped cement the ideological and personal ties that grew between the top leadership of the Taliban and Al Qaeda. In an impoverished, unpoliced, ungoverned state with no stake in international society, Al Qaeda could establish bases to strengthen and train its global networks.

That network's most spectacular act of terrorism, on September 11, revealed the dangers of allowing so-called humanitarian emergencies or failed states to fester—not only to neighboring countries but to the world. An American administration that came to power denouncing efforts at "nation building" and criticizing reliance on international organizations and agreements has now proclaimed that it needs to ensure a "stable Afghanistan" to prevent that country from ever again becoming a haven for terrorists. The United States, along with every other major country, has committed itself to supporting the reconstruction of Afghanistan within a framework designed by the United Nations.

"Administration," Not "Government"

The Agreement on Provisional Arrangements in Afghanistan Pending the Re-establishment of Permanent Government Institutions—to give the December 5, 2001 Bonn agreement its full and accurate title—resulted directly from this new level of commitment and political will by both Afghans and major powers. Most reports on this agreement treat it as a peace agreement, like those that have ended armed conflicts elsewhere. But in Bonn the UN did not bring together warring parties to make peace. The international community has defined one side of the ongoing war in Afghanistan—the alliance of Al Qaeda and the Taliban—as an outlaw formation that must be defeated. In Bonn the UN brought together Afghan groups opposed to the Taliban and Al Qaeda, some possessing power and other forms of legitimacy, notably through Muhammad Zahir Shah, the former king of Afghanistan. They set themselves the central task of protecting human security: starting the process of establishing—or, as the Afghans insisted, in recognition of their long history, re-establishing—permanent government institutions.

This agreement thus differs from many others that, as critics have noted, sometimes amounted to the codification of de facto power relations, no matter how illegitimate. This agreement does recognize power, especially in the allocation of key ministries to the relatively small group that already controlled them in Kabul thanks to the United States military campaign. In most respects, however, the Bonn agreement attempts to lay a foundation for transcending the current rather fragile power relations through building institutions.

The Interim Authority of Afghanistan established by the agreement will include three elements: an administration, a supreme court, and a special independent commission to convene the Emergency Loya Jirga (national council) at the end of the six-month interim period. It also requested an international security assistance force, one of whose major purposes is to ensure the independence of the administration from military pressure by power-holding factions.

The Bonn agreement does not contain a supreme or leadership council composed of prominent persons. Such institutions in previous Afghan agreements gave legitimacy to de facto power holders, including those whom some call warlords, as well as leaders of organizations supported by foreign countries. Some of the discontent with the agreement derives from the fact that it does not give recognition to such leaders. Many Afghans seem to consider this a positive step.

Instead the agreement emphasizes the administration. The term "administration" rather than "government" indicates its temporary and limited nature, but it also emphasizes that the role of this institution is actually to administer—to restore services. The presence of the supreme court as well as measures defining an interim legal system require this administration to work according to law; the chair of this administration, Hamid Karzai, has also emphasized this. Some had hoped that this administration would be largely professional and technocratic in character, and that is certainly true at least of its women members. In Afghanistan as elsewhere, women can usually obtain high positions only by being qualified, whereas men have other options for advancement.

Some little-noticed elements in the agreement are designed to strengthen the ability of the administration to govern through laws and rules and provide for transitions to successively more institutionalized and representative arrangements. The international security assistance force should insulate the administration from pressure by factional armed forces. At the insistence of the participants, the judicial power is described as "independent." The Special Independent Commission for Convening the Emergency Loya Jirga has many features to protect it from pressure by the administration, including a prohibition on membership in both. The Special Representative of the Secretary-General (SRSG) for Afghanistan is also given special responsibility for ensuring its independence.

The agreement confronts the country's monetary crisis by authorizing the establishment of a new central bank and requiring transparent and accountable procedures for the issuance of currency. This measure is partly aimed at ensuring that the authorities will be able to pay meaningful salaries to officials throughout the country, thus re-establishing the administrative structure that has been overwhelmed by warlordism. Appointments to the administration are to be monitored by an independent Civil Service Commission. Although this body will face severe constraints, it is aimed at curtailing arbitrary appointments, whether for personal corruption or to assure factional power. The Civil Service Commission will be supplemented with a formal Code of Conduct, with sanctions against violators. For the first time, the Afghan authorities will establish a Human Rights Commission, which will not only monitor current practice but also become the focal point for the extremely sensitive discussion about accountability for past wrongs. The SRSG also has the right to investigate human rights violations and recommend corrective actions.

The agreement provides for the integration of all armed groups into official security forces. Although this is not what specialists refer to as a "self-executing provision," other measures will reinforce it. The international security force will assist in the formation of all-Afghan security forces. Monetary reforms and foreign assistance to the authorities may enable the latter to pay meaningful salaries to soldiers and police, providing an incentive for them to shift their loyalties from warlords. The latter may become generals, governors, politicians, or businesspeople, as institutions are built and the economy revives.

Whose Afghanistan?

Building these Afghan institutions will constitute the core task of protecting human security in Afghanistan. The agreement provides a framework. But implementation in such a war-torn and devastated society will largely depend on how the international donors and the UN system approach the task of reconstruction.

As donors, agencies, and nongovernmental organizations rush in, they risk losing sight of the central task: building Afghan institutions owned by and accountable to the people of Afghanistan. The Bonn agreement states that the SRSG "shall monitor and assist in the implementation" of the agreement, but it does not establish a UN transitional administration in Afghanistan. It vests sovereignty in the Interim Authority. The Afghan participants at the meeting scrutinized every provision that provided for international monitoring or involvement to ensure that the new authority would be fully sovereign. The lessons of the past two decades in Afghanistan and elsewhere are that only accountable and legitimate national institutions, although open to the outside world and subject to international standards, can protect human security.

There is a real risk that the actors in the reconstruction market, as they bid for locations in the bazaar that is opening in Afghanistan, may harm, hinder, or even destroy the effort to build Afghan institutions. Donors and agencies seeking to establish programs need to find clients, and it is often easier to do so by linking up directly with a de facto power on the ground. Such uncoordinated efforts have reinforced clientelism and warlordism in Afghanistan for years in the absence of a legitimate authority. Programs must now be coordinated to ensure that they work together to reinforce the capacities and priorities of Afghan institutions. At the January 2002 conference on reconstruction in Tokyo, Chairman Karzai asked the donors to coordinate, and the conference established an "Implementation Group" chaired by the Afghan administration in Kabul, to monitor, the effort. The group has yet to meet, but bilateral donors and NGOs are already racing to duplicate projects, and Afghan ministers spend so much time traveling abroad and meeting delegations that they have little time for their primary task: reestablishing governance.

The growing international presence, with high salaries and big houses, is already overwhelming the new administration and distorting the economy. Rents for large houses in central Kabul have risen from $100 to $10,000 per month; Afghan NGOs can no longer afford office space in the center of the

Aid Pledged for
Afghanistan's Reconstruction (in millions)

Iran Over the next five years	$560
Japan Over the next two and a half years	$500
European Union In the first year	$495
United States Over the next year	$297
Saudi Arabia Over three years	$220
Pakistan Over five years	$100
India Line of credit announced in Nov.	$100
Britain In 2002	$86
South Korea Over the next two and a half years	$45
Total Pledged	**$2.4 billion**

Note: Aid pledges were delivered at the January 2002 International Conference on Reconstruction Assistance to Afghanistan that was held in Tokyo.
Source: *The New York Times*, January 22, 2002.

capital. When the mujahideen took power in Herat in 1992, the city had ten qualified Afghan engineers working in the municipality. Before long it had only one, since the other nine went to work as drivers for UN agencies, where they earned much higher salaries. These are just some examples of how the normal operation of the international aid system can actually deprive countries of the capacities they need.

If the vast sums that seem to be flowing toward Afghanistan are to help reinforce rather than undermine the fragile institutions established in the Bonn agreement, international actors must establish new bodies to monitor and control the disbursements in partnership with the Afghan authorities. The expenditures must follow the priorities they set in consultation with the SRSG, not the multiple priorities set by the agendas of various countries or agencies. The international community may have to sacrifice some of its immediate interests, but as it has learned only too bitterly, it is worth paying a modest price to protect the self-determination and human security of the people of Afghanistan. The international community's own security depends on it.

PART III

Economic Liberalization

12. India's Economic Liberalization: The Elephant Comes of Age

December 1996

SHALENDRA D. SHARMA

When the Indian government unveiled its ambitious economic liberalization program in mid-1991, it was widely believed to be a nonstarter. Earlier attempts had not amounted to much, and scholarly paradigms held that a "developmental" authoritarian state of the East Asian variety (not India's weak democratic regime) was a sine qua non for the implementation of bold "market-friendly" macro-economic policies. However, this time India has proved the pundits wrong. Not only has liberalization dismantled the command economy structure and ended decades of economic isolationism, it has also produced sustained economic growth and fostered a new self-confidence and optimism. Indeed, liberalization has become such an indelible part of contemporary India's developmental ethos that it is now considered irreversible.

While India's postliberalization economic growth has not been as spectacular as that of China and the newly industrializing countries (NICs) of East and Southeast Asia, it has nevertheless been steady and respectable. Unlike the explosive "tiger economies" of East and Southeast Asia or China's overheated "dragon economy" that have captured the global imagination, the Indian economy has been more like a lumbering elephant slowly emerging from the shadows. Sooner or later, the world will have to come to terms with its formidable presence and power. Indeed, as the world's sixth largest economy (after the United States, Japan, China, Germany, and France), and endowed with a rapidly expanding middle class of some 250 million, a huge domestic market, a large pool of educated and skilled labor, and resilient democratic institutions, India has the potential to be an economic colossus by the early twenty-first century.

Prelude to Liberalization

In early 1991 India was caught in an economic crisis of exceptional severity. Battered by rising oil prices because of the Persian Gulf War, the already floundering economy hit bottom. The central government's budget deficit rose to an unprecedented 8.5 percent of GDP; the inflation rate, which had fluctuated within single digits throughout the 1970s and 1980s, soared to 17 percent; the external debt mushroomed from $20.6 billion in 1980 and 1981 to over $70 billion; and the debt-service ratio increased to a debilitating 32 percent of GDP.

By the second quarter of 1991, the rapidly deteriorating fiscal situation had resulted in the downgrading of India's credit rating in international financial markets. This further eroded the confidence of foreign creditors, including nonresident Indians with sizable deposits in Indian banks, and triggered a panic run on the foreign exchange reserves. India was left with a paltry $1.2 billion in reserves, an amount barely sufficient to pay for two weeks of imports. On the verge of defaulting on its foreign debt, in mid-June India was given a major reprieve by foreign creditors and saved from the humiliation of default by drawing emergency loans from the IMF. In July, the Reserve Bank of India transferred part of the nation's gold stock abroad to the Bank of England on a temporary basis, allowing it to maintain its structural-reform conditionality and minimal external financial liquidity and debt-servicing obligations. The Reserve Bank had never before undertaken such drastic measures, even during serious economic difficulties in the 1950s and mid-1960s.

In the summer of 1991 it was impossible to find anyone optimistic about India's future; many seasoned India watchers were already writing the country's obituary. Some feared the Latin Americanization of India, while others concluded that the subcontinent was fated to be a perennial economic basket case, a "caged tiger" mired in "a million mutinies."

India, however, has defied the odds. Not only have the country's democratic institutions shown remarkable resilience, but its economy has undergone a miraculous transformation. No doubt there must have been much satisfaction within the Finance Ministry when *The Economist* changed its pessimistic tune in its March 5, 1994, issue and admitted that

India's $250 billion economy, already the second largest on the Asian continent, "could soon rival China as a new economic force."

Indeed, there is good reason to be bullish on India. In less than five years the country has achieved macroeconomic stability and sustained growth. The annual GDP growth rate rose from 1.2 percent in 1991–1992 to nearly 5.5 percent in 1994–1995, and the targeted growth of 6.5 percent in fiscal 1996–1997 is not unrealistic. The budget deficit has been reduced to a manageable 5 percent of GDP. Inflation is down to a modest 7 to 8 percent and interest rates (while still high) have declined from 22 percent to 17 percent, with further reductions forecast for fiscal 1996–1997. Foreign exchange reserves were up to a healthy $22 billion in mid-1996, and the vigorous 21 percent growth in exports during the first 10 months of 1993–1994 has greatly reduced vulnerability to external shocks.

Most encouraging has been the steady rise in foreign direct and portfolio investment—from a paltry $30 million in 1990 to approximately $5 billion by the second quarter of 1995. Blue-chip corporations that include General Electric, Siemens, Proctor and Gamble, Mercedes-Benz, General Motors, Kellogg, Pepsi, Nestle, Honda, and Suzuki are establishing or expanding their Indian operations by increasing capital investments and acquiring majority stakes in their Indian joint ventures. For example, Coca-Cola, which was ignominiously forced out in 1977 by Prime Minister Indira Gandhi's hard-line nationalization policies, has returned to the lucrative Indian market by taking over the three most popular soft-drink brands. The pace of change has been so dizzying in some areas that the once sleepy town of Bangalore has been transformed into a noisy high-tech mecca, a veritable "Indian Silicon Valley" where high-tech heavyweights like IBM, AT&T, Intel, Sun Microsystems, Texas Instruments, Digital Corporation, Motorola, Hewlett Packard, Phillips, and Polaroid have set up shop to cash in on India's abundant engineering talent.

In addition, the sustained diversification and expansion of financial services, especially banking and stock-market portfolios, clearly indicate that domestic and foreign investors are no longer jittery about India. Despite a wide-ranging securities scam in the Bombay Stock Exchange in 1992, Indian businesses and commercial interests have been able to raise some $6 billion from new issues in the Indian capital markets. Moreover, the Indian stock market, with over 7,000 listed companies, has become one of the most active in Asia in terms of daily trading volume. Foreign financial investors have poured over $1 billion into India's stock markets. This sustained economic activity will undoubtedly enable the Indian government to meet its still considerable debt obligations while devoting its resources to pressing developmental needs.

The Legacy of the License-Permit Raj

India's remarkable economic turnaround is the result of a bold and carefully orchestrated macroeconomic liberalization program undertaken in the midst of the June 1991 crisis by the new government of Prime Minister P. V. Narashima Rao. In his maiden budget speech to parliament, Finance Minister Manmohan Singh, the chief architect of liberalization, declared in his iconoclastic fashion that the fiscal crisis was symptomatic of a deeper economic malaise and that nothing short of a fundamental economic restructuring would stop the fiscal hemorrhage and release India's "unbound economic potential." More bluntly, he informed his fellow citizens that neither the government nor the economy could live beyond its means. He announced that the time had come to convert the regulated, inward-looking Indian economy to a more market-friendly, outwardly oriented model.

The foundations of India's inward-looking command economy were laid in the immediate postindependence period by Prime Minister Jawaharlal Nehru. Deeply influenced by Soviet central planning, Nehru believed that state-guided, planned economic development committed to "a socialistic pattern of society" would foster rapid economic growth, self-reliance, and the eradication of mass poverty. However, more than four decades of active dirigisme produced only disappointing results. Under the guise of planned development, India's interventionist state erected an elaborate system of corporatist structures, irrational protocols, quantitative regulations, and "control instruments" (such as prohibitively high tariffs, licensing-cum-barriers on imports of technology and capital goods, and restrictions on foreign investment and collaboration). Government restrictions permeated all levels of the public and private sector, creating one of the most comprehensively controlled and regulated economies in the noncommunist world. Under this system, all categories of import goods—consumer, intermediate, and capital—were subject to discretionary controls.

With few exceptions, consumer goods imports were banned completely. Capital goods imports fell into two categories: restricted items, and those permitted under "open general licensing." The latter category was a misnomer since these imports were subject to many restrictions, such as requiring an importer to be the "actual user" of imported machinery who could not sell the machinery for up to five years after purchase. Imports of intermediate inputs fell into two categories, with the stringency of control ranging from "banned," "restricted," "limited permissible," to open general licensing. In addition, before planning business expansion, entrepreneurs were required to obtain licenses from bureaucratic watchdogs, such as the Capital Goods Committee, that could indefinitely delay or reject outright applications for licenses without explanation.

Aptly labeled the "license-permit raj," this pernicious system was purposely structured to facilitate central planning and command mandates. It did so by granting arbitrary powers to a hierarchy of influence-peddling politicians, bureaucrats, and overly obsequious apparatchiks. This in turn spawned parasitical rent-seeking activities that inhibited economic competition and severely undermined innovation, production, efficiency, and, ultimately, economic growth. Moreover, indiscriminate import-substitution and policy-induced distortions such as excessively protectionist trade policies and overvalued exchange rates contributed to the emergence of a highly concentrated oligopolistic business and industrial structure characterized by managerial ineptitude, declining productivity, and mounting losses.

Not surprisingly, the economy grew between 1951 and 1984 at about 3.5 percent annually—a rate lower than that of developing countries as a group (which grew at 5.2 percent), and substantially lower than that registered by China and many other countries in East and Southeastern Asia. By the time the economic crisis hit in 1991, India was finally ready for its own perestroika.

Rao's Perestroika

Immediately after taking office, the Rao administration implemented a package of structural reform measures designed to stabilize the economy and lay the foundation for sustained economic growth. The core of the liberalization program, the "austerity budget," made deep cuts in government expenditures and devalued the enormously overvalued rupee by 22 percent against the dollar. The program also implemented monetary policies to allow production, prices, interest rates, and wages to find their "natural equilibrium" through the interaction of supply and demand. It presented a strict timetable to deregulate the financial markets and phase out all forms of quasi-autarkic regulations and bureaucratic controls. The World Bank (which just weeks earlier had been highly critical of the Indian government) responded by giving its "seal of approval" and making available substantial amounts of assistance, including a $500 million structural adjustment loan. The IMF soon followed, making $1.7 billion available.

Over the past five and one-half years, the Indian economy has undergone significant changes. The New Industrial Policy (NIP) has effectively dismantled the ubiquitous industrial-licensing regime, thereby abolishing all government control over firms' investment and production decisions, including ownership, location, local content, technology fees, and royalties. In addition, with the exception of a small list of "strategic industries," all sectors previously reserved for public enterprises are now open to private investment. Civil aviation, mining, power, and energy are open to private domestic and foreign investors. With the liberalization of telecommunications and pharmaceuticals, and further liberalization of the coal industry in 1995, the primary remaining investment restrictions are on railways.

NIP has also rationalized foreign direct investment by providing "automatic approval" registration with the Reserve Bank of India for all foreign investments of up to 51 percent of equity; provisions for expeditious clearances for investors seeking equity shares exceeding 51 percent are already in place. Today foreign investors incorporated in India are treated the same as domestic investors; they can invest in any sector and also remit dividends abroad without any restrictions. That India is a member of the World Trade Organization, has joined the Multilateral Investment Guarantee Agency, and is currently negotiating bilateral investment treaties with several countries, will help promote a competitive economic environment for all and ensure foreign investors fair treatment, especially legal security for market transactions and safeguards on intellectual property rights.

Complementing NIP is an aggressive program to tame the "white elephants"—India's approximately 225 public sector enterprises. Unlike the former Soviet Union, the Indian government has been pursuing a judicious, multipronged gradualist strategy that includes privatization of state-owned enterprises (SOEs) and the liquidation of chronically "sick" or unviable enterprises; reducing monopoly privileges and budgetary support (that is, subsidies and tax breaks) for all public sector enterprises; market sales of SOE equities; subjecting public sector firms to market discipline and accountability by creating a competitive environment for private and public enterprises; and establishing the National Renewal Fund (financed in part by the World Bank) to prevent the most vulnerable workers in SOEs from bearing a disproportionate share of the necessary adjustment costs.

The government's gradual liberalization of India's trade and exchange regime is of no less significance. The rupee has been made fully convertible and stable at an exchange rate of 31 to the dollar, which is already making Indian exports more competitive and imports costlier. As for trade liberalization, licensing requirements on all imports (with the exception of a short list of "final consumer goods") have been eliminated, and it is expected that even this list will be reduced. The government has already slashed customs duties, greatly streamlined customs procedures, and abolished unnecessary regulations in order to expedite export shipments.

As part of its trade reform, the government reduced the maximum import tariff from 85 percent to 65 percent at the beginning of 1994 (it was more than 300 percent in June 1991). The 1995 budget introduced additional tariff reforms, reducing the average tariff to about 27 percent, and it now stands at 22 percent. Fully aware that these rates are still high by international standards, the Finance Ministry has promised to reduce tariffs and customs duties to levels comparable to those of East Asian countries by 1997.

Recognizing that an efficient banking system and functioning capital markets are essential for the success of liberalization, the government has introduced far-reaching financial sector reforms. India's heavily regulated banking system is dominated by several large public sector banks that control 85 to 90 percent of all deposits. This system is undergoing a phased process of modernization that includes deregulation and increased competition with the entry of new foreign and private banks into the market. Capital markets are also being modernized under the aegis of the Securities and Exchange Board of India (SEBI). Established in February 1992, SEBI has introduced the basic regulatory framework within which a healthy stock market can operate.

The Challenges Ahead

The important achievements since 1991 notwithstanding, India still has a challenging ways to go. It must improve its public savings and reduce the fiscal deficit. While India's private savings performance is strikingly comparable to that of Malaysia and other successful East Asian economies, its public savings performance (that is, the excess of central and state government revenues over current expenditure plus the gross profits of public enterprises) has been much worse and is deteriorating. In the 1980s it was around 3 percent of GDP; it currently stands at zero. Correcting this situation is critical to the restoration of the public sector's capacity to invest and to accommodate higher levels of private investment. Greater investment, especially in infrastructure and social services, is imperative if India is to achieve and sustain rates of growth and poverty reduction comparable to those of the other high-performing countries in Asia.

Much more needs to be done if India is to become competitive. Restrictions on consumer goods imports and agricultural commodities trading are still important obstacles to the full integration of India into the global economy. Similarly, reformers must further downsize publicly owned banks and insurance firms and encourage new entrants in the field. Agriculture, which employs about two-thirds of the workforce and accounts for 30 percent of GDP, has generally been bypassed by the reforms. To end market distortions and inefficiencies in the agricultural sector, the government must eliminate subsidies on items such as fertilizers, irrigation, electricity, and rural credit that have been eating into development expenditure and causing a decline in public sector agricultural investment.

The hard reality is that agriculture cannot be kept insulated from market reforms. As China's experience shows, extending the liberalization process to agriculture has the potential to accelerate the growth momentum of the economy and to increase its efficiency and productivity.

Again, looking at China's experience, the time is ripe for the Indian government to abandon its ethos of export pessimism and create special economic zones and open cities to encourage employment and penetrate global markets. With a vast pool of unskilled and skilled labor and a large and expanding internal market, such zones would provide dividends for both India and foreign investors. Cities like Bombay (now Mumbai), Bangalore, Cochin, Madras (now Chennai), and Calcutta could serve as magnets for foreign investment and as export bases for India. Given its geographical location as the crossroads between Asia, the Middle East, and Europe, India has the potential to become an important center of international commerce and business. If this potential is to be realized, India must avoid overvalued exchange rates, keep inflation and budget deficits low, and help exporters with measures such as providing automatic access to foreign exchange and providing access to intermediate inputs and capital goods. The East and Southeast Asian economies often provide automatic rediscounting of export financing, sometimes at subsidized interest rates. The certainty of access to such credit encourages entrepreneurs to undertake new export ventures and helps them penetrate foreign markets.

Moreover, following the example of Southeast Asia's newly industrializing economies, India's reformers must provide more incentives for export-oriented foreign investors. The Southeast Asian NICs have been highly successful in wooing export-oriented foreign direct investment by waiving investment restrictions and offering special incentives. In Indonesia the proportion of approved investment going into export-producing enterprises increased from 38 percent in 1986 to 70 percent in 1991. In Thailand the proportion increased from 10 percent in 1971 to more than 50 percent in 1988. Shifting the focus of foreign investment from import substitution to exports has generated substantially more exports and investment. Also, India must aggressively seek full membership in the Association of Southeast Asian Nations and the Asia Pacific Economic Cooperation council, and associate status with the European Union.

Finally, in a country where 34 percent of the population lives below the poverty line, it is imperative that the reforms protect public expenditure programs benefiting the poor, strengthening these programs where necessary. Of course, not all public service spending merits protection: some of it is inefficient and regressive, and such spending should be analyzed to verify that the poor are actually benefiting and that investments are concentrated where the social returns are highest.

Pragmatic Progress

In its assessment of East Asia's remarkable economic growth, the influential World Bank study, *The East Asian Miracle,* concluded that the East Asian economies achieved high growth by "getting the basics right." For India, this means the pursuit first and foremost of prudent market-guided macroeconomic policies, with only selective state intervention—or interventions that are circumscribed and reversible. To its credit, the new United Front administration of Prime Minister H. D. Deve Gowda has resisted pressures from the left to undermine economic liberalization. Gowda, who facilitated economic reforms as chief minister of Karnataka, is a pragmatist whose policies will not diverge much from his predecessor's. By appointing the original reformer, P. Chidambaram (an articulate advocate of "fast-track reform") finance minister, the government is sending a clear message that there will be no fundamental changes to the country's macroeconomic policies. As Kipling noted long ago, when the lumbering elephant begins to move at a measured gait, all sensible men and beasts get out of the way. The tigers must now contend with the elephant—and Kipling always placed his bets on the elephant.

13. Reforming India's Economy in an Era of Global Change

April 1996

JOHN ADAMS

India's economic achievements have been varied and impressive in the half-century since it gained independence in 1947. Structurally, the nation has become more industrial and less agricultural. Steel, chemicals, machinery, rail equipment, defense goods—the products of a mature industrial economy—have become available, in large part through government-led investment. Along with China, Brazil, South Korea, and Mexico, India is one of the giant economic engines of the emergent third world, and ranks among the dozen largest national economies on the planet. In the last five decades the nation's output has increased fivefold. In 1950, 360 million Indians produced $50 billion of goods and services; in 1995, 925 million Indians produced $250 billion.

If there have been successes in developing the economy and making the typical Indian family better off, there have also been disappointments. Using a conservative count, 200 million people survive only meagerly in terrible poverty. Two-thirds of all women are illiterate. Clean water, adequate sanitation, and basic health care are absent from many villages and urban slums. Any overall judgment of India's record will thus depend on how the items on the plus side of the ledger are tallied against those on the negative side. While there is no way to conclude the debate definitively, it is beyond question that the scope and scale of India's economy have been vastly transformed.

The Accomplishments before Rao's Reforms

Since 1991, India has experienced an ongoing wave of significant economic policy reforms. Careless rhetoric emanating from the media, and sometimes from putative experts, avows that these initiatives were mandated by inferior economic performance in prior decades, especially the failure of an excessively autarkic socialism. This interpretation is false; the facts are exactly the reverse.

This becomes clear when India's record of economic growth is divided into three phases. From 1950 through 1980, India was committed to planning; with New Delhi and state governments invested heavily in industry and infrastructure, including irrigation and power. This period of the "Socialist Pattern of Society" generated respectable rates of economic growth (allowing for some unevenness attributable to the monsoons' effects on agriculture and mild fluctuations in industrial production). Agricultural output expanded by almost 3 percent per year on average after independence. In the 1970s, annual industrial growth was 4.5 percent per year, while exports grew at 5.9 percent. GDP climbed at a 3.4 percent annual rate, and GDP per capita rose by 1.2 percent a year. These are respectable numbers for a large, very poor economy; only in the shadow of the incredible advances of South Korea and Taiwan can they be made to appear deficient.

For reasons that are not yet fully understood, India's growth rate accelerated dramatically in the 1980s. This Golden Decade featured a pattern of self-reinforcing expansion that represented a leap to an unprecedented economic trajectory. All components of the economy behaved admirably. Agriculture continued solidly on course, with its growth rate bumping up to 3.4 percent a year, despite disheartening monsoons between 1986 and 1988. Industrial production rose by 6.9 percent annually from 1980 to 1991, accompanied by an export surge that averaged 7.4 percent per year. GDP expansion averaged 6.5 percent annually and GDP per capita climbed at a healthy rate of 3.5 percent, roughly tripling the rate of the prior three decades. India, along with Pakistan, suddenly had one of the world's most rapidly expanding economies.

Unfortunately, the rapid economic growth in the 1980s was accompanied, at the end of the decade, by a descent into an episode of fiscal and monetary mismanagement that was untypical of India's postindependence economic leadership. Generally, the Planning Commission, the Ministry of Finance, and the central bank of India have adhered to conservative tenets in managing the nation's fiscal deficits and supply of money and credit. In contrast to many third world (and some first world) governments, macroeconomic policymaking by the responsible Indian authorities had been comparatively immune to the expedients politicians often advocate to cultivate popular support, especially when elections near. Inflation was normally held to single digits, the budget deficit was controlled, and sufficient foreign exchange was available to sustain the value of the rupee.

After 1985, India's economic managers relaxed their hold on the nation's supply of money and credit and were inattentive to a mounting fiscal deficit. By the end of the decade, excessive borrowing was financing both the internal budget deficit and the external payments shortfall arising from the excess of imports over exports. Political infighting marred and ended first Prime Minister V. P. Singh's and then Prime Minister Chandra Shekhar's brief terms of office. The Persian Gulf War in 1990 led to a higher energy import bill, caused a decline in worker remittances from the Middle East, and was the final tug in a rapidly unraveling financial situation. The budget deficit equaled 10 percent of GDP in 1990, annual inflation surged to over 10 percent, and foreign reserves fell to only $2 billion, scarcely enough to cover one month's imports.

Radical Rao

In May 1991, following Prime Minister Rajiv Gandhi's assassination, Indians went to the polls and brought the Congress Party back to power—barely. Economic issues did not figure heavily in the election debates, which centered on other topics: political stability, Hindu nationalism, and job and college quotas for disadvantaged castes. As it had done before, the Congress leadership found consensus and refuge in selecting a noncontroversial senior figure, P. V. Narasimha Rao, a southerner from Andhra Pradesh state, as party head and prime minister.

Recognizing the need to seize control of the national purse and reestablish confidence, Rao assembled a team of experienced pragmatists, headed by Finance Minister Manmohan Singh. The rupee was devalued, controls on private investment were relaxed, and foreign investment rules were modified to enable foreign firms to hold controlling interests (51 percent) in joint undertakings. Neither members of the Congress nor the opposition voiced concern over these sharp departures from prior practices, which had seemed immutably grounded in India's state-directed program of self-reliance. In the normally highly charged crucible of Indian politics, economic policy suddenly appeared quarantined from criticism or serious debate.

The financial tightening Rao and his team instituted quickly brought inflation under control, began to correct the government's overspending, and triggered the refilling of foreign-exchange coffers. Public investment slowed and private investors, faced with uncertainties and changing rules, cut back on capital spending. Contrary to conventional wisdom, India's economy was stalled, not energized, by the catharsis of Rao's reform. The economic surge of the 1980s was over.

GDP grew only 0.9 percent in 1991, agricultural output was off by -2.3 percent, and industrial output fell 0.8 percent. In 1992 and 1993, the economy stabilized; annual GDP grew 4.3 percent and agriculture resumed expanding at 4 percent per year, but industrial output climbed at a sluggish 3.2 percent rate. Compared to the more than 6 percent annual GDP growth path of the 1980s, the three-year slump between 1992 and 1994 cost the Indian economy some 10 percentage points of potential GDP gain, or about $20 billion. Only in mid-1994 did industrial growth fully resume and GDP expansion move back above 5 percent.

By late 1995 the economy had regained its robustness. Industry was growing at approximately 8 percent annually, and aggregate GDP growth was about 6 percent. Export growth, which had been strong after 1991, was by the summer of 1995 running 20 percent ahead of 1994. Entering 1996, it is fully evident that India has returned to the high growth path of the Golden Decade.

Not a Morality Play

It is often said that India embarked on a course of policy reform because the policies followed between 1950 and 1991 failed. This observation is usually grounded, with more or less sophistication, in a contrast between the inherent disadvantages of state-guided economic development programs and the avowed virtues of the market system and private initiative. Scrutiny of that period belies this observation.

After 1950, the sustained effort entailed in pursuing the Socialist Pattern of Society transformed the economy structurally, laid the material basis for national security, fed the nation, and generated acceptable overall growth. During the Golden Decade of the 1980s, India was one of the world's fastest growing nations. That growth, and targeted assistance and work programs, appreciably lowered the fraction of families living below the poverty line. The post-1991 reforms came on the heels of exceptional growth, and were followed by three years of stagnation. Reforms are advancing at a measured pace, taking the form of dispensations from the still-powerful center and its legendary bureaucracy, driven more by necessity than conviction. Significantly, New Delhi has not taken any abrupt steps to privatize state enterprises, but rather seeks to make them more efficient and earn profits for public reinvestment.

That the reform process escaped the usual superheated rhetoric and street actions that have customarily displayed the sharp cleavages among India's political parties and social strata almost defies explanation. Nothing in the lead-in to the 1991 election suggested that a Rao-led Congress Party would implement drastic policy changes and redraft India's economic strategy. In parliament the opposition neither challenged the Rao-Singh initiatives nor offered coherent alternatives. And as the country moves toward the April 1996 polls, a similar torpor prevails. The Hindu nationalist Bharatiya Janata Party (BJP) talks vaguely of a return to Gandhian *swadeshi*-ism, or patronizing and giving preference to Indian industry, but no one takes this option seriously. At the same time, the leader of West Bengal's ruling Communist Party, Jyoti Basu, has legitimized the pursuit of domestic and even foreign capital to rejuvenate the state's senescent industries.

The political leadership's placid response can be accounted for only by placing economic reform in the broader context of the global changes that are so pervasive and irresistible as to move most of the policy adjustments beyond debate. Little can be gained, inside or outside India, by trying to impose a morality-play scenario on unfolding events, one in which capitalism vanquishes socialism.

India and the Four International Imperatives

Prime Minister Rao's Congress government faces uncertain prospects in the upcoming parliamentary elections, but regardless of the outcome, India's economic policies will be shaped domestically by the need to deliver sustained rapid growth whose dividends must be broadly shared. Yet the nation's range of options is increasingly curtailed by a set of compelling international imperatives that sharply restrict the leadership's former discretion to pursue a uniquely Indian path.

These forces and their implications may be clustered under four headings: the technological imperative, the institutional imperative, the size imperative, and the communications imperative. Responding effectively and promptly to these global pressures is essential as the Indian government reconfigures economic policies and as Indian business managers strive to seize the advantages they offer. Failure or delay will condemn most Indians to sustained impoverishment and heighten the risk that a discredited political system will fragment or dissolve, leaving a billion people in disarray akin to that embroiling Zaire or Afghanistan.

An international economic imperative exists when a nation is presented with advantages so evident, or costs so oppressive, that lines of action are plainly drawn. Conforming to the most-favored-nation clause is necessary to reap the considerable advantages of participation in the World Trade Organization; this is an illustration of an institutional imperative. Designing, producing, and marketing automobiles is best achieved in a large-scale corporate enterprise, an example of the size imperative. Examples of the communications imperative have become ubiquitous: few governments are willing to devote the time and resources to discover every satellite dish, videocassette player, or Internet connection to protect state telecommunications monopolies or restrict access to foreign ideas and impure entertainment.

In his budget messages between 1991 and 1995, Finance Minister Singh recharted India's economic course. Controls on private investment have been removed or relaxed. By 1994, mining, most manufacturing sectors, electricity, airlines, telecommunications, and banking had been substantially opened to private domestic investors. Foreign companies were welcomed more selectively. In early 1992, the government abandoned the maze of licenses controlling the import of intermediate and capital goods. The average tariff rate was slashed from 87 percent of import values in 1991 to 33 percent in 1994. In April 1995, items such as coffee, audiotapes, personal computers, and sporting goods were added to the list of consumer imports no longer requiring official approval. New private banks have been sanctioned since January 1993, and all banks have been given greater latitude to make loans and set interest rates. Personal and corporate tax rates have been lowered and simplified. The rupee is now convertible.

Most components of India's package of reforms are associated with one or more of these four international imperatives, which are also responsible for India's readiness to court foreign multinationals after years of disdain. Consider technology. Under the policy of self-reliance, India had been reluctant to approach foreign companies for new technologies, fearing colonial-type dependence; many Indians also shared an overt hostility to the presence of multinationals on Indian soil. Between 1950 and the 1980s, India absorbed and developed the technology to create a large industrial economy. But by 1990 the nation probably had more technology gaps in more areas, such as pharmaceuticals, computers, industrial materials, and telecommunications, than in 1970.

Neither the government nor the private sector could spend sufficient funds to catch up in all fields of science and engineering. India's GDP of $250 billion roughly equals what the United States, Germany, and Japan together spend annually on research and development. To match this total, India would have to devote its entire national product to research and technology. The country had little choice other than to change its attitude if it was to stay near the technology frontiers across the spectrum of modern innovations.

India's new outlook on private investment from overseas was quickly manifested in the government's reception of foreign delegations. In May 1994, United States Secretary of Commerce Ronald Brown led a delegation of 26 chief executive officers of major American companies to India. Although the amount is largely symbolic, $7 billion in tentative investment deals were announced, covering power plants, oil and gas exploration, satellite communications, and cable television. In early 1996, a 300-member Canadian delegation initialed 78 commercial and investment contracts dealing with the transport, highway, telecommunications, and petroleum industries. At the same time Britain and India completed discussions on a science pact aimed at small and medium-sized Indian firms. In addition, the government's foreign investment committee cleared 58 proposals from Microsoft, Motorola, Siemens, General Electric, BASF, and Nokia, among others. International business and economic magazines and newspapers now highlight India as a hospitable environment for foreign investment.

The Institutional Imperative and ENRON

As a legacy of its British colonial experience, India acquired not only the English language but a system of government and law that remains broadly consistent with Western practices. Property rights and contract adjudication, for example, take forms familiar to Western businesses. This common heritage puts India in a favorable position to respond to the institutional imperative. The homogenization of legal and business practices lowers the transaction costs business incur exporting, importing, and completing financial transfers across international boundaries.

Unlike China, India is a participant in the World Trade Organization, the successor to the General Agreement on Tariffs and Trade. When the final Uruguay round of GATT talks was concluded in 1994, it contained provisions that concerned Indians, such as those treating pharmaceutical and seed patent rights. Mild anti-GATT protests were staged in New Delhi but they did not deter the government from accepting the accord and initiating changes in India's outmoded patent laws, thereby bringing them in line with international practice.

India's central and state governments do not yet have in place well-established procedures to conclude negotiations with foreign investors, or to resolve disputes that may arise. The noisiest contretemps over a large foreign investment project arose in August 1995, when a newly elected government in Maharashtra, India's most industrial state, revoked an agreement with the United States-based Enron Corporation, which had already begun construction of a $2.8 billion power plant north of Bombay. The 2,015-megawatt facility was intended to help close the large gap between electricity demand and supply in the region. Maharashtra's former Congress Party government, with the strong support of its counterpart in New Delhi, had signed an agreement with Enron, but the state's new chief minister, Manohar Joshi, head of a BJP-led coalition, said its terms were unacceptable. This set off a chain reaction in other states that had active or pending power projects with foreign participation and chilled India's investment climate. By November negotiations with Enron had been reopened on pricing, costs, ownership, and environmental protection. In January 1996 final terms were agreed to, including a 22.5 percent cut in the price per kilowatt hour and a 30 percent ownership stake for Maharashtra's electricity board, which governs the local distribution system.

The Enron affair offers several lessons. India's states are going to become more significant players in soliciting foreign investments, yet they lack experience in negotiating with large multinationals such as Enron, with its $2 billion in annual sales; setting rules to which all parties adhere will be critical to future successes in obtaining needed infrastructure and technologies. A key element in resolving the Enron dispute was the initial contract, which called for arbitration (in London) in case of a default. By breaking the original agreement the Maharashtrian government had exposed itself to a $200 million liability, an amount it did not have and could not raise.

In fairness to the government, it should be noted that some experts had voiced concerns about the high rates to be charged and the project's cost, and there were plausible grounds for reopening the discussions. This could have been done quietly but political posturing and the opportunity to chide the Congress Party for making a bad deal proved irresistible. At root, Maharashtra state needed the power to maintain its leadership in Indian industry and finance. Enron presumably saw profit in the project, even as reframed, and wanted a good image in future dealings with India.

Enron executives were remarkably soft-spoken and patient during the dispute, a stance they shared with those at Kentucky Fried Chicken. Two of the chain's restaurants were closed in late 1995 by municipal authorities in Bangalore and New Delhi who claimed, respectively, that the meals contained excessive additives and that the facilities were unsanitary. Quick court decisions overturned these politically motivated charges. At least in these cases, India's judicial system reacted promptly and decisively to correct unjustifiable actions. Compared to China, India is far more advanced at developing and playing by a set of rules, and this fuller accommodation to the institutional imperative will work to India's advantage when international firms compare prospects for investments in the two Asian giants.

Expanding Business Size

To a degree not appreciated by all Indians, their economy occupies only a small and not yet influential niche globally. India's involvement in the world's trade and investment flows remains minuscule. Its population of over 900 million accounts for one-seventh the world's people, but the country provides only 0.6 percent of global exports and its share of capital flows is even less. Indian firms and banks are for the most part much smaller than their counterparts in developed economies.

India's largest aluminum producer, HINDALCO, has annual sales of about $285 million; Alcoa, in contrast, has annual sales of $13 billion. The total sales of Chrysler ($52 billion), Exxon ($111 billion), AT&T ($80 billion), and General Electric ($44 billion) exceed India's total national income. Several conclusions follow from these observations. India's economy is still comparatively small, its large population base offset by poverty and low productivity. Its farms, shops, and business firms are likewise undersized. In contrast the large-scale corporation, which is a remarkably effective way to marshal inputs, labor, and machines for production, is underrepresented in India.

Bigger is not always better, but expanding India's economy and increasing the country's participation in global trade and investment flows will require the emergence of much larger private business organizations. This scale imperative will confront a deep-seated antipathy to large firms and sympathy for small producers. Mahatma Gandhi strongly endorsed handicrafts and domestic production. After independence, the state discriminated in favor of small-scale enterprises, reserving about 900 products for that area and providing favored treatment in terms of government purchases, taxes, and labor regulations. The Monopoly and Restrictive Trade Practices Act of 1969 made it even more difficult for large firms to expand capacity within the already constrictive planning regime.

Put simply, the country's economic development will require that India overcome a popularly ingrained fear of business size and remove statutory hindrances to expansion and mergers. For better or worse, a corporate sector of giant domestic and foreign firms will bring in its train a large infusion of advertising, brand names, and standardization in a country still not fully at ease with such practices.

The Telecommunications Link

Today consumers will simply not be denied access to multiple television channels, telephones, popular music, news, and computer networks. Business transactions are facilitated by cheaper and better means of communication. Especially in a democracy committed to freedom of expression, there is intrinsic merit to opening all media to public access. In India there are 4 television receivers per 100 people, compared to 21 in South Korea and 15 in Malaysia; there are 8 telephone lines per 1,000 people, compared to 357 and 112, respectively. Until recently the Indian government controlled television and radio broadcasting and programming. In early 1995 the Supreme Court overturned that monopoly in deciding a case brought by the Cricket Association of Bengal and the Board of Control for Cricket in India, which had sought a contract with foreign telecasters. The court held that free speech was being obstructed and called for the immediate establishment of a public regulatory authority to oversee wide public access to the media.

Recognizing that government enterprises have failed to provide the country with minimal, much less state-of-the-art, telecommunication services,

New Delhi has embarked on a dramatic course. The intent is to eliminate the 8 to 10 years of waiting now required to obtain a telephone line for an office or home. By March 1997 there is to be at least one public telephone for each of India's 600,000 villages; only 200,000 communities are currently served by at least one telephone line. Domestic and foreign firms will enter markets alongside existing Department of Telecommunications operations; this will help allay union fears of job losses in the state sector. In 1994 the government took steps to establish a telecommunications regulatory system and opened bids on service areas for wired and cellular services. The first round of auctions yielded a potential $45 billion in fees for the government. AT&T, U.S. West, Nynex, British Telecom, Telekom (Malaysia), and France Telecom were among the international participants.

Unfortunately, the bidding process had an unexpected outcome. A small entrant, Himachal Futuristic Communications Ltd., won the right to provide service in nine regions, most with bids substantially outreaching the next highest. Doubts about the company's financial and technical capacities led to government intervention, limiting any firm to three licenses. Opposition parties in parliament erupted in a firestorm of criticism and leveled accusations of impropriety. The government stood firm, but the muddied situation caused some foreign firms to stay out of a January 1, 1996, round of bidding. Nonetheless, there is no doubt that India is committed to moving toward the telecommunications frontier as soon as possible.

What Remains to Be Done

As the world's largest democracy takes stock after 50 years of freedom, there remains a long list of matters that will require resolution. In most of these areas advancements will occur not so much by reflexive reactions to compelling international pressures and opportunities but through concerted domestic action via constructive governance.

Despite its strong commitment to socialism, India has made disappointing strides in reducing illiteracy, improving education, and enhancing health. The literacy rate has risen from 18 percent in 1950 to only 50 percent in the 1990s, and girls lag at all levels of schooling. Over 186 million people do not have access to potable water supplies and 644 million do not have sanitary facilities. Life expectancy has climbed from 40 to 61 years during independence, but infant mortality remains high. Although the rate of population growth has been falling and is probably now at or just below 2 percent annually, India's population is expected to reach 1.5 billion or so by the middle of the next century. Reducing the birthrate by improving women's health is a worthy goal. Continued economic and social progress requires urgent improvement in all these areas.

The nation's infrastructure, especially its roads, is in need of massive investment. Housing and urban amenities have slipped far behind needs. A new delineation of responsibilities between the state governments and New Delhi must be worked out, along with appropriate tax and revenue divisions. A much more industrial and much more urban India will also face more worrisome environmental burdens. Air pollution is already severe in the major cities. Rivers are contaminated by agricultural runoff, industrial wastes, and untreated sewage. Forests and wildlife are under great stress.

In the 1990s India has abandoned or modified many of its economic precepts in reaction to dramatic changes internationally. Pursuing economic growth and social gains will require further adjustments; mistakes will no doubt be made and corrected. What might we expect in the near future?

Over the next decade or more, the Indian economy will grow at or above 6 percent, with higher rates of industrial and export expansion. The nation's involvement in world trade will widen and increased foreign investment will flow in. The private sector will be especially dynamic. As it redirects its attention toward infrastructure, education, and other social needs, the government will score measurable gains, although more slowly than many would like. State governments will assume more active roles in economic affairs, including international relationships. Only unexpected political or ethnic turbulence, or an imprudent military adventure, will derail India's economic locomotive.

14. India's Economic Liberalization: A Progress Report

April 2003

SHALENDRA D. SHARMA

D espite incremental and frustratingly piecemeal implementation, India's economic liberalization project has finally dispelled the specter that had haunted the country for so many years after independence: the stagnant 3 percent "Hindu growth rate." Indeed, with an average annual growth rate hovering above 6 percent, India was one of the world's fastest-growing developing economies in the 1990s.

The driving force behind economic revival is this ambitious reform program put into place after a severe balance of payments crisis in 1991. That year—in the face of a quickly deteriorating fiscal position, increasing external debt (especially short term), accelerating capital flight, and rapid depletion of foreign reserves—the Indian government, on the verge of defaulting on its foreign debt, was forced to seek emergency assistance from the IMF. In return, Prime Minister P. V. Narashima Rao's government promised to enact a wide range of macroeconomic reforms designed to "convert India from . . . [an] inward-looking economy into a market-friendly, outward-looking one."

The reform program that followed broke decisively with more than four decades of pervasive government planning and regulation that had earned India the dubious distinction of being the most controlled economy in the noncommunist world. The reforms have included the abolishment of state monopoly in virtually all sectors of the economy, significant liberalization of industry and trade, deregulation of the financial system, improvements to supervisory and regulatory systems, cuts in tariffs, and the introduction of policies favorable to privatization and foreign direct investment (FDI).

One of the most dramatic changes has been the liberalization of trade policy. Under the highly restrictive pre-1991 trade regime, government authorization was required for the import of virtually all goods; imports of manufactured consumer goods were completely banned. Maximum tariff rates exceeded 300 percent and the average tariff rate in 1990–1991 stood at 87 percent—the highest in the world. By 1994 the average tariff rate had declined to 33 percent and was approximately 20 percent in 2000.

Major change has also come to the industrial sector. Before the reform period, a long (and continually growing) list of industries, including iron and steel, heavy machinery, oil and petroleum, air transport, mining, and telecommunications, was reserved solely for the public sector, under the intrusive eye of the Monopolies and Restrictive Trade Practices Act. In a short period of time this heavily protected industrial sector has witnessed the virtual abolition of the industrial licensing system and other regulatory impediments. (Compulsory licensing is now required mainly for environmental, safety, and strategic reasons.) Moreover, many sectors of the economy previously reserved for state control have been opened for private investment, including power, telecommunications, mining, ports, transport, and banking. Substantial progress has also been made in phasing out remaining quantitative restrictions on agricultural, textile, and industrial products.

Prior to 1991, strict restrictions on FDI had reduced it to a trickle; since 1991 controls on FDI and portfolio investment have been significantly relaxed. Automatic approval of foreign investment of up to 51 percent of shareholding is now permitted for a wide range of industries (and since 1996 the list of industries in which FDI is permitted has been further widened, with 100 percent foreign equity and ownership permitted in some sectors). In September 1992, portfolio investment was allowed for registered foreign institutional investors, and Indian companies were permitted to raise capital from abroad by issuing equity in the form of global depository receipts and other debt instruments. The reforms in the financial sector have not only forced Indian companies to improve the quality of their products, but have enabled many to restructure their activities through mergers and acquisitions.

Banking has been subject to gradual reform since the early 1990s. Regulation and supervision of the banking system have been strengthened. In the past two years, a series of measures to reduce the number of nonperforming loans (especially in public sector banks) and to restructure three public sector banks has been implemented. The Reserve Bank of India—

the country's central bank—has also strengthened prudential requirements, including raising minimum capital and capital adequacy ratios to
conform to international standards. Equally important, greater competition in the banking sector and improvements in the capital and debt markets have reduced reliance on central bank financing.

"An Idea Whose Time Has Come"

Cumulatively, these reforms have reawakened among India's entrepreneurs
what John Maynard Keynes once called the "latent animal spirits," thereby
giving a sharp boost to growth. Nowhere is this dynamism more evident
than in the information technology (IT) industry and the service sector.
Ten years ago, India's computer industry had total sales of $150 million. In
2002 its exports were more than $6 billion—or 13 percent of India's total
exports. Indeed, India's IT industries now have a proven track record and
an international reputation for quality. The city of Hyderabad is known as
Cyberabad, and soon Indian companies such as Infosys, Wipro, and
Satyam could be household names around the world. India also accounts
for a third of the world's software engineers.

Robust exports of food and capital goods, garments, engineering tools,
and refined petroleum products have also contributed considerably to
India's growth in recent years. But it is the country's rapidly expanding
services sector that has provided growth and stability in the post–September 11 period, which has been characterized by uncertainty, financial market turmoil, and a sharp global economic slowdown. Services currently
account for 40 percent of India's GDP, 25 percent of its employment, and 30
percent of export earnings.

And what about the balance of payments crisis that drove India to reform? For the sixth consecutive year, India has recorded a surplus, despite
increases in oil prices, a sharp downturn in international equity prices, and
successive increases in interest rates in the United States and Europe. Foreign exchange reserves have risen steadily from $42.3 billion in March 2001
to a record level of nearly $72.4 billion in January 2003, which is equivalent
to almost 14 months of estimated imports for the current year. Reserves are
now more than four times the level of short-term external debt, providing
India with a substantial buffer. In fact, India's external debt situation has
improved significantly in recent years as a result of effective external debt
management. The foreign debt–GDP ratio decreased from 28.7 percent at

the end of March 1991 to 20.8 percent at the end of March 2002. The debt–service ratio declined from a peak level of 35.3 percent of current receipts in 1990–1991 to 16.3 percent in 2000–2001. For the first time, the World Bank has classified India as a "less-indebted country."

The economic growth catalyzed by the reforms has benefited (albeit unevenly) all sectors of society, so that India can finally point to a positive change in the country's stubborn poverty problem. Reaffirming that the link between economic growth and poverty reduction is unambiguous, the latest official surveys indicate that poverty levels have fallen from about 40 percent of the population to roughly 28 percent during the second half of the 1990s. This translates into a net reduction in rural poverty of some 60 million people between 1993 and 2000. (In rural India, poverty fell to 27 percent of the rural population, while urban poverty fell from 32 percent to 24 percent of the urban population.)

Victor Hugo once noted that "there is one thing stronger than all the armies in the world, and that is an idea whose time has come." The idea of market reforms that swept the world some two decades ago is now part of India's development vocabulary. Although supporting reforms was once considered politically incorrect, every major political party recognizes the need to "deepen" the reforms. The differences in opinion that occasionally arise are about the pace and ordering of reforms. Fears that changes in governments will undo what has been achieved or bring the reform process to a halt are without merit.

Funding the State . . .

The accomplishments of the past decade, while impressive, are dwarfed by what remains to be done. Of growing concern is the failure to maintain the economic momentum achieved through the early 1990s. Many had concluded that India's potential growth rate under reform is about 8 percent annually, but recent experience has fallen short of that: growth has shown a decelerating trend since 1997. Prolonged droughts, international sanctions following nuclear testing in 1998, high energy prices, and the devastating earthquake in the state of Gujarat in late January 2001 that killed approximately 20,000 people have all contributed to the slowdown. But the main reasons are egregious domestic macroeconomic distortions, a slackening in the pace of reforms in particular, and half-hearted attempts to follow through with the more difficult, yet crucial second-generation reforms such as financial regulation and labor law modernization.

The heart of the problem is India's peculiar system of fiscal federalism, which makes it impossible to reduce the skyrocketing fiscal deficits of the central and state governments. Specifically, under India's deeply flawed fiscal system, the central government allocates credit to state governments through a "formula" that is unrelated to whether state governments put their funds to productive use. Not surprisingly, state governments, in their eagerness to win elections, often make fiscally irresponsible campaign promises, and then pay for them with funds allocated by New Delhi. Currently, the combined federal and states' deficit exceeds 10 percent of GDP—the highest level since 1990. As a result, general government debt has risen to almost 65 percent of GDP. This huge fiscal deficit has placed tremendous upward pressure on interest rates and has also discouraged private investment.

To redress this problem, several state governments have signed memoranda of understanding on fiscal reform programs with New Delhi, and the process of reining in expenditures by reforming food subsidies and prices for petroleum has begun. Attempts continue to reduce the government's stake in state-owned enterprises, which remain a drain on resources. To enhance the revenue base, efforts are under way to improve tax collection.

. . . and Reforming Regulation

Additional challenges to further reform are India's infrastructure and regulatory bottlenecks. India's roads, railways, telecommunications, electric power, air transport, and ports need expansion as well as improvement in the quality of service. These issues can be best addressed through regulatory reform and increased investments. Although this area has been opened to private investment—including foreign investment—the authorities have been unsuccessful in creating a fully supportive environment for the private sector. For example, as part of the reform program, private investors are expected to generate electric power for sale to state electricity boards, which oversee transmission and distribution. But because of the boards' poor administrative capacity, along with the loss (or theft) of power during transmission and low electricity tariffs for many categories of consumers, private investors have concluded that the boards simply cannot guarantee payment. Indeed, many private investors have yet to be paid, while others are now demanding terms guaranteeing purchase of electricity by both the federal and state governments before they invest. Resolving this problem is critical; no sector of the economy can achieve successful transformation without an adequate and reliable supply of power.

Another critical part of the economy—the agricultural sector, which employs 60 percent of India's population—has also been ill served by the reform process. Declining public investment in irrigation, soil conservation, water and flood management, and rural infrastructure (coupled with only a modest rise in private investment in agriculture) has contributed to the deceleration in agricultural growth in the second half of the 1990s. The decreased public investment in agriculture can be traced to the poor fiscal position of state governments and the maintenance of generous support for inefficient subsidies. For example, as much as 0.7 percent of GDP goes into fertilizer subsidies. The major beneficiaries of this subsidy, however, are the poorly managed domestic fertilizer industry and high-income farmers.

Further exacerbating agricultural problems are outdated laws and regulations. The government's guaranteed price support for food grains—crucial in the 1960s and 1970s to give farmers the incentive to produce more food grains—has outlived its usefulness. Today, price controls are maintained for staples to ensure remunerative prices for farmers. As a result, support prices have been fixed higher than market prices, encouraging overproduction. This has led to an increase in the stock considered necessary to ensure food security (60 million tons in mid-2002, as opposed to a more reasonable 17 million tons).

Although the central and state governments have justified the maintenance of high support prices on the grounds that it allows them to procure and subsidize the sale of certain commodities to low-income families through the public distribution system, these claims are not entirely valid. It is well known that this system does not adequately distribute food to the needy. Yet, procurement by government agencies continues to increase—in large part to maintain the support prices (agriculture is also shielded through import and export controls, including tariffs and export restrictions). The abolition of the price support system is not likely in the near future, but it clearly needs to be better aligned to market demand if farmers are to be encouraged to shift from overproduced food grains like wheat and rice to other staples.

Next Steps

The Indian economy still remains relatively closed—at least by standards of the fast-growing economies of East Asia. Tariff levels are among the highest in the developing world; FDI remains low (FDI in India averages 0.5 percent of GDP; in China it is 5 percent of GDP); and currency restrictions need to be lifted. Domestically, privatization of state-owned businesses must be accelerated, regulation of the financial sector improved, labor laws modernized, and investment in primary education strengthened.

A government planning commission has reported that growth rates of between 8 and 9 percent annually over the next decade are required to reduce India's poverty rate to around 11 percent. The per capita income levels in China and other East Asian countries that were roughly comparable to those in India in the 1960s are now much higher. Renewing the momentum of reform, and thereby broadening and reviving growth, is essential if India is to achieve its economic goal of breaking out of the third world.

PART IV

Democratization

15. Bangladesh: Can Democracy Survive?

April 1996

CRAIG BAXTER

In 1990 two opposition leaders, generally opposed to each other as well as to the government of President Hussain Muhammad Ershad, joined together to force the resignation of Ershad and restore democracy. Five years later the two leaders, Prime Minister Begum Khaleda Zia of the Bangladesh Nationalist Party (BNP) and Sheikh Hasina Wajid of the Awami League, were on a collision course that puts the prospects for democracy in Bangladesh in doubt. The collision came on February 15, 1996, when Begum Zia's party won an almost uncontested election to parliament after Sheikh Hasina's party and other opposition groups boycotted the poll.[1]

The two leaders and their parties agreed to cooperate in order to depose Ershad, set up a caretaker government, and hold free and fair parliamentary elections. They differed, however, on what should follow. Prime Minister Begum Zia and the BNP wanted to retain the presidential system of government initiated by Mujib in 1975 and continued by military leaders Zia and Ershad (it was even said that Begum Zia wanted the Ershad system without Ershad). Sheikh Hasina and the Awami League wanted a return to parliamentary government, although it was her father who had ended that system.

The two parties opposed each other in the 1991 election and each received about 32 percent of the vote. The BNP, however, won the largest number of parliamentary seats, 140 of the 300 directly contested. The Awami League trailed with 88.

---

1. Prime Minister Begum Zia, the head of the BNP, is the widow of Ziaur Rahman ("Zia"), who was the key leader of the country from 1975 until his assassination in 1981. Sheikh Hasina Wajid, the head of the Awami League, is the daughter of Sheikh Mujibur Rahman ("Mujib"), who led Bangladesh to independence from Pakistan in 1971, served as prime minister from 1972 to January 1975, and then as president until his assassination in August 1975.

Even though Ershad had been forced to resign as president and was jailed (and even though before the election there had been talk of barring the party from the poll) his Jatiya Party won 35 seats. Other than demanding Ershad's release from jail, the Jatiya Party's platform differed little from that of the BNP. The Jamaat-i-Islam won 18 seats. The Jamaat wants to transform Bangladesh into an Islamic state in which sharia (Islamic law) would be imposed—and under which the two women who led the major parties might be disbarred from holding political office.

The election did not give the BNP a majority. But there were 30 women members to be elected indirectly by the parliament (the allocation of additional seats for women is a carryover from Pakistan, where it was assumed that women were unlikely to win in the general election). Women could also contest the directly elected seats, which Begum Zia and Sheikh Hasina did successfully. The BNP and the Jamaat agreed to support each other and were able to sweep the women's election, with the BNP winning 28 of the seats and the Jamaat the other 2. This gave the BNP an absolute majority of 168 of 330 seats.[2]

Begum Zia was sworn in as prime minister on March 20, 1991. Her cabinet included several ministers who had served in her husband's cabinet, along with retired civil servants and military officers. The constitution permitted 10 percent of the ministers to be drawn from outside parliament—a clause often referred to as the "technocrat" provision—which Zia used to make several appointments.

The Shift to a Parliamentary System

While the BNP oficially favored the continuation of the presidential system, support for this was far from unanimous in the party. Many cabinet ministers preferred a parliamentary system under which the president would have powers that were principally ceremonial. But it was the close popular vote in the 1991 election that shifted BNP opinion on this issue. If votes obtained by allies of the Awami League in seats the Awami League left open (that is, did not contest) are added to the Awami League total, the Awami League outpolled the BNP in the election. This made it more likely that the BNP would lose a presidential contest, since some or all of the opposition parties

2. Although the Jamaat was opposed to women holding high office, it was not opposed to women being represented.

might agree on a single candidate to oppose the BNP candidate, Begum Zia. A split government would, in the Bangladesh context, pose a much greater problem than a similar arrangement in France did during the last years of François Mitterrand's presidency; the opposition's tolerance level is very low in Bangladesh.

The BNP decided that a parliamentary system was the better course. Both the BNP and the Awami League proposed constitutional amendments to change the system. Because a two-thirds vote is needed to amend the constitution, the BNP could not force its version on the parliament. Compromise, a rare commodity in Bangladesh, was necessary.

A parliamentary commission made up of members of the major parties met and managed to reach an agreement on amending the constitution. One key sticking point was the continuation of the rule that 10 percent of the cabinet could be appointed from outside parliament, a point the Awami League finally accepted.

Parliament passed the compromise amendment on August 6, 1991, and Bangladesh returned to a parliamentary system. Begum Zia was sworn in again as prime minister under the new system on September 19.

On October 8, the parliamentary speaker, Abdur Rahman Biswas, was elected president by parliament for a five-year term. Even this created some controversy. Begum Zia apparently feared that some BNP members might vote against Biswas if a secret ballot were held. She arranged for a presidential ordinance to be issued by the acting president, Shahabuddin Ahmed, that allowed the vote to be held publicly. There were no defectors under this method of voting.

The amendment to change the form of government was the first and last compromise in parliament. The compromise had raised the hope that there would be cooperation between the government and the opposition, but this was not to be. The BNP used its majority to push through every bill the government proposed. The opposition often walked out of parliament when it felt that its views were not being listened to, much less considered. At the same time, whatever agreement there had been between the BNP and the Jamaat quickly evaporated. The BNP was willing to accept the Jamaat votes in the women's election, but it was firmly opposed to the Jamaat's Islamization plans.

Religious and Political Unraveling

In 1993 communal violence between Muslims and Hindus in what is now Bangladesh broke out for the first time since 1964. The fighting stemmed from the destruction of the Babri Masjid mosque at Ayodhya in India in December by groups associated with the Hindu nationalist Bharatiya Janata Party. The violence was confined mainly to Dhaka and Chittagong, and was soon controlled by the police. The Jamaat denied any involvement; smaller, violent Islamic groups were found responsible.

A Bangladeshi novelist and physician, Taslima Nasreen, further aroused the anger of the extremist Islamic groups when she wrote a novel, *Shame*, criticizing the actions of Muslims against Hindus in the post–Babri Masjid period. The extremists said that this and other actions by Nasreen, including a newspaper interview in Calcutta, were blasphemous, and they demanded her death. Fearing for her life she left Bangladesh —perhaps with the connivance of the government—and arrived in Sweden on August 10, 1994.

On January 30, 1994, the BNP suffered a setback in city corporation elections when the party lost the mayoral contests in both Dhaka and Chittagong to the Awami League, although it won in Khulna and Rajshahi. The loss of Dhaka was especially galling since the BNP had won all 13 seats from Dhaka district (of which the city is the major part) in the 1991 parliamentary election, even defeating Sheikh Hasina in the contest for one of those seats. There was also a substantial drop in the popular vote from the 1991 election.[3]

On March 20, 1994, a by-election for a parliamentary seat in the district of Magura was held. The seat had been held by the Awami League, but the BNP was declared the winner. The Awami League cried foul, claiming that the voting had been rigged. The BNP denied the charge and its stand was upheld by the Election Commission. A senior civil servant who was involved in the matter told this writer that the only violation of election rules came when some members of the Awami League refused to vacate a government rest house. In his view, the Awami League had simply chosen the wrong candidate. There has been no solid proof that vote-rigging took place. Whatever may be the case, the charge led to a series of demands by the opposition that seriously endangered the 1996 election.

3. See Nizam U. Ahmed, "Party Politics in Bangladesh's Local Government," *Asian Survey,* vol. 35, no. 11 (November 1995).

Another event that rocked the political scene in 1994 was the Golam Azam case. Azam was allegedly guilty of war crimes and actions resulting in the deaths of many who favored an independent Bangladesh in the 1971 war. After the war he fled to Pakistan. He then returned to Bangladesh and became the leader of the Jamaat.

The charges against Azam were pursued using two strategies. One was to demand that he be tried for the alleged war crimes. Awami Leaguers were among those who made this demand. Azam was placed under arrest but a formal trial was never held. He has since been released from jail, but a group of citizens did convene a trial—which, of course, had no legal standing—and "convicted" him. His claim to Bangladeshi citizenship was also challenged. The government charged that in fleeing Bangladesh and taking up residence in Pakistan, Azam had lost his Bangladeshi citizenship. The case went to the Supreme Court, which ruled on June 22, 1994, that Azam was a Bangladeshi citizen as defined in the constitution because he had been born in territory that had since become Bangladesh.

The Awami League continued its protests over the alleged election fraud in Magura, joined by the Jatiya Party and the Jamaat, along with several other much smaller parties, in what is surely a strange alliance. Ershad's Jatiya Party is not a natural ally of the Awami League—the league had played a major role in ousting Ershad and demanding his arrest and trial for various crimes. And the Jamaat had just pursued the Golam Azam case, in which the Awami League was opposed to the Jamaat. The only bond among the parties is their strong opposition to Begum Zia and the BNP.

The Seeds of Distrust

A parliamentary government requires a certain level of respect, consideration, and cooperation between the government and the opposition, and this includes consultation between the prime minister and the leader of the opposition. This was seen once since the 1991 election: when the BNP and the Awami League compromised on the change from a presidential system to a parliamentary system. After this the BNP used its majority to pass legislation with little or no discussion with the opposition on or off the house floor.

But if the BNP majority failed to fulfill the parliamentary ideal of taking into account the objections of the opposition, those parties forming the opposition have done no better in acting as a "loyal opposition" that respects the government of the day. When the opposition demanded that the government resign before the 1996 election, it was clear that the ingredients necessary for a functioning government were not present in the Bangladeshi parliament.

The opposition's demand that the government resign before the 1996 election became specific, with the time period set at 90 days prior to the election. In that 90-day period the administration would be in the hands of a "neutral caretaker government" whose primary purpose would be to conduct the poll. The opposition made it clear that the record of Magura as they saw it disqualified the BNP government from conducting the election since it could not be trusted to do so in a free and fair manner.

The demand soon became non-negotiable. Sheikh Hasina said several times that she would meet the prime minister only after the demand had been accepted; of course, then there would be little left to talk about. The demand statements themselves were sketches about what form the caretaker government would take.

On May 5, 1994, the opposition began a boycott of parliament to support its demand. Prime Minister Zia said she would resign from her post 30 days before the election. As one foreign visitor, a former speaker of the British House of Commons, noted, a compromise on 60 days ought to have been easy to make, but the opposition's demand remained non-negotiable.

The opposition began a series of demonstrations and *hartals* (general strikes) that disrupted the economy and left the government and the opposition no closer to an agreement. On December 28 the opposition resigned en masse from parliament. This may have been a foolish move; if a compromise had been reached it would most likely have required a constitutional amendment that could only be passed by a two-thirds majority of parliament.

The speaker refused to accept the resignations on the flimsy ground that he had not received individual letters of resignation from each resigning member. However, absenting oneself from parliament can lead to disqualification if the absence, without excuse, lasts for 90 sitting days. On June 20, 1995, the opposition seats were declared vacant. A constitutional amendment was no longer possible.

The Constitutional Impasse

The government continues to argue that the opposition's demand is not in accord with the constitution; but neither was the setting up of a caretaker government in 1990 fully within constitutional parameters.

The constitution requires by-elections for vacated seats to be held within 90 days of the vacancy. Thus, the by-elections for the resigned seats in parliament should have been held by September 18. But another clause provides that in case of emergency this period may be extended by another 90 days. Flooding in northern Bangladesh provided such an emergency and a new date was set for December.

It was clear that the opposition would not contest the by-elections. An uncontested election would be a farce, so the prime minister asked the president to dissolve parliament, which he did on November 24. This solved the by-election problem but did not settle the general election impasse.

Throughout this period, foreign emissaries made many attempts to help solve the deadlock between the government and the opposition. The Commonwealth of Nations sent its secretary general and a former governor general of Australia to help. Western ambassadors in Dhaka tried to persuade the two parties to reach a compromise so that a free and fair election could be held within the time limit prescribed by the constitution. None of these efforts have been successful.

The Election Commission set February 15 as the date for the general election. The election had already been postponed twice because of opposition complaint that it did not have time to select its candidates (this itself was a strange complaint, since the opposition insisted that it would not take part in the election unless its original demand for the BNP government's resignation was met). In addition, the election date fell during the Muslim holy month of Ramadan, hardly a good time to campaign or vote.

The February 15 election was not a true measure of the support of the people for the various parties. The opposition, with the exception of a few very small parties, boycotted the poll. Unsurprisingly, the BNP took most of parliament's 300 seats. Bangladesh has thus returned to the situation in 1988, when Ershad held an election that was boycotted by the opposition and an unrepresentative parliament was installed. The 1996 parliament will be as representative. The opposition has threatened constant strikes against the new government. Bangladesh will, no doubt, be swept up in turmoil for some time to come.

The Economy: "A More Hopeful Story"

The BNP government's performance in the economic field has been quite good. Annual GDP growth has been about 5 percent, with recent growth in the industrial sector hovering around 15 percent. The privatization program, begun slowly under Zia and accelerated under Ershad, has continued, although the number of state-owned enterprises turned over to the private sector remains small.

Investment capital is not abundant. Labor unions also are concerned about unemployment because private owners are not likely to keep redundant workers on the payroll. The government has tried to meet the demands of the International Monetary Fund in matters such as reducing the budget deficit, lowering tariffs, freeing foreign exchange, and improving the collection of taxes. The inflation rate has been reduced to a manageable rate of 7 to 8 percent. Attempts to attract foreign direct investment continue, but a shortage of natural, human, and financial resources in Bangladesh makes this a questionable project. More, but still insufficient funds have been devoted to education, health delivery, and population planning.

In writing about the economy of Bangladesh, the December 25, 1995, *Economist* noted that even with the many reports of poverty in Bangladesh, there is "a more hopeful story." It pointed out that many participating in the country's economic expansion are women, and many of them are employed in the garment industry. "Bangladesh is now one of Asia's more open economies with import tariffs averaging 26% and no industrial licensing controls."

A Thing of the Past

The cooperation in 1990 between the BNP and the Awami League in the ouster of Ershad is clearly a thing of the past. The hostility between the government and the opposition and between the leaders of each has jeopardized Bangladesh's democracy. One of the leading commentators in Bangladesh, Mizanur Rahman Shelley, said in the October 24, 1995, *Independent* (Dhaka) that, "The lack of a worldwide civil society...is why people of struggling Bangladesh are caged by 72- and 96-hour hartals that virtually close down the impoverished country. The reason for their predicament is the impractical stubbornness of their leaders to come to terms as to how a civil society should resolve its problems in a civilized manner."

Bangladeshi leaders need a strong dose of the medicine prescribed by Shelley if democracy and development are to continue. Unfortunately, many Bangladeshis agree with shopkeeper Joynal Abedin, who told the January 14 *New York Times* that, "Our politicians think only about power, about their own greed."

16. Pakistan at Fifty: A Tenuous Democracy

December 1997

SAMINA AHMED

W hen Pakistan gained independence after the dismemberment of the British Indian empire in 1947, the people of the newly independent state were hopeful that their own country would give them the rights and freedoms denied by a colonial order. For most of Pakistan's history, however, the rights of the people have been usurped by authoritarian rulers. Although Pakistan at 50 does have all the trappings of a democratic regime—an elected government, functioning representative institutions, and a formal adherence to constitutional rule—democratic norms and governance continue to elude a weak and fragile state. Not only is the legitimacy of state institutions contested, but linguistic, regional, ethnic, and sectarian divisions threaten Pakistan's fragile national cohesion. Moreover, with the economy in shambles, the managers of the state have proved themselves incapable of providing a better life for Pakistan's citizens.

Democracy was formally restored in 1988 after more than a decade of military rule that had seen state policies fuel ethnoregional and sectarian tensions and widen economic disparities. Nine years later, Pakistan's political leaders and parties have failed to establish a stable democratic order. Economic stagnation and underdevelopment, political infighting, corruption, and ineptitude have led to widespread popular disillusionment and even despair. A public opinion poll published by *The News* (Islamabad) in September 1997 found that a vast majority of respondents believed sectarian conflict and lawlessness would rise; only 5 percent were optimistic that Pakistan would even survive.

As public confidence in the state and its institutions has declined, elements of Pakistan's opinion-making elite have begun to question the democratic system, claiming that an ineffective and irresponsible elected leadership cannot achieve political stability and economic growth. Pakistan's political history, however, reveals that authoritarian state structures, weak democratic institutions, and the absence of democratic values and norms have all contributed to the crisis of the state after 50 years of existence.

Military-Guided Democracy

In its first decade, Pakistan was ostensibly a democratic state. Yet none of the preconditions for a democratic order existed. There was no elected leadership or representative political institutions. The absence of democratic values and institutions was partly the legacy of Pakistan's birth. Political institutions in the former colonial state were weak, while its state apparatus was overdeveloped. Moreover, the Muslim League leadership that had spearheaded the struggle to form the Muslim-majority state lacked mass support in the areas that now constituted Pakistan. Since the political leadership was incapable of or uninterested in attaining popular support, it soon became dependent on the civil and military bureaucracies to retain power and suppress domestic dissent.

The inherited state apparatus at first propped up the political leadership and then supplanted it. As a result, during the so-called parliamentary period between 1947 and 1958, there were no elected parliaments, and governments were formed and dismissed by the civil bureaucracy with the military's support. When General Ayub Khan decided in 1958 to oust the nominal political leadership, a period of direct military rule followed in which no political dissent was allowed and any pretense of representative rule was discarded.

Internal tensions and popular demands for democracy resulted in Ayub's replacement in 1969 by General Yahya Khan, who held Pakistan's first general elections. The results of the 1970 elections, in which the Awami League, an East Pakistani opposition party, emerged victorious, were rejected by the West Pakistan–based Punjabi-Pakhtun dominated military; civil war, Indian military intervention, and the breakaway of East Pakistan soon followed.

After its defeat in the 1971 Indo-Pakistani war and East Pakistan's secession and recognition as the independent state of Bangladesh, the military withdrew to the background, transferring power to Zulfiqar Ali Bhutto, the head of the Pakistan People's Party (PPP), which had won a majority of seats in West Pakistan in the 1970 election. Authoritarian rule was replaced by a democratic order of sorts, but this new dispensation contained its own contradictions. Although Bhutto had a significant base of popular support, he was unable to challenge the military's dominance. Moreover, encroachments on provincial autonomy and Bhutto's disregard of democratic norms weakened his government's legitimacy. His growing dependence on the military to forcibly suppress political dissent spelled the end of a brief democratic episode. Following allegations of rigging the 1977 elections, the Bhutto government was dismissed and martial law imposed.

During the next 11 years, General Zia ul-Haq's military regime discarded democracy. Dissent was forcibly repressed and political parties were banned. Since popular legitimacy eluded the military regime, Zia tried to consolidate its domestic hold by co-opting a section of the political leadership, appointing a nominated parliament and prime minister. When Zia died in a plane crash in 1988, the military high command decided, once again, to direct affairs from behind the scenes, ostensibly restoring democracy.

The military's refusal to accept civilian supremacy has distorted and diluted the democratic character of the political order in place since 1988. For example, after the PPP's victory under Benazir Bhutto—the daughter of Zulfiqar—in the 1988 elections, it was not allowed to form a government until it had consented to a power-sharing agreement that ensured that the armed forces' institutional interests and the military's formulation of sensitive internal and external policies would not be challenged. Thus the first Benazir Bhutto government and all those that have followed have relinquished some of their authority in return for military support.

Whenever a government has attempted to challenge the military's dictates, it has been removed. Thus governments may have been formed by the will of the people, but the popular mandate has not been respected. No elected government has survived a full term, and even the electoral process has been tampered with. In 1990, for example, Prime Minister Benazir Bhutto's two-year-old PPP government was removed by the president at the military's behest, and the elections later that year resulting in the victory of Nawaz Sharif's Islamic Democratic Alliance (IDA) were rigged. In 1993, the military's displeasure with Sharif led to his removal. Benazir Bhutto was again elected prime minister, and the military was, once again, instrumental in dismissing her government in 1996. February 1997 saw Sharif, now head of the Pakistan Muslim League-Nawaz (PML-N), elected prime minister again. The military's constant interventions have led to a progressive weakening of democratic institutions, creating doubts about the democratic character of Pakistan's current political dispensation.

Distorted Democracy

Long years of authoritarian rule have left the political leadership unable to work collectively to strengthen and maintain democratic institutions and values. For example, since it came to power this February, Sharif's Muslim League has used its overwhelming majority in parliament to push through successive amendments that have distorted the spirit of the 1973 constitution. This behavior mirrors that of the government's predecessors, since most Pakistani governments have disregarded constitutional governance and norms. Pakistan's founding fathers did not even feel the need for a constitution; the first was drafted as late as 1956 by Iskader Mirza, an unelected president who represented the interests of the dominant civil-military bureaucracies. The declaration of martial law in 1958 led to the abrogation of this document. In 1962 the military regime promulgated its own constitution, which had as little legitimacy as its authors.

Both the 1956 and 1962 constitutions created highly centralized state structures dominated by a strong executive. Nominal legislatures and state intolerance of political dissent retarded the growth of a political party system and perpetuated patron-client relationships. The judiciary, lacking independence and autonomy, was unable to provide justice; thus the rule of law was undermined.

Following Pakistan's breakup in 1971 and the withdrawal of direct military rule, the political leadership, headed by Zulfiqar Bhutto's PPP government, drafted the 1973 constitution. This document created a parliamentary democracy based on a federal structure, the separation of the three branches of government, and the provision of fundamental rights to citizens. While Bhutto's authoritarian style subsequently undermined the fundamental rights guaranteed by the constitution, the existence of a constitutional doctrine formally defining governmental limits and responsibilities did reinforce democratic norms, including the rule of law.

The 1973 constitution was, however, distorted in spirit and form by Zia ul-Haq's attempt to gain legitimacy and suppress dissent and democratic aspirations. While the constitution was not abrogated, a 1985 amendment providing constitutional cover to all acts and ordinances of martial law changed its character. Thus Islamic legislation discriminating against women and minorities became a part of the constitution, directly contradicting the doctrine of fundamental rights. The military regime's political preferences were also constitutionally enshrined. Parliamentary democracy was weakened by Article 52, which gave an indirectly elected president—a position held by Zia himself—the power to dismiss a representative prime minister and national and provincial legislatures.

The distorted constitutional framework inherited by elected governments after the restoration of democracy in 1988 prevented the consolidation of democratic institutions and norms. Since the long period of authoritarian rule had also deeply polarized the body politic, the Pakistani political leadership failed to join hands to remove the 1985 amendment. When in power, the two major political parties, the PPP and the Muslim League, have supported the abrogation of the 1985 amendment; when in opposition, they have advocated keeping the amendment, since it is seen as a device to dismiss the government of their political opponent. With the assistance of willing political partners, successive military chiefs have used the 1985 amendment to remove elected governments, manipulating democratic politics and the direction of political development.

The military has long been deeply hostile to the PPP, which had been the mainstay of organized political opposition during the Zia years. In a military-directed "constitutional coup," the president dismissed the PPP government of Benazir Bhutto in 1990, using his powers under the 1985 amendment. When Bhutto's successor and the military's chosen civilian partner, Prime Minister Sharif, attempted to assert his authority, he too was removed by the president at the military's instigation using Article 52 in 1993. A temporary alliance with the military high command brought Bhutto back to power but not for a full term since she was, as noted earlier, once again removed by the president at the military's bidding in 1996.

Not surprisingly, the top priority of the current Sharif government is survival. Using its overwhelming majority in parliament, the government has pushed through successive constitutional amendments to strengthen its position. This April, with the support of the PPP opposition, the ruling party passed the thirteenth amendment to the constitution, depriving the president of his powers to dismiss assemblies and sack governments. While the passage of this amendment has received strong domestic support, the July 1997 fourteenth amendment—an antidefection bill—has been strongly criticized.

Dissension within the ruling party's ranks prompted Sharif to push through the fourteenth amendment, by which a parliamentarian can lose his or her seat if he or she breaches party discipline, votes against the party line, or abstains from voting in a manner that violates party policy. No judicial recourse will be available to a legislator declared a defector by a party's disciplinary committee.

The fourteenth amendment has led to concerns that members of parliament will be held hostage by their party leadership, unable to voice dissenting opinions or vote their conscience. This emasculation bodes ill for democratic politics, especially in view of the Muslim League's majority and a weak and ineffective parliamentary opposition.

Relying on the Judiciary

While the legislature has become increasingly subservient to the executive, democracy has been strengthened by an assertive judiciary. In the past, especially during periods of direct military rule, the judgments of superior courts had undermined democratic norms by condoning authoritarian intervention. Since the restoration of democracy, some judgments of the superior judiciary, such as its decision to uphold the dismissals of PPP governments in 1990 and 1996, have been internally queried; moreover, the judiciary rejected the president's dismissal of Sharif's Muslim League administration in 1993, which led to the restoration of the Muslim League government. (The military high command, however, then forced the prime minister and president to resign, which led to the government's dissolution.)

At the same time, the judiciary has aggressively asserted its constitutional role, upholding the rule of law and reinforcing democratic norms. Superior court rulings and findings have condemned transgressions by state institutions of the fundamental rights of citizens. Judges on the panel examining the circumstances behind the killing of Murtaza Bhutto, Benazir Bhutto's brother, for example, held police and state agencies responsible for acts of premeditated violence.

The superior judiciary has also taken governments to task for resorting to coercive measures to stem ethnic and sectarian conflict. The supreme court upheld the dismissal of the Bhutto government in 1996 partly on the grounds that it had allowed human rights violations and "extrajudicial" killings in Sindh province. In July 1997, the chief justice of the supreme court took suo moto action on "indiscriminate killings," crime, and violence in Karachi, the capital of Sindh. The hearings are under way.

Nor is the judiciary prepared to accept executive interference with its independence. Thus another judicial justification for the dismissal of the

Bhutto government was its contempt for the superior judiciary and political interference in judicial appointments. Just as the assertiveness of the judiciary led to a clash between the two branches of government in 1996, there are indications of growing tensions between the superior judiciary and the Sharif government.

Reacting negatively to judicial assertiveness, including the examination of ethnic management policies in Sindh, the Sharif administration has begun to challenge the judiciary's autonomy. In September the government initially decided (though it later reversed itself) to reduce the number of supreme court judges in an attempt to circumvent the chief justice's recommended promotions to the bench. Despite warnings from the bench that executive interference will undermine democratic governance, Sharif has declared that the parliament, in which the ruling party has a large majority, will exercise its constitutional powers to determine the size of the supreme court.

This confrontation between two key institutions of a fragile democratic order bodes ill for political stability. The removal of yet another elected government, no matter how inept, would likely destabilize democracy. Judicial assertiveness in upholding the rule of law and fundamental human rights will promote and maintain democratic norms, but only if democratic governance survives and is strengthened.

Internal Schisms

Ethnic and sectarian violence poses a far greater threat to the Sharif government than judicial disapproval since it has rendered elected governments vulnerable to authoritarian intervention. The breakdown of law and order in Sindh—especially ethnic violence in the province's urban areas—was used by the military as a justification for dismissing the PPP governments in 1990 and 1996. Proponents of authoritarian rule claim that the failure of elected representatives to subdue substate extremism proves the ineffectiveness and inadequacy of democratic politics in Pakistan.

But Pakistan's political history reveals that ethnic divisions and sectarian tensions are directly related to the absence of representative rule and democratic norms. Successive regimes have failed to provide institutionalized mechanisms to accommodate ethnic and regional demands in a pluralistic society, transforming the internal competition for political power and socioeconomic benefits into conflict between substate actors.

In pre-1971 united Pakistan, political and economic power was monop-olized by a predominantly West Pakistan–based, and mainly Punjabi, civil and military bureaucracy that operated through highly centralized state structures; this resulted in widespread alienation among the Bengalis of East Pakistan. Since Bengalis constituted over 54 percent of the popula-tion, the predominantly Punjabi, politically dominant military saw demo-cratic institutions as a threat to its interests. Even in West Pakistan, ethnic grievances mounted as the Sindhi, Baluch, and (to a lesser extent) the Pakhtun populations were deprived of representative and participatory avenues for articulating grievances and voicing demands. (In 1971, the Yahya regime's refusal to transfer power to the East Pakistan–based Awami League resulted in the bloody civil war and the breakup of Pak-istan.)

In present-day Pakistan, Punjabis form a majority of the population and continue to dominate the military and civil bureaucracy. Only superfi-cial attempts have been made to provide adequate representation to ethnic minorities such as the Sindhis and the Baluch. The 1973 constitution did address some ethnoregional demands by creating a federal framework, but it has failed to accommodate regional demands for greater autonomy and control over provincial resources. As ethnic grievances have increased, au-thoritarian rulers, apparently having learned little from the East Pakistan experience, have relied on coercion to suppress regional and ethnic de-mands. Even when elected governments have been in power, the military has retained control over sensitive policy areas, including ethnic relations. Its dependence on ethnic manipulation, divide-and-rule strategies, and the use of force have exacerbated internal divisions.

In Sindh, for example, the Zia regime considered the Sindhis a threat since they had spearheaded resistance to military rule. To contain Sindhi dissent, the minority Urdu-speaking Muhajir community—migrants and their descendants from India's west and north—were extended state sup-port. Since Pakistan's formation, Muhajirs, who mainly settled in the urban centers of Sindh, had received state patronage while ethnic Sindhis were neglected. Muhajirs were, for example, over-represented in the civil bu-reaucracy and provided preferential access to economic resources. During the administration of Zulfiqar Ali Bhutto—himself a Sindhi—attempts to redress the grievances of the Sindhis caused Muhajir estrangement, mani-fested in language riots. Under Zia's military rule, when Sindhi alienation was at its height, Sindhi-Muhajir relations deteriorated even further as the Muhajirs sided with the military regime. Following the formation of Altaf

Hussain's Muhajir Qaumi Movement (MQM) in 1986, Sindhi-Muhajir tensions resulted in periodic outbreaks of violence.

During the first terms of the PPP and PML-N governments, the military continued to dictate ethnic policy in Sindh, based on a combination of coercion and co-optation. When ethnic violence increased, especially in Sindh's capital, Karachi (Pakistan's only port and main industrial and commercial center), the military conducted operations, first against the Sindhis, and then against an increasingly assertive Muhajir leadership. The military-sponsored split of the MQM, which created a splinter group called the MQM-Haqiqi, contributed to ongoing Muhajir infighting that has claimed more than 400 lives in the first six months of 1997 alone.

Thus elected governments have been dismissed for their failure to maintain law and order in Sindh, but democratic governance and democratic politics themselves have been the victims of the military's interventionist policies. Electoral alliances in the Sindh provincial government and in the federal government, such as the coalition between the first PPP government and the MQM, have failed because of direct intervention on the part of the military. In 1997, Sindh is once again ruled by a precariously balanced alliance, this time between the Muslim League and the MQM. As Muhajir infighting engulfs Karachi, MQM leader Altaf believes that the MQM's branch of the Muslim League is incapable or unwilling to address its concerns, including the alleged support extended by military-dominated intelligence agencies to its MQM-Haqiqi rivals.

The Sharif government also faces an upsurge of sectarian violence between Pakistan's 80 percent Sunni Muslim majority and 18 percent Shiite Muslim minority, particularly in urban Sindh and Punjab; this has prompted the administration to deploy paramilitary forces in a number of cities. While sectarian tensions have periodically erupted throughout Pakistan's history, communal violence has become endemic since the 1980s, when the Zia dictatorship used religion to legitimize military rule, patronizing selected Sunni religious groups who were then pitted against the regime's political opponents. The confrontation with state-sponsored Sunni religious extremists resulted in a Shiite backlash and the formation of Shiite armed factions. After the restoration of democracy, successive governments have tried to contain sectarian violence with little success, since groups across the sectarian divide are well armed and motivated.

The situation is complicated by the links between Pakistan's internal and external security dilemmas. Ethnic and sectarian groups have easy access to sophisticated arms, a direct result of Pakistan's involvement in neighboring Afghanistan's civil war (yet another legacy of the Zia era). Cross-border traffic in narcotics also provides funds for extremists and has promoted the criminalization of Pakistani politics. A speedy resolution of the Afghan crisis and a strict policy of nonintervention would clearly help elected governments buttress internal stability. The military, however, continues to dictate policy toward Afghanistan.

The Sharif administration's proposed remedy, the Anti-Terrorist Act of August 1997, is unlikely to help the government contain ethnic and sectarian violence, and may have grave implications for democracy. The act gives the military and civilian law-enforcement agencies unprecedented powers to search and enter or arrest without a warrant and to use force against "suspected" perpetrators of violence. It also waives the constitutional bar against self-incrimination. No legal action can be taken against any person for any act committed in good faith under the antiterrorist law. Special courts dealing with criminals charged under the act must dispose of cases within seven days, and appeals can be lodged only in a specially constituted appellate tribunal, which again must give its judgment within a week.

The act has been severely criticized by the political opposition, lawyers, and human rights activists, who fear that granting extraordinary powers to the police, paramilitary forces, and the military will undermine fundamental human rights guaranteed by the constitution and turn Pakistan into a police state. The political legitimacy of the ruling Muslim League is likely to erode as the antidemocratic provisions of the act are applied. And it will not bring an end to sectarian and ethnic strife, which depends on the government's political resolve to address internal grievances and uphold the rule of law.

Questioning Democracy

A shift from democracy to authoritarianism is unlikely to occur in the immediate future due to a number of internal and external imperatives. In the external sphere, the military establishment is aware of the changes in the international environment. With the end of the cold war and the decline in Pakistan's strategic utility, its main allies, such as the United States, will not approve of a reimposition of military rule, and major aid donors such as Japan could withdraw badly needed assistance and investment.

Internal factors will, however, play a more significant role in preventing direct military rule. The military's ostensible support for democracy has helped democratic governance regain some of its lost legitimacy, and Pakistan's circumscribed democracy has helped strengthen civil society; democratic norms are gradually taking root. In the past nine years a fiercely independent press has critically monitored the government's actions, promoting public awareness of democratic values and the dangers posed to civil society by authoritarianism. Human rights groups such as the Human Rights Commission of Pakistan are playing a crucial role in assisting the democratic process, as are several professional organizations, including those representing lawyers, women, and minorities.

Any attempt to remove the formal infrastructure of representative government is likely to be strongly resisted. Even the judiciary, which in the past accepted the executive's bidding, is unlikely to condone such a change. Yet the present political order's built-in distortions could prevent the consolidation of democratic institutions and norms. The growth of political consciousness among the Pakistani public is not paralleled by a commitment of its elite to democratic ideals. Thus a deeply polarized political leadership has become more committed to sustaining or attaining power, even at the cost of sacrificing democratization.

Successive elected governments have advanced the military's interests in the belief that the military establishment holds the ultimate political veto. In the 1997–1998 budget, for example, social spending has been cut while defense expenditures have increased and formally constitute 26 percent of the budget. At the same time, substate violence continues to threaten the security of Pakistan's citizens but there is little awareness in the political leadership of the urgent need to find sustainable solutions based on accommodation and bargaining as well as strict adherence to the rule of law.

The political leadership's lack of commitment to democratic politics is demonstrated by the Sharif administration's deeply flawed policy of *ehtesab,* or accountability, which is intended to end political corruption but is unmistakably partisan in nature, selectively targeting political opponents with little regard for legal due process. For her part, the main opposition leader, former Prime Minister Benazir Bhutto, has called for the dismissal of the elected leadership and the formation of a "national" government in which the bureaucracy, the armed forces, and the intelligence agencies are given representation. Sharif claims that "We have democracy and we should be thinking of strengthening" it; but unless the political leadership realizes that its very survival lies in collaborative efforts to consolidate a representative, pluralistic, and participatory system strong enough to withstand military intervention, democracy in Pakistan will remain vulnerable.

17. India's Vision—and the BJP's

December 1999

DAVID STULIGROSS

On October 13, 1999, Atal Bihari Vajpayee was sworn in as prime minister less than a week after the results from India's most recent national elections were announced. The extent of his winning coalition's victory bodes well for a stable national regime. His inauguration, which marked the culmination of another democratic election in this multiethnic nation of nearly 1 billion people, stood in stark contrast to the mechanics of political change in neighboring Pakistan, where, only the day before, the military had once again seized power in a coup.

The Elections and their Results

India's current electoral round started with a cup of tea. In April 1999, J. Jayalalitha, leader of the All India Anna Dravida Munnetra Kazhagam (AIADMK) Party, indicated her displeasure with the governing Bharatiya Janata Party–led coalition that included the AIADMK by meeting with Subramaniam Swamy, a renegade member of parliament. Within weeks the AIADMK withdrew support from the government but was unable to form an alternative government with the Congress Party. Since no coalition could claim a majority, parliament was dismissed and, after the government's budget was passed as presented, no lawmaking occurred between April and October. The existing Bharatiya Janata Party–led administration continued in office until the elections could be held.

Those elections, which began in early September, were held in a series of staggered state votes that ended in early October. It was by far the largest and most complex democratic process in the world: nearly 370 million citizens (fully 60 percent of eligible voters) in 537 constituencies chose among 2,850 candidates who represented some 160 parties (approximately 1,750 independent candidates ran as well). When the votes were tallied, representatives of 39 parties and 5 independent candidates had earned parliamentary seats. Twenty-four of these parties had been members of a preelection coalition, the National Democratic Alliance (NDA), led by the Bharatiya Janata Party. The BJP alone earned 184 seats, and the entire NDA earned 303 seats, 31 more than a simple majority. At the same time Congress, the other national party, demonstrated its strength in three of the five simultaneous state elections; it has formed governments on its own in Arunachal Pradesh and Karnataka and leads a coalition government in Maharashtra.

Three aspects of electoral dynamics suggest a stable run for the NDA. First, for the first time in a decade, a coalition has assumed office on the strength of a preelection alliance. Voters had the opportunity to consider the common NDA election manifesto before the election, and were thus aware of its agenda. Second, aside from the BJP, no National Democratic Alliance party can pull down the alliance by itself. The second-largest alliance member, the Telugu Desam Party (TDP), controls only 28 seats. Third, a fall from within would be made still more difficult if the NDA passes a constitutional amendment, proposed in its manifesto. Under the amendment, parties seeking to topple the government would first be required to demonstrate their ability to create an alternative majority coalition. This provision would reduce the kind of political opportunism that generated the current round of elections.

Nonetheless, Vajpayee's new coalition government faces three challenges. First, India's relationship with Pakistan, and security questions more generally, are floating to the surface of the average Indian citizen's political consciousness. Second, the Bharatiya Janata Party, the coalition's leading party, is increasingly torn between two development visions that unite and divide the Indian public in different ways: social nationalism and economic liberalism. Third, because they represent particular constituents with defined bread-and-butter concerns, the coalition parties that make up the government will compete with one another to direct scarce government resources toward their own constituents.

The Politics of Regional Security

International attention to South Asian regional security issues has evolved far more quickly in the past two years than have the issues themselves. In May 1998, India and Pakistan became declared nuclear powers and began the process of nuclear weaponization. One year later the world witnessed a military conflict between these declared nuclear powers when members of the Pakistani army and a disparate collection of insurgents from Afghanistan and Pakistan crossed the Kashmir Line of Control—the cease-fire line that divides the disputed territory between Pakistan and India—and occupied Indian bunkers. Normally these bunkers, which offer limited protection against the brutally cold winters in the high Himalayas, are vacated annually by Indian soldiers, only to be taken over subsequently by unwelcome guests of one stripe or another; in 1999, however, the extent and coordination of the Pakistani army–led occupation was unprecedented. This prompted an Indian air and infantry response, leading to the loss of nearly 3,000 lives, with India bearing the bulk of the casualties.

From the Indian perspective the confrontation was a response to a Pakistani military initiative, but that initiative has not generated a significant change in Indian security policy. To the extent that an Indian domestic change has occurred, it has been in the direction of a convergence of opinion among political parties and within the Indian public in favor of India vigilantly defending the Line of Control and pursuing diplomatic initiatives aimed at formalizing the current de facto arrangement as a permanent solution.

The intensity and breadth of this opinion has evolved over the past decade. In 1989, during the run-up to an earlier round of parliamentary elections and as Indian-Pakistani tensions were escalating, Prime Minister Rajiv Gandhi delivered a major Kashmir policy speech—to the utter disinterest of his audience in the southern city of Madras.[1]

In contrast, in 1999 people throughout the country demonstrated their support of India's Kashmir defense in two ways. First, millions of Indian citizens—including those in the south—attended rallies and contributed to bereavement funds for slain Indian soldiers. Second, a proposal for a 10 percent "Kashmir tax" gained wide support across the social, ideological,

---

1. The newspapers reported on the substance of the speech; Arun Swamy convincingly recorded the audience's disinterest. See Arun Swamy, "The Nation, the People, and the Poor: Sandwich Tactics in Party Competition and Policy Formation, India, 1931–1996," Ph.D. dissertation (Berkeley: University of California, Department of Political Science, 1996).

and geographic spectrum. Indian citizens, at the rhetorical level at least, are willing to pay to defend Kashmir, and that expense is substantial. Even in peacetime, India's Department of Defense spends $255 million annually to defend the Siachen Glacier, one small but expensive portion of Kashmir. While lower defense expenditures might enable India to avoid the painful bureaucratic and political changes required by the occasional loan from the International Monetary Fund, no political party, even if it chose to do so, could cast the tradeoff in these economic terms and still win votes.

Indeed, with one important exception, the national consensus on the security question deflated the issue's importance in the October 1999 elections. Early in the campaign, BJP aspirants claimed that the party's leadership was required to ensure a continued Kashmir defense. Leaders in the Congress Party retorted that under the BJP the government had bungled its intelligence operations: infiltrations that might have begun as early as November 1998 were not observed or reported until April 1999. Opinion polls showed that the charges sparked public interest for perhaps a week, but voters soon rejected the accuracy and relevance of both sides' charges. The issue completely fell from the electoral scene three weeks before polling was complete.

The exception, a back way into the security issue, took the form of competing characterizations of Congress Party president Sonia Gandhi. Gandhi is a member of the Gandhi dynasty: husband Rajiv, mother-in-law Indira, grandfather-in-law Jawaharlal Nehru. She is also an Italian-born, Indian-naturalized citizen. Although it is legal for a naturalized citizen to become India's head of state, debate raged within the country about whether a foreign-born leader would demonstrate appropriate judgment or command necessary authority in international negotiations.

The extent to which voters considered the dynastic and citizenship issues cannot yet be gleaned from electoral data, but the debate itself affected Congress's electoral fortunes before a single vote was cast. In May 1999, Sharad Pawar said he could not support Sonia Gandhi's prime ministerial ambitions. He was promptly expelled from the party and, together with two other Congress Party leaders expelled on similar grounds, formed a new party, the Nationalist Congress Party (NCP).

Sharad Pawar claimed early on that his NCP would remain "equidistant" from Congress and the BJP. Although rapprochement with Congress may seem simpler than a national alliance with the BJP, in the initial stages he has kept his promise. Along with the national elections, 5 of India's 25 states held elections as well; 2 of these were Maharashtra (India's most industrialized state) and Meghalaya (a small northeastern state). The NCP allied with the Congress to form a government in Maharashtra, and with the BJP to form a government in Meghalaya, thus putting into practice, as political scientist Arun Swamy observes, the NCP equidistance principle.

Competing National Visions

The Sonia Gandhi-as-foreigner issue is but a trivial example of a deep-rooted contest to define what it means to be an Indian citizen. The Congress Party, during its decades of uninterrupted national leadership, institutionalized aspects of competing notions of national incorporation: "assimilation" of individual citizens who share and contribute to a common notion of Indianness, and "integration" of communities whose very distinctiveness contributes to an evolving sense of what it means to be Indian. The BJP, in contrast, has placed both rhetoric and policy at the individual level and has made assimilation a top priority. This message has a demonstrated appeal: the BJP won 184 seats from 18 states and union territories. The party's days of relying on a narrowly defined urban base, especially in western India, are long past.

To be sure, the BJP's social vision in its purest form is extraordinarily broad, encompassing virtually all aspects of Indian society; it is a nationalist party, not a sectarian one. Also, accommodations made during the course of coalition-building since 1996 have taken the three most contentious issues of the BJP assimilationist agenda off the table.[2] Further, the BJP's proposed economic reforms attract voters (and coalition parties) who might not support the BJP social agenda. Nevertheless, fears linger. Competition between BJP leaders—whose top priority is a social agenda—and those who put economic development first continues to tear at the

---

2. These include promulgation of a common civil code for all Indians (currently, members of each religion are bound by laws—such as marriage, divorce, and inheritance—informed by their own religious traditions); a common degree of autonomy for all states (currently, for reasons associated with the terms of accession at independence, the state of Jammu and Kashmir has considerably more budgetary and policy autonomy than other states); and erection of a Hindu temple on a disputed site in Ayodhya (although it is hard to detect any broad, nation-building principle behind this agenda item).

party. Three moments in 1999 point to internal tensions the party must address in coming years.

First, some of the most severe Hindu-Christian violence in recent years occurred during the spring of 1999, with tribal communities in the states of Gujarat and Orissa as the focal points of the brutality. Both tribespeople and foreign missionaries were massacred. The broad BJP vision of "Hindu culture" can accommodate tribal communities that retain their traditional religions, but the vision is less clear about the national obligations of tribespeople who have converted to Christianity. More strident supporters of Hindu nationalism—members of Hindu social groups such as the Rashtriya Swayamsevak Sangh (RSS) and the Bajrang Dal—are quite clear that tribespeople who wish to convert to a "modern" religion must choose an Indian one, namely Hinduism. Christian evangelists, they believe, use coercive, or at best nonspiritual incentives in their appeals for new converts. This is an odd objection, however, for groups that include murder among their counterevangelistic methods.

As is often the case, this round of social violence was prompted by grassroots economic concerns. In Gujarat, tribespeople are increasingly successful at gaining agricultural employment as commercial farms extend into their traditional lands; lower-caste agricultural communities explain their underemployment by using social discrimination arguments, and the logic resonates. At the same time, tribespeople who are not employed on commercial farms observe the continuing "encroachment" of these farms on "their" land and use discrimination rhetoric to bolster support among "sons of the soil." Economic competition comes to wear communal garb. The BJP faces internal tensions because leaders who wish to address social dissension propose different solutions than those who wish to address underlying economic issues.

What is the relationship between the party, the government, and the violence? Surely the United States State Department's equating the BJP, the RSS, and Bajrang Dal mischaracterizes reality, but many analysts looked equally askance at reports by commissions of inquiry that absolved the BJP-led Gujarat state government and Bajrang Dal religious activists in Orissa of involvement in the killings in their states. The BJP undoubtedly has a nationalist agenda, yet debates rage within the party as to the content of that agenda. And there is no question that, in other contexts, civil society is expected to strengthen and deepen rather than weaken democratic processes. Further, it is increasingly clear that a tremendous variety of Indian citizens approve of the BJP's developmental vision. However, if social groups feel that implementation of the BJP vision in practice undermines their ability to cohere as a group or improve their economic conditions, individually or collectively, they are likely to rebel.

Such a democratic rebellion constitutes the second social moment. Limited evidence suggests that the Muslim communities, directed by their mullahs, effectively engaged in strategic voting during the 1999 election, particularly in the state of Uttar Pradesh (UP). In 1998 the BJP earned 54 of UP's 84 parliamentary seats; in 1999 this total dropped to 30. The BJP total was expected to fall because of increasing disaffection with the state-level BJP government and increasing tensions between the state and national units of the party. The puzzle is that two essentially state-level parties, the Samajwadi Party (SP) and the Bahujan Samaj Party (BSP), captured 14 new seats. Conventional wisdom held that the BJP's decline in seat terms would be smaller and that the Congress, which gained 10 seats, would be the main beneficiary of the BJP decline.

By far the dominant change in UP politics was the BJP vote share, which plunged from 36.2 percent to 28.2 percent. Reports in the press indicated that Muslim leaders directed their followers to vote for the party most likely to beat the BJP. Surely not all, and perhaps even not most, of UP's Muslim community, which makes up 16 percent of the state's population, heeded the call, but perhaps enough did to tip the electoral balance. The fascinating aspect of this strategy is that Muslims were not directed to vote *for* a party or an ideology, but *against* one. This is a weak form of expressing a politicized religious voice, but, if corroborated, it would be one of the strongest managed by the Muslim community in north India since independence.

The third social moment of 1999 takes the form of an alliance decision by one of the BJP's coalition partners, the Telugu Desam Party (TDP), led by Chandrababu Naidu in the state of Andhra Pradesh. Naidu is a strong proponent of the BJP's economic liberalization platform and, as chief minister of Andhra Pradesh, has enacted some of India's most far-reaching economic programs along with increased government support in areas such as health and education. He also faced the challenge of an apparently resurgent Congress as Andhra Pradesh headed simultaneously for state assembly and national parliamentary polls. The TDP calculation weighed the value of BJP support generally against potential alienation from the sizable Muslim population of Andhra Pradesh. (Muslims, to an extent comparable to other communities, have expressed confidence that Naidu's economic reforms will benefit them, at least in the medium term.)

Naidu's compromise was to hammer out a seat-sharing arrangement with the BJP (each would not run candidates in the other's constituencies), but he would not be an active partner in the BJP government. The arrangement proved to be exceptionally strong: the alliance earned 36 of the state's 44 parliamentary seats; the TDP alone earned 179 of the state's 294 assembly seats and has formed a state government on its own strength.

Pursuing Economic Development

The politics of economic development have shifted as state-level parties have become more prominent actors at the state and national levels. When Congress dominated national politics, it used central government resources to solidify its support in states where it was also in power as well as to developmentally outflank state governments controlled by other parties. The BJP is trying the same strategy, but it is hamstrung both because it must mediate between its own interests and those of the NDA's 23 other parties and because central government resources are rapidly dwindling.

The relationship between governance and development has evolved over the past half-century of Indian independence. India's first prime minister, Jawaharlal Nehru of the Congress, focused developmental efforts on two broad constituencies. Education policies, food subsidies, and political legitimacy for the poorest of the poor communities (especially the former untouchables and the tribal population) provided a wide electoral base. At the same time, loosely following Soviet developmental models, Nehru promoted a vision in which large-scale industries, tightly regulated by government, would become India's "modern temples" and engines of economic development. This combination of focused development and broad electoral support effectively shut out a growing spectrum of socially and economically mobile middle classes from the national development debate, not only because of their relatively small size at the time but also because they were in competition with one another. Middle-class developmental issues focused on social and economic concerns that did not reach the national level.[3]

---

3. See Arun Swamy, "Parties, Political Identities, and the Absence of Mass Political Violence in South India," in Amrita Basu and Atul Kohli, eds., *Community Conflicts and the State in India* (New Delhi: Oxford University Press, 1998), pp. 108–148.

These concerns did reach the state level, and by the mid-1960s the Congress came under increasing attack from relatively coherent state parties that succeeded in defeating the party at the state level. Every state has been governed at least once by some party other than Congress, and today Congress is in power in only 9 of India's 25 states. Many of these non-Congress parties have attempted to ally with one another, and during three brief periods—1977–1979, 1989–1991, and 1996–1998—succeeded in forming a national government. All three times the coalitions directed their developmental attention toward decentralizing power. During their most recent national tenure, state governments were given greater rights of taxation and a larger proportion of centrally collected revenues.

While granting developmental autonomy to the level of government most aware of developmental needs has its advantages, the political aspect of the trend deserves emphasis as well. Developmental autonomy enables parties leading state governments to more effectively administer the projects that benefit their constituents and thereby strengthen their position relative to India's national parties, the BJP and Congress, in their states. Reduced national treasuries limit the ability of parties leading the central government to implement a nationally sensitive development policy or to directly benefit the citizens who elected them, particularly those in states where other parties are in power.

The BJP, like the Congress when it was in power between 1991 and 1996, has firmly resisted institutional changes. Further decentralization is not a part of the NDA manifesto. Yet each of the NDA members seeks to extract its pound of flesh in the form of centrally administered development projects directed toward its state. Andhra Pradesh and Tamil Nadu seek greater irrigation resources since, 30 years after the Green Revolution, more than 60 percent of India's farmland remains dependent primarily on rainfall; Bihar and West Bengal want greater agricultural development resources; all states desire more power production in order to fuel continued industrial growth.

Their concerns are genuine; although the economy is performing well in comparison with other countries, which were affected more seriously by the 1997–1998 international financial crisis, signs of strain exist. Real GDP growth has been phenomenal this decade, rising to 7.8 percent in 1996 and projected to remain above 5 percent through 2000. This growth has been fueled by a remarkable and constant annual domestic savings rate of more than 23 percent throughout the decade (compared with the United States, where net savings rates are consistently close to zero). This increase also was sparked by industrial development in the first half of the decade, but industrial growth peaked at 12.7 percent in 1996–1997 and has fallen to only 4 percent in 1998–1999.

Agricultural development has picked up much of the slack, but the dominant factor in agricultural growth is rainfall. India has been blessed with a string of 11 good monsoons, but this trend will not last forever. Further, development has been unevenly distributed, and poor consumers are feeling the brunt of liberalizing—but not yet liberal—marketplaces. Throughout the decade, retail prices have risen nearly twice as quickly as wholesale prices. The 1999 rates are 6.9 percent and 13.1 percent, respectively. Strictly, this reflects competition between producers and retailers for consumer rupees, but, not surprisingly, consumers look to the government to protect them from painful market adjustments.

Unfortunately, the government is woefully short of cash. The central government (and most state governments as well) has run a persistent budget deficit for more than a decade. By 1999 government expenditures exceeded direct and indirect tax revenues by 53 percent. Nearly all the difference is made up by domestic loans, and interest payments on these loans now comprises 28 percent of the central budget, or a whopping 53 percent of revenues. The government simply does not have the resources to meet the claims of its constituent members. This problem transcends party politics; any alternative government would face the same constraints, but different governments might make different choices.

On the day before the votes were counted—but before the new NDA government was installed—the BJP caretaker government made a tough economic choice that illustrates the coalition management problems it is likely to face in coming years: it boosted the government-controlled price of diesel fuel by 40 percent. The price rise was intended to increase government revenues and to "rationalize" the market by removing what essentially was a transportation subsidy. Immediately the truck drivers' union announced a national strike; it argued that competitive pressures would not allow it to pass on the price rise to customers and would thus force the drivers out of business. Retailers of consumer goods, especially perishable food items, immediately raised their prices—as much as 25 percent in some regions—in anticipation of a shortage. The prime minister, however, stood firm before the outcry by the truck drivers and consumers reacting to the retail price increases.

Although this issue remains unresolved, the political tension is clear. Parties whose constituents' specific interests are threatened by nationally sensible policies must make a choice: stick with the government in the hope that it will benefit their constituents, or support their constituents' short-term needs in the anticipation that other parties might topple the government, which would force new elections in which voters might punish them at the polls.

Prime Minister Vajpayee and the BJP can press several advantages as they try to guide such calculating politicians toward a stable regime. The October 1999 electoral verdict provided the NDA with the strongest electoral mandate in recent years. In addition to the alliance's majority, Vajpayee himself was the overwhelming favorite for prime minister, even in states where the BJP did not perform well. Also, a realistic alternative to the current coalition would be hard to cobble together; competition is intense not only among NDA members but also among the 15 parties that constitute India's parliamentary opposition as well. Still, although the NDA may enjoy stability, it faces challenges at it seeks to transform its electoral victory into a set of tangible security, social, and economic developmental results.

18. Pakistan's Coup:
Planting the Seeds of Democracy?

December 1999

AHMED RASHID

On the evening of October 12, Prime Minister Nawaz Sharif dismissed Pakistani army chief General Pervez Musharraf and appointed as his successor the head of the Interservices Intelligence and a close family friend, Lieutenant General Khawaja Ziauddin. Exactly one year earlier Sharif had forced Musharraf's predecessor, General Jehangir Karamat, to resign as army chief after he, like Musharraf, had criticized the poor performance of Sharif's government.

This time, however, the army moved quickly to defend its chief and preserve the unity of the most powerful institution in the country. Within a few hours the military had taken control of the entire country and placed Sharif, Ziauddin, and over 200 cabinet members, politicians, and senior bureaucrats under house arrest. In the early hours of the morning General Musharraf told the nation in a televised address that Sharif "had played around with state institutions and destroyed the economy" and had tried to "destabilize, politicize, and divide the armed forces."

Two days after the coup, Musharraf declared an "emergency." He suspended the constitution and legislature, removed the heads of all political institutions, and restricted the courts from considering the constitutionality of the new military government. He said the military would rule Pakistan through a National Security Council and a cabinet of technocrats until the army could return the country from the present "sham" democracy to a "true" democracy. It was martial law save for the name.

This, the fourth imposition of military rule in Pakistan, appeared to many foreign observers as, at worst, a battle lost between democracy and dictatorship, and at best as an overreaction to the failure of democracy, one that did not warrant army intervention. Pakistanis saw it quite differently. The bloodless coup met with overwhelming public support. Leaders across the political spectrum hailed the army for "saving" Pakistan. Not a single member of Sharif's Pakistan Muslim League (PML) condemned the coup or supported Sharif, demonstrating how isolated the prime minister had become from public opinion and from his own party.

Internationally, the coup's ramifications were potentially immense; the army's grip on foreign policy has contributed enormously to Pakistan's recent problems. This was the first military takeover in a nuclear-weapon state, which only five months earlier had nearly provoked a war with its nuclear-armed neighbor, India, by sending troops and Kashmiri militants into the Kargil region in the Indian-held sector of Kashmir. On its western border the army has long supported the Taliban, which controls 90 percent of Afghanistan, a collapsed state that has become a base for international terrorists, massive opium production, light weapons, and the harshest brand of Islamic fundamentalism ever experienced in the Muslim world— a fundamentalism increasingly popular in Pakistan.

At home the implications of the coup for the army are no less serious. Pakistan is a fragile state, teetering on the edge of bankruptcy and beset by Islamic fundamentalism, ethnic and sectarian warfare, and rapacious politicians unable to provide good governance in the 51 years of the country's troubled history. For an army that has suppressed civil society in three earlier martial laws, General Musharraf has set himself the most unusual of tasks. The army's success will depend not merely on a return to democracy as demanded by the United States and other Western countries, but on the crafting of a genuine civil society in Pakistan so that democracy becomes meaningful and development oriented and not just a means for politicians to plunder the state. The army is well aware that this is Pakistan's last chance for survival as a modern nation-state; it also understands the risk it has taken on. By seizing power, the army, the country's last viable institution, has taken responsibility for the nation's survival and its people's future.

The Coup's Seeds

Pakistan has been ruled by the army for nearly half its lifetime, but none of the military's interventions have been successful in the long term; they have only helped deepen the fissures in Pakistani society. Superficially, today's martial law follows the same pattern as two earlier periods of martial law in 1958 and 1977, when long periods of chaotic, corrupt, and authoritarian civilian government led to military interventions.

But those martial laws were premeditated and led by ambitious generals, Ayub Khan and Zia ul-Haq, who implemented highly ideological agendas in which a return to democracy did not figure. Both regimes ended disastrously: Ayub Khan was overthrown by his own army after a bloody mass movement in 1968 and Zia ul-Haq was killed in a plane crash in 1988. The third martial law, which was imposed after Ayub's fall in 1968, led to war with India and the loss of East Pakistan, which was reborn as Bangladesh. Historically, military rule has not provided solutions but has added to Pakistan's problems.

The October coup was different from previous military interventions. Although the army certainly had contingency plans, the coup was an act of self-defense to maintain the institutional integrity of the military and to prevent civil war among the generals. Moreover, because Sharif had concentrated all power in himself—in the process disposing of all democratic checks and balances, undermining state institutions, abusing and amending the constitution repeatedly, and destabilizing the economy—the public had widely demanded that the army act.

The October coup bought to an end 11 years of civilian rule that had begun with Zia's death. During those 11 years, Pakistan has seen 11 governments, 4 of which were elected and none of which completed a full term in office. Sharif and his bitter rival, Benazir Bhutto, had each been twice elected to office and twice booted out for widespread corruption and incompetence. Bhutto's two governments were marked by rampant corruption that undermined state institutions and the economy. Sharif's were marked by the same, with the addition of attempts to concentrate power.

Because of the president's authority to dismiss a government, each removal was imperfect but constitutionally acceptable; each time the army took a back seat as interim governments were formed to hold fresh elections within the constitutionally mandated 90 days. But each dismissal also prompted widespread public calls for a longer period of rule by the interim government so that it could carry out an across-the-board accounting of corrupt politicians. The desire of many people and the army was to end the vicious cycle of Bhutto–Sharif, who headed the two largest parties in the country but had been at each other's political throats for 15 years, and enable a new generation of more forward-looking politicians to come to the fore.

The army thus reflected public opinion by wanting good civilian government. But the army also contributed to undermining civilian governments with its control over foreign policy toward India and Afghanistan, its huge budgetary demands, its innate conservatism, its lack of economic understanding, and the role of the military intelligence agencies.

The seeds of the latest coup can be traced to November 5, 1996, when President Farooq Leghari, with the backing of army chief General Karamat, dismissed Prime Minister Benazir Bhutto. The army and the public demanded accountability and a longer period of interim government to achieve that accountability. Leghari declined, struck a dubious deal with Sharif, and ordered elections within 90 days. Sharif swept back to power with 134 of the 204 seats contested in the National Assembly. Public frustration at the politicians and the lack of choice was reflected in the lowest turnout in Pakistan's history; only 32 percent of the voting population took part in the polls (in contrast, 60 percent turned out in India's recent polls).

Sharif's Pakistan Muslim League party took only 17 percent of the general vote, but the first-past-the-post electoral system gave his league two-thirds of the seats in parliament, making him the most powerful prime minister in Pakistan's history, with sufficient parliamentary votes to amend the constitution at will.

The Sharif government's slide into gross political mismanagement, corruption, and authoritarianism does not bear full repetition here, but it was because of that slide that the prime minister's relations with the army deteriorated. During his tenure as army chief between 1996 and 1998, General Karamat prepared contingency plans for military rule three times when the regime teetered on the brink of dissolving during several constitutional deadlocks that paralyzed the country. But each time Karamat refused to intervene, unwilling to interfere with the democratic process. Sharif went on to cower the bureaucracy, the judiciary, the police, parliament, the opposition, banks, and business.

Then, at the very moment Sharif needed international support to avert a default on the country's foreign debt—after the West had imposed economic sanctions on Pakistan because of its nuclear tests—Sharif picked a fight with the IMF, the World Bank, and international investors over foreign-funded electricity power projects. This move destroyed local and foreign business confidence in his government.

Karamat publicly spoke out about the deteriorating situation on October 5, 1998. Addressing the Naval War College in Lahore, he said: "Unlike countries with economic potential, we cannot afford the destabilizing effects of polarization vendettas and insecurity-driven expedient policies."

Unable to accept any criticism, Sharif forced Karamat's resignation just two days after the speech. Karamat chose to go quietly rather than invoke any contingency plans, hoping his example would inspire Sharif to change his ways and prevent a division in the army. Instead, his departure galvanized Sharif to make what one Western ambassador described as "a megalomaniac and paranoid bid for power." The prime minister misread Karamat's departure as the army's surrender and absolute weakness in the face of his power. Karamat's Lahore speech, which was simply a plea for good governance, ultimately formed the basis of Musharraf's actions a year later.

Musharraf: From Aiding to Ousting the Government

General Musharraf was third in line to become army chief and owed his elevation to that post after Karamat's dismissal to Sharif. With little hesitation and despite criticism from within the military, Musharraf plunged the army into helping the government deal with the problems caused by the many state institutions and services that were on the verge of collapse. In his most dramatic move he inducted 70,000 troops into the state-owned electricity generation company to collect unpaid bills. He declined to repeat Karamat's criticism and hoped—again—that by a different example the army would encourage Sharif to move away from his confrontational politics and pursue nation building.

Encouraged by Musharraf's obedience and aid, Sharif redoubled his repressive campaign against all sectors of civil society that dared criticize him. This time the press, human rights advocates, lawyers' groups, and other developmental nongovernmental organizations were targeted. To keep the growing power of the Islamic fundamentalist parties in check, he promised them a bill to allow the imposition of sharia (Islamic law), which, if passed, would have overturned the country's legal system and constitution. He then encouraged the mullahs to launch a witch hunt against liberals who opposed the bill.

During this time, Sharif retreated behind a close coterie of family friends and former employees, ignoring the cabinet and parliament—and the army. The most powerful men around Sharif were his father, Mohammed Sharif; his brother Shahbaz Sharif, the chief minister of Punjab province; his former family lawyer and the minister of justice, Khalid Anwar; his former business partner Saif ur Rehman, head of the powerful Accountability Cell (charged with investigating political corruption); Ishaq Dar, the former accountant of his industrial conglomerate, Ittefaq Industries, who served as minister of finance and commerce; and a sycophantic mediaperson, Mushahid Hussain, the minister of information.

As president, Sharif had chosen retired Justice Rafiq Tarrar, a rigid Islamic fundamentalist, fellow Punjabi, and friend of his father's with no political experience or public exposure. With the help of another family friend, Lieutenant General Ziauddin, he emasculated the Interservices Intelligence, the army's most powerful foreign and domestic intelligence agency, and tried to divide the generals by enticing some to be totally loyal to him rather than the army chief.

Sharif's ad hoc style of decision making was leading to the country's international isolation and seriously undermining the economy, while the prime minister's vendettas—including attempts to crush the press and silence journalists critical of him—were alienating every sector of society. The army's frustration intensified as national security and the army's image abroad began to be affected. When the army and Sharif decided to carry out five nuclear tests on May 28, 1998 in response to India's tests earlier that month, Sharif ignored the army's requests to prepare economic and foreign policy measures that would counter the expected international outcry. The result was an economic debacle that bought Pakistan to the verge of default on its foreign debt of $32 billion as the United States and other nations imposed sanctions on Pakistan in response to the testing.

It was the Kargil campaign that created the greatest friction. The army had deemed a military operation in Kargil necessary to revive the 10-year-long Kashmir insurgency that was being beaten back by huge Indian troop deployments and military action, a position with which Sharif agreed. When Sharif was first briefed by the army in January 1999 about executing the Kargil operation, he gave the go-ahead but then told nobody in the government, made no economic or foreign policy preparations for the resulting international fallout, and decided on his own to invite Indian Prime Minister Atal Bihari Vajpayee to Lahore in February 1999. By inviting Vajpayee and talking peace with India while Kargil was in the offing, Sharif and the army ensured that Pakistan's credibility abroad was badly damaged. Ultimately, the manner in which Pakistan was forced to withdraw from Kargil after President Bill Clinton intervened at Sharif's request infuriated both the public and the military, which had seen the intervention escalate into a large Indian military response that included the possibility of Indian intervention in Pakistan.

While Sharif tried to lay the blame for Kargil on the army, Musharraf insisted that Sharif was on board and made all the key decisions. Meanwhile, the country's long political and economic crisis had worsened. In September, 19 diverse opposition parties united to form a "Grand Democratic Alliance" and began a series of rallies across the country demanding Sharif's ouster. The Jamaat-e-Islami, the country's most powerful Islamic party, launched its own effort to topple Sharif, while the Jamiat ul-Ulema-i Islam and several extremist groups belonging to the Deobandi sect of Sunni Islam began a third movement.[1]

For the army the last straw was two separate visits to Washington by Shahbaz Sharif and Ziauddin, where they criticized Musharraf and the army. The United States State Department appeared to side with Sharif when it issued a terse statement on September 20, warning the army not to carry out any unconstitutional act. The army felt humiliated by Sharif's attempt to create external support for his faltering regime and denigrating the army in the process.

Musharraf now went public. He criticized the government for failing to maintain law and order after 40 people died in sectarian killings around the country. Then, on October 8, he removed Lieutenant General Tariq Pervaiz, the commander of the Quetta Corps (one of the country's nine corps), for holding a private meeting with Sharif, which was against army regulations. The removal infuriated Sharif, who was trying to make inroads among senior generals in preparation to sack Musharraf.

As tensions escalated, Musharraf warned several of the nine corps commanders who were loyal to him that he would not be removed from office by force because Sharif was trying to divide the army. The 111 Brigade of the 10th Corps based in Rawalpindi outside Islamabad—the traditional coup-making unit—was put on 15-minute-readiness notice. Ultimately, it was Sharif who moved first and not the army.

1. The Deobandis arose in British-ruled India during the nineteenth century as a revivalist Islamic movement within the Sunni sect that aimed to regenerate Muslim society as it struggled to live within the confines of a colonial state. The Deobandis hoped to revive Islamic values based on learning, spiritual experience, and sharia. The Deobandis hold a restrictive view of the role of women and reject Shiaism.

When Musharraf addressed the nation on the night of the coup, his words reflected the acute slide the country had taken since Karamat's speech a year earlier. "We have lost our honor, our dignity, our respect in the comity of nations. Is this the way to enter the new millennium? We have hit rock bottom. We have no choice but to rise and rise we will." Musharraf had come full circle in just 12 months: from going out of his way to help the Sharif government to ousting it from power.

The seven reform objectives and six guidelines to revive the economy that Musharraf announced covered most aspects of what Pakistanis desire and expect. But Musharraf gave no timetable on how long the army would stay in power. The question uppermost in people's minds is whether the army can deliver on its promises. Continued public support for the coup will depend on whether the army can fulfill its own agenda.

The External Dimensions of Internal Change

An army coup at the end of the twentieth century is an anachronistic and, to the international community, unacceptable means by which to rebuild a country. While the domestic crisis in itself is dire, two paramount issues will determine the army's international acceptability and its success or failure at home: foreign policy and the economy.

Musharraf, who is 56, also faces an image problem that he must overcome. Born in New Delhi to a family of Urdu-speaking migrants who settled in Karachi, Musharraf does not belong to the powerful Punjabi power brokers who have dominated Pakistani politics and the army. His ethnic origins are an advantage in the troubled province of Sind, but a disadvantage in Punjab. Abroad, Musharraf is held responsible for the Kargil debacle, which branded him as an adventurous hard-liner, mesmerized by military tactics but seemingly unaware of strategy or diplomacy.

Yet Kargil was only possible because of Pakistan's nuclear status. The army believed that India would not retaliate against a Pakistani intrusion into Indian Kashmir by widening the conflict and crossing the international border because of the risk of nuclear war. Some Western but especially Indian commentators pointed out that Kargil was virtual nuclear blackmail by a newly nuclear-weaponized state to achieve tactical foreign policy aims. The ensuing deadlock in India–Pakistan relations and the dangers inherent in a nuclear and missile race between the two countries are now major destabilizing factors in the region.

Meanwhile, the army and Sharif's support for the ruling Taliban in Afghanistan has also alienated Pakistan from the rest of the region. Iran, Russia, India, and four Central Asian states (Tajikistan, Kyrgyzstan, Kazakhstan, and Uzbekistan) support the anti-Taliban movement known as the Northern Alliance and accuse Pakistan of abetting Taliban-style terrorism and fundamentalism in their countries. Pakistan's closest allies, China and Turkey, have also recently taken strong exception to the Taliban. (In China's case, Uighur Muslim militants from Xinjiang province have been given sanctuary by the Taliban.) Russia has recently accused the Taliban and Pakistani militants of involvement in the Islamist movements in Dagestan and Chechnya.

For the United States and Europe, the sanctuary given by the Taliban to the Saudi terrorist Osama bin Laden and some 400 Arab extremists, along with the Taliban's refusal to extradite them, has become the principal threat from Afghanistan and a major factor in the West's pressure on Pakistan to change its policy toward that country. Pakistan is one of only three nations that have recognized the Taliban government and is now the only country in the world that continues to support it after Saudi Arabia and the United Arab Emirates cut off aid this year because of the bin Laden issue.

Changing policy on Afghanistan will be difficult for an army that, since the capture of Kabul in 1992 by the Afghan mujahideen, has been wedded to trying to return to power in Afghanistan the majority Pashtun population at the expense of Afghan minority ethnic groups. This policy itself has been complicated as the Taliban has developed extensive links inside Pakistan with Deobandi extremist parties and their religious schools; the truck and transport mafia that is the linchpin of drugs and consumer goods smuggling between Pakistan, Afghanistan, and Central Asia (and the main source of revenue for the Taliban); as well as business groups, police, and bureaucrats in the two Pakistani border provinces of Baluchistan and the North West Frontier Province.

Some 80,000 Pakistani militants have trained and fought with the Taliban since their emergence in 1994, providing a huge militant fundamentalist base for a Taliban-style Islamic revolution in Pakistan. The Taliban have thus established close ties not only with the military but with many sectors of Pakistani society, which now pose a threat to Pakistan's stability.

The army's domestic agenda cannot be carried out fully until it changes its Afghan policy. If the army wants to crack down on sectarianism, it will have to force the Taliban to hand over Pakistani and foreign extremists to whom the Taliban have given sanctuary. To control the fundamentalists at home, the army has to end the supply of weapons and training the Taliban provide. To revive the economy, it will have to end the smuggling trade that in 1998 was worth $2.5 billion and has crippled Pakistani industry and created huge losses in customs revenue.

Afghanistan also affects foreign policy with India. Many Pakistani and Kashmiri militants fighting in Indian Kashmir train on Taliban-controlled territory rather than inside Pakistan. Successive governments and the army have been unable to change Afghan policy partly because an Afghan settlement is now held hostage by the Kashmir dispute with India and the Kashmiri struggle for self-determination, which is the cornerstone of Pakistan's foreign policy. If it were to squeeze the Taliban, the army would also face the much more difficult issue dealing with Kashmir and Pakistan's future relations with India.

In short, nearly every aspect of Musharraf's domestic agenda touches on Afghanistan. But to reduce Pakistan's support to the Taliban will almost certainly create a backlash from the well-armed Deobandi extremists at home, which only the army is strong enough to keep under control.

Arresting the Economic Meltdown

Any economic revival in Pakistan also depends on exporting more to Pakistan's neighbors than to the West, where Pakistani goods are increasingly uncompetitive. In 1998 exports fell by 13 percent, the largest drop in 30 years. Pakistan's exports—unfinished textiles, leather, rice, carpets, and some consumer goods—have barely changed in composition or value added since the 1960s. The only markets for these poor-quality goods are countries on an equal or lesser economic footing than Pakistan: India, Afghanistan, Iran, and the countries of Central Asia. But to access Central Asia and Iran, Pakistan needs to promote an Afghan settlement, while accessing India requires normalizing relations.

Any economic revival will also depend on first restoring local investor confidence and then encouraging foreign investment by reengaging the IMF and the World Bank, which during Sharif's tenure suspended loan programs worth $1.56 billion and $500 million, respectively. Investor confidence will not return unless there is peace on Pakistan's borders, law and order inside the country, and the army is seen as a responsible agent of change and modernization.

Pakistan is in dire economic straits. With a foreign debt of $32 billion and foreign exchange reserves that have not been more than $1.6 billion for the past five years, Pakistan spends 67 percent of its budget servicing interest repayments on its debt. Annual GDP growth has fallen from 6 percent to well under 4 percent over the last two years. But with population growth at 2.8 percent a year, real growth is just 1 percent. Aside from exports, Pakistan's two other sources of foreign exchange, foreign investment and remittances from overseas Pakistani workers, have also shown a sharp decline in the past two years. With Pakistan in its fourth year of a severe recession, one-third of the country's industry is shut down, state-owned banks are bankrupt, agriculture is stagnant, and prices are rising while rampant unemployment helps fuel Islamic militancy.

According to the State Bank of Pakistan, the country's ruling elite owes a staggering $4 billion in nonperforming and defaulted loans to state-owned banks. Nine of the biggest defaulters were members of the last cabinet and include members of the Sharif family. Musharraf's first task is to force defaulters to pay this money back. Any economic recovery will eventually raise public and international questions about the military's own enormous budget (45 percent of the total 1999–2000 budget), which now includes a full-fledged nuclear weapons program. But the military cannot afford to cut its budget unless there is movement toward peace with India. Economic revival is thus closely intertwined with foreign policy.

Pakistan's Last Hope?

As the army develops its policies on governing Pakistan, there will be intense internal debate within the military. The army stands fully united behind Musharraf, who is considered a liberal, but his key military advisers—his kitchen cabinet of generals—are almost equally divided between what can be only inadequately described as secular liberals, diehard conservatives, and even Islamic hard-liners. The more conservative generals will likely favor the status quo and may not support a major reevaluation of policy toward Afghanistan and India or even toward the Islamic parties. Thus Musharraf will have to maintain the momentum of change, while keeping his generals with him.

At the heart of the problem for the army remains the fact that the near collapse of the Pakistan state has become intertwined with the need to engage in a domestic cleanup that includes revived foreign and economic policies. Little can be done on one front without impinging on the other two fronts; in short, no single issue on Musharraf's agenda can be tackled in isolation.

The army must also rebuild public faith in civil society if a return to democracy is to be truly effective. Unlike in the past, the army will have to work with and strengthen the judiciary, chambers of business and commerce, the press, developmental nongovernmental organizations, and human rights groups. It will have to introduce ordinances to change some of the worst aspects of human rights abuses, which have led the international community to criticize Pakistan. Only then will civil society be prepared to allow the army a permanent stake in a future democratic setup—which it will demand and may well be necessary—through the National Security Council. The army, contrary to anything it has ever done in the past, will have to institutionalize checks and balances to allow a vibrant democracy and civil society to flourish. In short, the army has to sow the seeds for true democracy.

Chronology of Recent Events

1994 Events

Afghanistan

June 26—Forces loyal to President Burhanuddin Rabbani oust troops under the command of Prime Minister Gulbuddin Hekmatyar and General Abdul Rashid Doestam from Kabul, the capital; in 2 days of heavy fighting 28 people have been killed and about 210 wounded. The 2 sides have been fighting since January 1.

Bangladesh

Aug. 3—Writer Taslima Nasrin appears before the High Court in Dhaka on a charge of offending the religious sentiment of Muslims; she is granted bail but goes back into hiding because of death threats from Muslim fundamentalists. Nasrin was quoted as saying the Koran should be "thoroughly revised" to eliminate encouragements to discrimination against women.

Dec. 29—Announcing an agreement with the parliamentary opposition, Prime Minister Khaleda Zia says she will resign 1 month before the next general election, which must be called by 1996. Opposition legislators walked out of parliament 10 months ago, paralyzing Zia's government; yesterday all but 7 of the 154-member opposition in the 330-seat body resigned.

India

June 4—India launches a ballistic missile in a test flight over the Bay of Bengal; the government says the new weapon does not contravene international agreements limiting long-range missiles.

Aug. 8—In Srinagar, the capital of Jammu and Kashmir state, the government pulls back troops surrounding the Hazratbal mosque, the region's holiest Muslim shrine; the troops had been stationed there after a standoff last fall over an alleged arms cache inside. The government also extends emergency rule in the state for 6 months; a bomb killed 9 people and wounded more than 50 in the city last weekend.

Sept. 29—Officials in New Delhi close schools and other public places as a precaution against the spread of bubonic or pneumonic plague; the pneumonic form of the disease broke out in the northern city of Surat last week, and has killed at least 69 people in 5 states.

Nepal

Jan. 13—In Kathmandu, the country's first stock exchange opens.

Sri Lanka

Sept. 5—The 2-week-old government of
Prime Minister Chandrika Bandaranaike Kumaratunga and the rebel
Liberation Tigers of Tamil Eelam have
agreed in principle to begin talks to
end the 11-year-old civil war in which
34,000 people have died, *The New
York Times* reports. Today the government said the emergency powers in
place since the early 1970s will end at
midnight in all but the main areas of
fighting in the north and east.

Oct. 24—At a rally in the capital city of
Colombo, Gamini Dissanayake, the
opposition United National Party's
presidential candidate in the election
scheduled for November, is killed in
an explosion set off by a suicide
bomber; about 50 other people die,
including 3 former cabinet ministers,
and more than 200 are wounded. No
group takes responsibility, but the
Liberation Tigers are suspected.

1995 Events

Afghanistan

Feb. 11—The main factions fighting in the
civil war, led by Prime Minister Gulbuddin Hekmatyar and President
Burhanuddin Rabbani, agree to form
a multiparty council that will serve as
a temporary government; the council,
which will have between 25 and 30
members, will oversee the disarmament of warring factions.

Feb. 14—The Taliban, a recently organized militia consisting mainly of fundamentalist religious students, drives

Hekmatyar from his headquarters at
Charasyab; the Taliban's estimated
25,000 fighters control about 40% of
the country.

March 12—President Rabbani announces
that his forces have pushed the Taliban militia to a point 9 miles south of
the capital in a major offensive that
has killed or wounded at least 1,000
people in the last week. The Taliban
has taken control of more than one-
third of Afghanistan.

India

May 11—A siege by the army of Muslim
militants at Hazratbal mosque, Kashmir's holiest shrine, ends today after
the burning of the shrine; it is unclear
which side set the blaze. At least 20
people are dead. Muslim separatists
have been waging a 5-year war to create an independent Muslim state in
Kashmir.

June 1—*The Far Eastern Economic Review*
reports that US Navy forces held joint
training exercises with Indian forces
in mid-May; these are the 2d set of exercises to be held since the US and
India agreed to hold joint exercises in
January.

Aug. 31—A bomb kills Beant Singh, the
chief minister of the state of Punjab,
and 12 others, in the state's capital of
Chandigarh; Sikh separatists are
blamed for the blast.

Nepal

Sept. 10—The Communist government is
dissolved after Parliament passes a no-
confidence vote, 107 to 88; opposition

parties accuse Prime Minister Man-mohan Adhikari and his government of abusing land reform programs and placing supporters in civil service positions.

Sri Lanka

April 14—In an attempt to end the 13-year civil war, President Chandrika Bandaranaike Kumaratunga makes several concessions to the Tamil Tigers, the separatist guerrilla group representing the Hindu Tamils that is fighting the Sinhalese Buddhist majority; a cease-fire has been in effect for 3 months.

1996 Events

Afghanistan

Sept. 27—Taliban rebels capture the capital city of Kabul and execute former President Najibullah and his brother, Shahpur Ahmadzai; Najibullah ruled until 1992, when he was forced from office.

Oct. 5—The Taliban launches an attack near the Panjshir Valley where forces loyal to Ahmad Shah Masud, a rival guerrilla leader, retreated after the Taliban took control of Kabul late last month.

Oct. 8—Troops loyal to faction leader General Abdul Rashid Doestam drive Taliban forces from their positions near the Salang Tunnel north of Kabul.

Oct. 10—Doestam and Masud sign an agreement creating a formal military alliance between their armies; Shiite leader Abdul Karim Khalily also signs the agreement, in which the 3 men pledge to establish a nonfundamentalist government in the 9 provinces in which they hold power.

Oct. 19—Masud's forces recapture Bagram air base from the Taliban, 30 miles north of Kabul.

Oct. 25—The Taliban claims it has overrun the northwest province of Badghis and parts of neighboring Faryab province in an offensive it launched October 24; on October 21 the Taliban said it had reached a peace agreement with Doestam.

Oct. 27—The armies of Doestam and Masud launch joint air and ground attacks on the Taliban near the De Sabz pass, 20 miles north of Kabul.

Oct. 30—Masud's forces advance within 8 miles of Kabul; Doestam's forces drive the Taliban back from Faryab into Badghis.

Bangladesh

Feb. 11—Two people are killed and 150 injured in protests to prevent parliamentary elections scheduled for February 15; opposition parties are boycotting the elections, saying that they are rigged to ensure the reelection of Prime Minister Khaleda Zia.

Feb. 29—*The Far Eastern Economic Review* reports that Prime Minister Khaleda Zia's Bangladesh National Party won 201 of parliament's 300 seats in the February 15 elections; voter turnout was about 10%.

March 3—Prime Minister Zia offers to step down to allow a nonparty government to conduct new elections; the opposition says the February 15 elections were conducted fraudulently.

March 27—Responding to the protests, Prime Minister Zia asks President Abdur Rahman Biswas to form a caretaker government until new elections can be held; Zia does not resign.

March 30—President Biswas dissolves parliament and sets up an interim government that will be headed by former Chief Justice Habibur Rahman.

India

Feb. 21—Urban Affairs and Employment Minister R. K. Dhawan resigns after being named in the $18 million bribery scandal that has forced the resignation of 6 of Prime Minister P. V. Narasimha Rao's cabinet ministers.

Feb. 29—A judge orders the arrest of 10 politicians charged in the bribery scandal. Among those arrested is L. K. Advani, leader of the opposition Bharatiya Janata Party (BJP); Advani is later released on bail.

May 23—Results from the April 27-29 general elections show no clear majority in the 537 parliamentary seats elected thus far. Of the 534 seats reported today, the BJP has won 160; the Congress Party 136; and the National Front-Left Front coalition 110.

June 1—H. D. Deve Gowda, a Janata Dal party member and Karnataka state chief minister, is sworn in as prime minister; he heads a 13-party center-left coalition government. On May 28, Prime Minister Vajpayee resigned from the post moments before an an-

ticipated no-confidence vote by parliament.

Sept. 21—Former Prime Minister Rao, accused of fraud, resigns as leader of the Congress Party.

Sept. 24—Sitaram Kesri, chosen yesterday to be the new Congress Party leader, reaffirms his party's support for Prime Minister Deve Gowda's center-left coalition.

Oct. 2—Officials say that the pro-India National Conference, led by former Chief Minister Farooq Abdullah, has won 54 of 81 seats in Jammu and Kashmir's 87-seat assembly; the elections are the first since a separatist rebellion began in 1990.

Oct. 9—Farooq Abdullah is sworn in as Kashmir's chief minister, ending 6 years of direct rule by the federal government; however, a strike called by the separatist All-Party Hurriyat Conference shuts down the capital, Srinagar.

Oct. 30—Hours after appearing in court on forgery charges, former Prime Minister Rao is charged with conspiring to pay legislators $100,000 to support his government in a 1993 no-confidence vote.

Dec. 12—Prime Minister Deve Gowda and Bangladeshi Prime Minister Sheikh Hasina Wazed sign a 30-year treaty to share water from the Ganges River. The river's flow has been a source of friction between the 2 countries since 1974, when India built the Farakka Barrage, a dam that Bangladesh says restricts too much water during the dry season and releases too much during the monsoon.

Dec. 19—Former Prime Minister Rao resigns as chief of the Congress Party's parliamentary delegation; Rao is the subject of 3 separate corruption investigations.

Pakistan

July 31—In a reshuffle, Prime Minister Benazir Bhutto appoints her husband, Asif Ali Zardari, and 14 others to her cabinet; their portfolios are not immediately announced.

Sept. 20—Murtaza Bhutto, the brother and a political opponent of Prime Minister Bhutto, and 6 of his followers are killed by police in a shoot out that police say ensued when their cars refused to stop at security checkpoints.

Nov. 5—President Farooq Leghari dismisses Prime Minister Bhutto and her government on charges of corruption, nepotism, abuse of power, intimidation of the judiciary, and the collapse of law and order. Malik Meraj Khalid, a former parliamentary leader, is sworn in as caretaker prime minister; elections are to be held on February 3. Bhutto is put under house arrest in Islamabad, and her husband, Minister of Investments Asif Zardari, who is widely regarded as corrupt, is arrested in Lahore.

Nov. 6—Bhutto is freed from house arrest.

Dec. 18—Prosecutors charge Bhutto's husband with the September 20 murder of the ousted prime minister's estranged brother and political opponent, Murtaza Bhutto.

1997 Events

Afghanistan

Feb. 24—It is reported that the Taliban has captured the Shibar Pass in heavy fighting and retaken positions in central Afghanistan from the alliance of forces led by Ahmad Shah Masud and General Abdul Rashid Doestam.

Oct. 5—The ruling Islamic fundamentalist Taliban movement orders Afghans to destroy all pictures of human beings and bans the drawing or painting of such images.

India

March 30—The Congress Party withdraws its support from the minority coalition government of Prime Minister H. D. Deve Gowda; Congress leader Sitaram Kesri cites what he calls the government's failure to prevent ethnoreligious fragmentation, but rivals accuse him of trying to create a political crisis to avoid being replaced as party leader.

April 11—The 10-month-old United Front coalition government of Prime Minister Deve Gowda loses, 292 to 158, a no-confidence vote in parliament.

April 13—Deve Gowda offers to step down as head of the United Front coalition to enable it to form a new government with the Congress Party.

April 19—The governing coalition names Foreign Minister Inder K. Gujral prime minister; Gujral is popular because of his success in improving India's relations with Pakistan, Bangladesh, and other neighbors.

May 6—A court indicts former Prime Minister P. V. Narasimha Rao on charges of bribing 4 members of parliament to support him in a 1993 confidence vote; Rao, who resigned as Congress Party leader last September, is the first Indian prime minister to face criminal charges.

July 17—An electoral college chooses K. R. Narayanan to become India's tenth president; Narayanan, who was born into Hinduism's lowest or "untouchable," caste, will replace Shankar Dayal Sharma on July 25.

Aug. 26—India rejects a US offer to mediate in its conflict with Pakistan over Kashmir; troops continue to exchange fire over the border.

Sept. 12—A court in New Delhi rules that there is enough evidence to prosecute former Prime Minister Rao, 4 cabinet colleagues, and 13 others; all are charged with criminal conspiracy and abetting bribery in a scandal over the alleged buying of votes in a 1993 no-confidence vote that Rao's government narrowly survived.

Nov. 29—Prime Minister Gujral resigns after the Congress Party withdraws support for his 14-party coalition. The crisis began earlier this month when a judicial report linked some leaders of the Dravida Munnetra Kazhagam, a southern regional party and coalition member, to the 1991 assassination of Congress Party leader and former Prime Minister Rajiv Gandhi; Congress leaders had threatened to topple the government if Gujral refused to oust the Dravida Party from the coalition.

Dec. 4—President Narayanan calls new elections for February and March, 3 years early, after concluding that the 14-party coalition that has governed India since mid-1996 had no hope of sustaining majority support in parliament.

Nepal

Oct. 4—The center-left government of Prime Minister Lokendra Bahadur Chand loses a parliamentary no-confidence vote, 107 to 94. The centrist Nepali Congress, which led the no-confidence motion, is expected to head a new coalition; this will be the 5th change of government since 1990.

Pakistan

Jan. 29—The Supreme Court upholds the November ouster of Prime Minister Benazir Bhutto and her government on corruption charges.

Feb. 13—Final results reported in today's *Far Eastern Economic Review* give the Pakistan Muslim League 134 of 217 seats in the February 3 parliamentary election; party head Nawaz Sharif, who was prime minister from 1990 to 1993 but was dismissed for corruption and misrule, will again become prime minister. Ousted Prime Minister Benazir Bhutto's Pakistan People's Party won only 18 seats.

Feb. 17—Sharif is sworn in as prime minister.

April 1—Both houses of parliament vote unanimously to eliminate the power of the president, who is appointed, to dismiss elected governments and name armed forces chiefs; the measure was introduced yesterday by Prime Minister Nawaz Sharif.

July 5—Asif Ali Zardari, the husband of former Prime Minister Benazir Bhutto, is indicted with 18 other people on charges of conspiracy to murder Bhutto's brother and political opponent, Mir Murtaza Bhutto, who was killed along with 7 colleagues in a police shootout in September 1996.

Sept. 22—In a speech to the UN General Assembly, Prime Minister Sharif invites India to begin talks on a "non-aggression pact" with Pakistan.

Nov. 20—The army chief of staff, General Jehangir Karamat, and Prime Minister Sharif overturn a cabinet decision to impeach President Farooq Ahmed Leghari; the impeachment move was prompted when Leghari declined to sign a measure giving Sharif legal protection. Yesterday Sharif was indicted on charges of contempt of court for suggesting that the chief justice of the supreme court had overstepped his authority.

Dec. 2—President Leghari resigns, saying Prime Minister Sharif's 9-month tenure has been an assault on the rule of law; Sharif has pushed through 2 controversial constitutional amendments, one stripping the presidency of the power to dismiss governments and call elections, and the other forbidding members of parliament to vote against their party on any issue.

Dec. 31—Mohammad Rafiq Tarar of the governing Muslim League is elected president today with 374 of 476 votes in the electoral college (which is made up of national and provincial legislatures); Pakistan People's Party candidate Aftab Shahban Mirani finishes a distant second.

1998 Events

Afghanistan

Aug. 8—Taliban forces capture the northern city of Mazar-i-Sharif, the last major city held by anti-Taliban forces.

Sept. 2—Iran begins a planned 3 days of military maneuvers on its border with Afghanistan; the maneuvers are believed to be in response to the detention of 47 Iranians by Afghanistan's ruling fundamentalist Islamic Taliban.

Sept. 15—In New York, the Taliban's deputy representative to the UN, Noorullah Zadran, asks the UN to mediate between Afghanistan and Iran; recent statements by Iranian leaders about the now confirmed August 8 killing of at least 8 Iranian diplomats and one journalist in Mazar-i-Sharif have included threats of military action. Alvaro de Soto, the UN assistant secretary general for political affairs, says that the UN will not intervene.

Sept. 30—Iran begins more military exercises on its border with Afghanistan, with approximately 200,000 troops participating; the Taliban say they have stationed 20,000 troops on the border in response to the exercises.

Bangladesh

Nov. 8—A Dhaka district judge convicts and sentences to death 15 former military commanders for the 1975 assassination of Sheikh Mujibur Rahman, the prime minister; the current prime minister, Sheikh Hasina Wazed, is Rahman's daughter and one of the few family members not killed in the assassination.

Bhutan

July 12—*The New York Times* reports that late last month Jigme Synge Wangchuck, Bhutan's king, dismissed an appointed cabinet and instructed the National Assembly to elect a new one; in another change, the assembly will now have the power to demand the king's abdication.

India

Jan. 24—The Congress Party says it is withdrawing former Prime Minister P. V. Narasimha Rao's candidacy for next month's elections, citing his inaction during sectarian riots that left more than 3,000 people dead after Hindu zealots tore down a mosque in December 1992; in addition, Rao currently faces 3 criminal charges involving vote-buying and forgery.

Feb. 28—Indians vote in the third and final stage of staggered national elections; at least 150 people have been killed in election violence, including 62 in the February 14 Coimbatore bombings.

March 4—Final results of last month's national elections are announced, with the Hindu nationalist Bharatiya Janata Party (BJP) and its allies winning 250 of the 543 parliamentary seats being contested; the Congress Party and its allies took 166 seats, and the United Front coalition, which led the previous government, 98.

March 19—BJP parliamentary leader Atal Bihari Vajpayee is sworn in as prime minister and a new cabinet is named.

April 20—Prime Minister Vajpayee dismisses Communications Minister Buta Singh, who faces charges of vote buying in parliament.

May 11—India conducts 3 underground nuclear tests at Pokharan, in the country's northwestern desert; the nuclear tests are India's first since 1974 and the world's first since 1996.

May 13—India carries out 2 more nuclear test explosions at Pokharan.

June 25—With US support, the World Bank resumes lending to India with a $543 million package of loans to the state of Andhra Pradesh; the aid is mainly humanitarian and thus exempt from sanctions the US imposed last month after India's nuclear tests.

Sept. 24—Speaking to the UN General Assembly in New York, Prime Minister Atal Bihari Vajpayee says India is prepared to sign the Comprehensive Test Ban Treaty (CTBT) by next September, when the treaty is scheduled to go into force if all 44 countries with nuclear reactors have ratified it; Vajpayee says India's signing of the treaty will be contingent on talks to lift sanctions imposed on India after its nuclear tests in May.

Oct. 22—The governing Hindu nationalist Bharatiya Janata Party withdraws a controversial proposal to make the study of Hindu scriptures compulsory for all schoolchildren; the proposal caused a furor at a conference of state education ministers today in New Delhi, with opponents saying it represented an assault on minorities and on the secular character of the Indian state.

Pakistan

Aug. 17—Former Prime Minister Benazir Bhutto, who was ousted in 1996 for corruption and misrule, appears in court in Lahore to face corruption charges.

Aug. 21—Pakistan lodges an official protest with the US over the US cruise missile attack yesterday on suspected terrorist camps in neighboring Afghanistan, saying the US neither sought nor received permission to send the missiles through Pakistani airspace.

Sept. 23—In a speech to the UN General Assembly in New York, Prime Minister Nawaz Sharif pledges that Pakistan will sign the Comprehensive Test Ban Treaty by September 1999, when the treaty is scheduled to go into force; Pakistan may not sign, he says, if India resumes testing or if international sanctions imposed on Pakistan after it conducted nuclear explosions in May are not lifted. Today Sharif met with Indian Prime Minister Atal Bihari Vajpayee, and the 2 agreed to resume high-level talks on the disputed territory of Kashmir, to put an end to sporadic artillery battles in the territory, to set up a hot line, and to improve transportation links between the 2 countries.

Oct. 7—Prime Minister Sharif replaces the head of the armed forces, General Jehangir Karamat, with Pervez Musharraf, another army commander; Karamat had criticized Sharif's government and recently proposed the creation of a national security council through which the military could have a role in policy-making

Oct. 9—The National Assembly votes, 151 to 16, to amend the constitution to give the government power to impose laws derived from its interpretation of the Koran and to override the "constitution, any law or judgment of any court"; to become law the amendment must win a two-thirds vote in the Senate, which unlike the assembly is not dominated by Sharif's Pakistan Muslim League.

Oct. 18—After 3 days of talks in Islamabad, Foreign Ministers Krishnan Raghunath of India and Shamshad Ahmed of Pakistan depart without a formal agreement on reducing military tensions between their countries or resolving the dispute over Kashmir; further talks are scheduled for February in New Delhi.

Dec. 19—Prime Minister Sharif says the US has agreed to pay Pakistan $466.9 million as reimbursement for 28 F-16 fighter planes that Pakistan paid for in 1989 but never received; the US cut off all military aid to the country in 1990 to protest its efforts to develop nuclear weapons; New Zealand has agreed to lease or buy the planes.

Sri Lanka

Sept. 30—Red Cross officials say more than 1,300 Tamil rebels and government soldiers have been killed in fighting in the past 3 days over control of a strategic highway linking

Colombo with the northern town of
Jaffna.

1999 Events

Afghanistan

March 14—In Ashgabat, Turkmenistan,
after 4 days of UN-brokered peace talks,
the Taliban government and the opposition agree in principle to a coalition government to include all of Afghanistan's
political forces and a shared executive,
legislature, and judiciary.

August 4—Taliban militia leader Mullah
Mohammed Omar offers amnesty and
protection of personal property to all
opposition fighters who will put down
their arms; Omar's offer follows a series of Taliban victories that have
given it control of 90% of the country.

Oct. 15—A spokesman for the opposition
Northern Alliance says that the alliance's forces have driven the Taliban
government's troops south and captured 2 districts in Faryab province;
200,000 refugees have fled northward
since the Taliban's offensive began
July 28.

The UN Security Council unanimously votes to impose economic sanctions on the Taliban government unless
it extradites accused terrorist Osama
bin Laden to the US within 30 days.

Oct. 29—Bin Laden says he will leave the
country only if he is escorted by government security forces and if his destination kept secret.

Nov. 2—US officials reject bin Laden's
offer to leave Afghanistan for an undisclosed location and say economic
sanctions will be imposed on the coun-

try if he is not extradited to the US by
November 14; the US has accused bin
Laden of masterminding the 1998
bombings of 2 US embassies in Africa.

Nov. 23—The Taliban says it will agree to
unconditional talks with the US over
bin Laden; the talks would be the first
official contact between the 2 countries since the Taliban came to power
in 1998.

Dec. 14—The US tells the Taliban government that it will be held responsible
for any millennium terrorist attacks
carried out by bin Laden and his international network of supporters; the
US has accused bin Laden of oversee-
ing previous terrorist attacks against
American targets.

Bangladesh

Jan. 26—Police say feminist writer
Taslima Nasreen has left for Sweden
after receiving death threats from Islamic militants; Nasreen had recently
returned to Bangladesh after 6 years
of self-imposed exile.

Bhutan

Dec. 20—UN representative Om Pradhan
reports that King Jigme Singye
Wangchuk has released 200 prisoners,
most of whom are ethnic Nepali, including all who had been considered
prisoners of conscience by human
rights groups. Thousands of Nepalis
have crossed the southern border in
the past decade, prompting anxiety
among Bhutan's small ethnic Tibetan
Buddhist population; in response, the
monarchy has forced the immigrants

back across the Nepali border, saying they are not Bhutan citizens; immigrant leaders have accused the government of ethnic cleansing.

India

Jan. 23—An Australian-born Christian missionary and his 2 sons are burned to death in their vehicle by a mob in Manoharpur, Orissa state. *The New York Times* reported today that, according to the Indian Home Ministry, 86 attacks on Christians and their schools and churches were reported to the police last year, up from 24 in 1997 and 7 in 1996.

Feb. 16—Om Prakash Chautala withdraws his Indian National Lok Dal party's support from the governing coalition, citing Prime Minister Atal Bihari Vajpayee's refusal to roll back a hike in the prices of subsidized grains and fertilizer; Chautala's party holds 4 seats in parliament.

April 17—Parliament votes 270 to 269 to approve a motion of no confidence in the government of Prime Minister Atal Bihari Vajpayee; the year-old government, led by Vajpayee's Hindu nationalist Bharatiya Janata Party, collapsed after its largest coalition partner, a Tamil Nadu–based party led by former actress Jayalalitha Jayaram, withdrew its support 3 days ago; Vajpayee will act as caretaker prime minister until a new government is formed.

July 21—Troops renew shelling of a small group of guerrillas in Kashmir's Kargil sector who have not honored the agreement to withdraw by today.

August 18—Sonia Gandhi, leader of the Congress Party, declares her candidacy for parliament in the southern district of Bellary; 10 minutes later Sushma Swaraj, head of the governing Bharatiya Janata Party, announces that she will run for the same seat; Swaraj says Gandhi's foreign birth makes her unfit to hold national office.

Sept. 5—National parliamentary elections, which will be held in 5 stages, begin; the elections were called in April after an alliance led by the Bharatiya Janata Party lost its majority; voting is scheduled to be completed by October 3.

Oct. 7—Election results show that the Bharatiya Janata Party of Prime Minister Vajpayee has won 294 of 543 parliamentary seats; opposition leader Sonia Gandhi's Congress Party earns 113 seats, its worst showing since independence; several new alliances are made between state-level parties and the BJP, bringing the number of parties in the centrist governing coalition to 24.

Dec. 24—Shortly after takeoff from Nepal, five armed men hijack an Indian Airlines plane headed for New Delhi; the hijackers release 27 of the 189 people on board, along with the body of a passenger killed during the siege, at a third refueling stop in the United Arab Emirates; the hijackers' identities and demands are not known.

Dec. 25—Hijackers of the Indian Airlines jet land for food and fuel in the southern Afghan city of Kandahar, where they demand that India release Pakistani religious leader Maulana Masood Azhar and 35 Kashmiri militants; the governing Taliban militia in Afghanistan says initially that it will not negotiate with the hijackers.

Dec. 31—After securing the release of 2 Kashmiri separatists and an Islamic cleric from the Indian government, the 5 hijackers free the 155 hostages who have been held in the Indian airliner for the past 6 days at the Kandahar airport; demands for $200 million made by the hijackers earlier this week had been dropped; negotiations were mediated by the Taliban despite its earlier refusal to become involved; the still-unidentified hijackers and the freed militants depart in a van after the Taliban gives them 10 hours to leave the country; the hostages will be flown to New Delhi.

Pakistan

Feb. 17—The 9-judge Supreme Court rules unanimously that special military courts set up by Prime Minister Nawaz Sharif in December to stem years of political, sectarian, and ethnic violence in Karachi are illegal; the ruling sets aside all decisions handed down by the military courts, including 13 death sentences (2 of which have already been carried out). The strife in Karachi has claimed more than 3,000 lives.

Feb. 20—Indian Prime Minister Atal Bihari Vajpayee meets with Sharif in Wagha, just over the Pakistani border from the Indian state of Punjab; Vajpayee, the first Indian prime minister to visit Pakistan in 10 years, arrived on the inaugural run of a new bus line over the normally closed border.

Feb. 21—Sharif and Vajpayee pledge to act immediately to reduce the risk of nuclear war and seek peace between India and Pakistan, which became declared nuclear weapon states after nuclear tests last May.

April 15—A special court in Rawalpindi convicts former Prime Minister Benazir Bhutto and her husband, Asif Ali Zardari, of accepting kickbacks from a Swiss company in the mid-1990s, and sentences them to 5 years each in prison and a collective $8.6-million fine; the court also bars Bhutto from holding political office.

Oct. 13—Hours after Prime Minister Sharif fires army chief General Pervez Musharraf, the military dismisses Sharif and his government; Musharraf says the bloodless coup is an effort to stop Sharif's destabilization of the military. Sharif, his brother Shahbaz, who is chief minister of Punjab province, and intelligence chief Lieutenant General Mohammad Ziauddin are taken into "protective custody," according to a military spokesman; Musharraf does not say if or when new elections will be held; last October Sharif chose Musharraf to replace General Jehangir Karamat, who had publicly criticized the prime minister.

Oct. 15—Musharraf declares martial law, suspends the constitution and parliament, and names himself head of state. Musharraf also dissolves provincial legislatures; the move comes a day after spokesmen for both the armed forces and President Muhammad

Tarar had said that a democratic civilian government would be reinstated shortly.

Oct. 17—In a televised address, General Musharraf says he will replace parliament with a National Security Council that will include the navy and air force chiefs and 4 unnamed experts in law, finance, foreign policy, and national affairs; a cabinet of ministers, also to be appointed by Musharraf, will preside under the council; Musharraf also says he will withdraw troops from India's border in Kashmir and pursue peace negotiations.

Oct. 20—The military says it is investigating former Prime Minister Sharif for corruption, including embezzling hundreds of millions of dollars from the nation's banks; a spokesman for General Musharraf says Sharif most likely will stand trial for defaulting on bank loans and for tax evasion.

Oct. 21—The military government appoints 4 regional governors—3 retired military officers and one judge—to the provinces of Punjab, Sind, North-West Frontier, and Baluchistan; the army also freezes the bank accounts of officials who served in the Sharif government.

Oct. 25—The military appoints 7 civilians to the government, 3 to the cabinet and 4 to the National Security Council, which will be the country's chief governing body.

Nov. 11—The new military government charges ousted President Sharif and 7 other former government officials with treason, hijacking, and kidnapping in connection with the October 12 incident in which Sharif refused landing rights to coup leader General Musharraf's plane; if convicted, the accused could face the death penalty.

Dec. 17—Former Prime Minister Bhutto and 5 other officials are charged with murder for allegedly ordering the police to fire on members of the Islamic fundamentalist Jamaat-I-Islami party during a June 1996 protest; a police investigation is expected to last several months.

Sri Lanka

Dec. 18—President Chandrika Kumaratunga is wounded in one of two bomb explosions at election rallies in or near the capital of Colombo; at least 18 people are killed and 150 others injured. At about the same time that a suicide bomber detonates explosives outside a rally by Kumaratunga's People's Alliance party in Colombo's town hall, a second blast occurs at the opposition United National Party's suburban rally; although no group has claimed responsibility, authorities suspect the guerrilla Liberation Tigers. Presidential elections are scheduled to be held December 21.

Dec. 22—President Kumaratunga of the People's Alliance party is sworn in for a second term after winning yesterday's presidential election with 51.2% of the vote; the United National Party's Ranil Wickremesinghe earns 43%. Election monitors report widespread voting violations and say results from the northern Tamil region should be nullified.

2000 Events

Afghanistan

Dec. 20—The ruling Taliban militia orders an immediate boycott of American and Russian goods in response to yesterday's UN Security Council ultimatum that the Taliban surrender suspected terrorist Osama bin Laden and close terrorist training camps within one month or suffer harsh new sanctions; the restrictions would include an arms embargo against the Taliban, a ban on international travel by Taliban officials, and further limits on international flights to and from Afghanistan. The Taliban says it will not hand over accused terrorist Osama bin Laden and withdraws from UN-mediated talks on ending the country's 20-year civil war.

India

Oct. 12—A special court sentences former Prime Minister P. V. Narasimha Rao, who served from 1991 to 1996, and a cabinet colleague to 3 years in prison for bribing members of parliament to vote for Rao's government in a 1993 no-confidence measure; they had been convicted of the charges last month. Rao, also fined $2,220, will remain free until a November 8 appeal deadline.

Nepal

Feb. 18—Eleven Congress Party ministers of the 33-member cabinet resign to join others within their governing party who are calling for the replace-ment of Prime Minister Krishna Prasad Bhattarai.

March 16—Prime Minister Krishna Prasad Bhattarai resigns after 69 of 113 parliamentary members of his governing Nepali Congress Party demand that he step down; the rebelling party members cite growing disorder, poor administration, and continued attacks by Maoist insurgents; Bhattarai had been prime minister since May 1999.

March 22—Girija Prasad Koirala is sworn in as prime minister for the fourth time since 1990, when the country became a democracy; Koirala was chosen president of the Nepali Congress by party members 4 days ago to succeed Bhattarai.

Pakistan

Jan. 26—Chief Justice of the Supreme Court Said-uz Zaman Siddiqi is fired after refusing to take a new oath of governmental allegiance barring judges in the Supreme Court, the high courts, and the federal shariah courts from challenging army decisions; 5 other judges of the 13-member panel also declined to take the oath.

Sri Lanka

May 8—President Kumaratunga rejects the guerrilla Liberation Tiger's proposal of a cease-fire in exchange for the withdrawal of nearly 40,000 government troops from the Jaffna peninsula.

Oct. 12—Results from parliamentary elections held 2 days ago show that the ruling coalition, which includes

President Kumaratunga's People's Alliance, has won 107 of the legislature's 225 seats, while the opposition United National Party has take 89; because a simple majority was not achieved, Kumaratunga has been negotiating with smaller parties today to forge an alliance that will allow her party to form a government.

2001 Events

Afghanistan

Feb. 21—UN officials say that nearly 1 million Afghans are at risk of famine by spring; economic hardship caused by international sanctions, severe cold, and prolonged drought has caused nearly 750,000 people to try flee the country in recent months; most are now being housed in camps in the northern and western parts of the country. Another 180,000 who have crossed into Pakistan are also facing serious conditions in refugee camps in that country.

Sept. 13—The Bush administration names Islamic militant Osama bin Laden as the prime suspect in the terror attacks that took place in the United States on September 11. The Saudi-born bin Laden and key elements of his alleged terrorist organization, al Qaeda, reside in Afghanistan, as permitted by the Islamic Taliban militia, which seized control of that country's government in 1996.

Sept. 14—Ahmad Shah Massoud, commander of the Northern Alliance opposition group, is killed in his headquarters in the country's northern region by 2 Algerian suicide bombers posing as journalists.

Sept. 25—Saudi Arabia breaks diplomatic relations with Taliban-governed Afghanistan; Pakistan is now the only country that recognizes the fundamentalist Islamic state.

Oct. 7—The US and Britain launch airstrikes against Afghanistan with long-range bombers and cruise missiles, targeting terrorist training camps, Taliban airfields, and communications centers; US government officials say the aerial campaign will be followed by ground operations to track members of suspected terrorist Osama bin Laden's Al Qaeda network; Taliban leaders repeatedly refused President Bush's demands to turn over the Saudi-born bin Laden, who has lived in Afghanistan since the mid-1990s and who is believed responsible for the September 11 terrorist attacks on the US that killed nearly 3,000 people.

Dec. 5—Negotiators at a UN-sponsored summit of 4 Afghan opposition groups in Bonn, Germany sign an accord on a post-Taliban political structure in Afghanistan that establishes an interim ruling council and schedules national elections within 2 years; the council, which will consist of 30 members, will govern Afghanistan for 6 months, after which a traditional assembly will decide on a permanent structure; Pashtun tribal leader Hamid Karzai is named interim administrator for the transitional government; the agreement also calls for the immediate assembly of a tempo-

rary group of multinational peacekeepers in the capital city of Kabul
and possibly other areas; the Afghan
factions include delegates of former
Afghan King Mohammad Zahir Shah,
the Northern Alliance, the "Peshawar
Group" (representing millions of
Afghan refugees in Pakistan), and the
"Cyprus Group" (representing an
Iranian-backed group of Afghan
exiles).
Dec. 6—The Taliban agree to surrender
Kandahar, their last major stronghold,
as opposition forces begin entering
the city; the whereabouts of Taliban
leader Mullah Mohammed Omar and
of Osama bin Laden, are unknown.
Dec. 16—US officials say that Al Qaeda
has been destroyed in Afghanistan,
and Afghan commanders declare victory over the terrorist network after
nearly 2 weeks of fighting in the
mountainous Tora Bora region.
Dec. 22—In Kabul, interim Afghan leader
Hamid Karzai and his cabinet are
sworn in for a 6-month term.

Bangladesh

Oct. 3—At least 3 people are killed and
more than 100 injured in protests
across the country following parliamentary elections held 2 days ago; unofficial results for 282 of parliament's
300 seats show that former Prime
Minister Khaleda Zia's Bangladesh
Nationalist Party won 185 seats, and its
ally, Jamaat-e-Islami, 16; former Prime
Minister Sheik Hasina's Awami
League earned 62 seats, and the
center-right National Islamic Unity
Front, 14. Protests began today after

Hasina's supporters accused Zia of
rigging the elections; international
monitors say the vote was fair.

India

March 15—Defense Minister George Fernandes resigns after the release earlier
this week of videotapes secretly filmed
over the past 8 months that indicate
Fernandes accepted a bribe from Internet journalists who had posed as
arms merchants. Railways Minister
Mamata Banerjee resigns from the
cabinet and withdraws her Trinamool
Congress party from the governing
coalition in protest of official corruption. Two days ago Bangaru Laxman,
president of the ruling Bharatiya
Janata Party, also resigned when the
same video, allegedly showing him
taking $2,100 from the journalists, was
made public. Fernandes and Laxman
deny wrongdoing; 4 Defense Ministry
officials named in the documentary
have been suspended.
July 16—A 3-day summit in the central
city of Agra between Prime Minister
Atal Behari Vajpayee and Pakistani
President Pervez Musharraf ends with
no agreement on the disputed territory of Kashmir; previous negotiations between the 2 sides broke off
more than 2 years ago.
Dec. 13—Five gunmen enter the federal
parliament building in New Delhi,
killing at least 7 people and injuring 18
others; 4 of the attackers are killed by
Indian security forces and the fifth
blows himself up; no lawmakers are
wounded and no group claims responsibility for the attack.

Dec. 24—India and Pakistan put their
border troops on high alert; in the
past 2 days, the 2 countries have
amassed troops near their borders,
and several exchanges of fire have
been reported along the Kashmir border; Pakistan freezes the assets of
Lashkar, although it says India has not
provided evidence of the group's involvement in the attack on the Indian
parliament; Indian officials say 3 border security troops were killed and 2
wounded when Pakistani soldiers
fired on an Indian border post in
Kashmir yesterday.

Dec. 27—India moves short-range missiles capable of carrying nuclear war-
heads to the Pakistan border,
according to Indian defense officials;
India and Pakistan close airspace con-
necting the 2 countries.

Nepal

Nov. 27—In the past 5 days, more than
280 people, including at least 80 security personnel and 120 rebels, have
been killed in fighting between rebels
and government forces in the western region. Yesterday King Gyanendra declared a state of emergency,
which suspended most civil liberties
and authorized use of the army; the
violence began when Maoist rebels
launched simultaneous attacks on
army barracks and police posts in
Solukhumbu district, ending a 4-
month cease-fire; the rebels say the
government failed to meet their demand for an election of a constituent assembly to draft a new
constitution; more than 2,000 people

have been killed in the 5-year insurgency.

Pakistan

April 6—The Supreme Court orders a
retrial for former Prime Minister Benazir Bhutto, overturning her 1999
conviction on charges of accepting
kickbacks from a Swiss company;
Bhutto, who served 2 terms as prime
minister between 1988 and 1996, has
been living in self-exile in Britain
and the United Arab Emirates since
1999; Bhutto still faces corruption
charges.

June 20—General Pervez Musharraf, the
country's military leader, dismisses
President Rafiq Tarrar and appoints
himself as his replacement; Musharraf
also dissolves the National Assembly
and the 4 provisional assemblies. As
president, Musharraf will continue to
hold the positions of army chief of
staff and chief executive.

Sri Lanka

July 25—Bandaranaike International Airport reopens in the capital city of
Colombo after yesterday's Liberation
Tiger attack on the airport that killed
at least 19 people, including 14 rebels,
2 army commandos, and 3 air force
personnel; several aircraft were damaged or destroyed.

Oct. 10—President Chandrika Kumaratunga dissolves parliament and
calls new elections for December 5
after defections from her People's Alliance coalition make a no-confidence
vote probable; the announcement

came after 9 lawmakers quit the coalition today, reducing it to 111 of parliament's 225 seats. A cabinet minister also resigned, the fourth in a month.

Dec. 7—Results from parliamentary elections held 2 days ago show that the opposition 3-party United National Front won 129 of parliament's 225 seats; the governing People's Alliance and its supporting parties earned 96. President Kumaratunga invites opposition leader Ranil Wickremesinghe, an archrival, to become prime minister; since the campaign began on October 21, 61 people have died in election-related violence, according to the Center for Monitoring Election Violence; European Union observers say the voting was marred by blockading of polls, attacks on voters and party workers by armed gangs, and ballot stuffing.

2002 Events

Afghanistan

Feb. 15—Interim leader Hamid Karzai says yesterday's killing of Civil Aviation and Tourism Minister Abdul Rahman was an "assassination" and that 20 members of his government, including 5 senior military and defense officials, were involved; Karzai says the killing is linked to a blood feud dating to the struggle against the former ruling Taliban government and that the top 5 suspects were part of a faction of the Northern Alliance with which Rahman had broken. Initial news reports indicated that Rahman had been beaten to death by as many as 100 Hajj pilgrims who stormed his plane at the airport in Kabul, the capital, after waiting for 2 days for a flight to Mecca, Saudi Arabia.

India

Feb. 27—More than 50 Hindus are killed and at least 18 others seriously injured when approximately 2,000 Muslims set fire to their train in western Gujarat state; the Hindu activists were returning from the northern town of Ayodhya where they had been demanding the government build a Hindu temple on the site of a destroyed mosque. Muslims want the mosque rebuilt. Prime Minister Atal Behari Vajpayee calls for the temple plans to be canceled and deploys thousands of security personnel in Ayodhya; the demolition of the Ayodhya mosque in 1992 sparked riots between Hindus and Muslims across the country in which more than 2,000 people died.

March 2—In the past 4 days, nearly 400 people have died in Gujurat as ethnic violence spreads to rural areas; officials place 50 cities and towns under curfew. More than 4,000 soldiers and other federal security forces arrive in the state to reinforce local police, who have killed 49 people since the fighting began.

May 14—Three gunmen enter an Indian military camp in the disputed state of Kashmir, killing at least 30 people and wounding 48 others before they are killed by Indian security forces; al-Mansoorain, a previously unknown rebel group, claims responsibility; Indian and Pakistani military forces have been in a standoff since a December 13 raid on parliament that New Delhi has blamed on Pakistani-based Kashmiri rebels.

June 10—New Delhi lifts a 5-month ban on Pakistani commercial aircraft flying over India, selects a new ambassador to Pakistan, and withdraws warships from Pakistan's coast to lessen tensions between the 2 countries; earlier this week, the US and Britain urged their citizens to leave India and Pakistan.

July 18—Results from a presidential vote held 3 days ago by the country's legislature show that scientist A. P. J. Abdul Kalam, former head of the country's nuclear missile program, has been elected president; Kalam, who is a Muslim in the majority Hindu country, will assume the largely ceremonial office on July 25.

Oct. 16—The government announces a limited withdrawal of as many as 700,000 troops from its border with Pakistan, but not along the Line of Control in Kashmir, which divides the disputed region into Indian- and Pakistani-administered areas. Over the past 10 months the 2 sides have amassed 1 million troops along their border in the latest confrontation over Kashmir; the buildup was prompted by a December attack on the Indian parliament for which New Delhi blames Pakistani-backed Kashmiri separatists; Islamabad denies involvement.

Nepal

Oct. 11—King Gyanendra appoints a new government headed by former Prime Minister Lokendra Bahadur Chand, leader of the rightist promonarchy National Democratic Party. Last week Gyanendra dismissed Prime Minister Sher Bahadur Deuba and his government after Deuba had asked for a one-year postponement of next month's parliamentary elections because of fears that Maoist rebels would disrupt them; Gyanendra postpones the elections indefinitely.

Pakistan

Jan. 16—Pakistan says that in the past 5 days it has detained 1,430 activists from 5 banned Islamic groups and shut down 390 of their offices in an effort to ease tensions with India; Pakistani officials say the groups' leaders remain at large; India has called for Pakistan to extradite for trial the leaders of the 2 groups they blame for the December 2001 Indian parliament attack. Pervez Musharraf, Pakistan's military leader, says that any Pakistanis accused of involvement in the raid will be tried in Pakistan.

Feb. 12—In the eastern city of Lahore, government authorities arrest Ahmed Omar Sheikh, a British-born Islamic militant identified as the main suspect in last month's kidnapping of American journalist Daniel Pearl. During questioning, Sheikh says Pearl is alive; Pearl has not been seen since he was kidnapped on January 23 from a Karachi restaurant.

May 1—Official results from yesterday's nationwide referendum show that 97.7% of voters approved the extension of President Musharraf's term for another 5 years; the government says that a turnout of over 50%, relatively high for the country, legitimized the results. Musharraf, a former army general who seized power in a bloodless coup in 1999, called for the referendum last month to override results of parliamentary elections scheduled for October; human rights groups say that the vote was marred by widespread corruption, and turnout was no higher than 25%.

July 15—An antiterrorism court held at Hyderabad prison, near Karachi, sentences British-born Sheik Omar Saeed to death for his role in organizing the kidnapping and murder of American Daniel Pearl, the Wall Street Journal reporter who was abducted in Karachi in January and murdered shortly afterward; 3 other religious militants are found guilty of helping in the conspiracy to kidnap Pearl and sentenced to 25-year prison terms. During his interrogation by police in Karachi, Saeed also claimed responsibility for at least 3 high-profile terrorist incidents in India since last September, including a terrorist bombing at the Srinagar parliament that killed 17 people and a shooting spree at the Indian parliament in New Delhi in which 13 people were killed.

August 21—Musharraf unilaterally redraws the constitution, imposing 29 amendments that expand his powers, including the ability to make further amendments at will, dissolve parliament, and appoint the country's military leaders and Supreme Court justices; the changes also institutionalize the political role of the military by allotting it seats on a newly created National Security Council, a civilian-military body that will monitor future governments. Musharraf declared himself president last year.

Oct. 13—Results from elections held 3 days ago, the first since President Pervez Musharraf seized power in 1999, show that the Pakistan Muslim League Quaid-I-Azam, a new party loyal to Musharraf, won 78 of 272 constituency seats in the 342-seat parliament; the Pakistan People's Party, led by exiled former Prime Minister Benazir Bhutto, received 62 seats, and the Mutahidda Majlis-e-Amal, a coalition of 6 conservative Islamic groups, earned 45 seats (compared with 2 at the last election); European Union observers said the election was seriously flawed because the military government gave preferential treatment to pro-government candidates, misused state news broadcasts, and locked out top political rivals. Since April, when Musharraf extended his self-declared presidency for 5 years through a referendum, Musharraf has issued a series of constitution-altering decrees, including giving himself the powers to fire the prime minister and dissolve the legislature, and requiring all candidates for public office to have a university degree, which excludes 90% of the country's mostly illiterate population.

Nov. 21—Zafarullah Khan Jamali, head of the progovernment Pakistan Muslim League–Quaid party, wins 172 of 328 National Assembly votes, to become prime minister; Fazlur Rahman, a Muslim cleric opposed to President Pervez Musharraf's cooperation with the US in the war on terrorism, receives 86 votes, and Shah Mahmood Quereshi of former Prime Minister Benazir Bhutto's Pakistan People's Party earns 70. Today's parliamentary vote became necessary after no party won a clear majority in October's general election; under constitutional amendments imposed by the president last summer, Musharraf retains ultimate power, including authority to dissolve parliament, but will relinquish day-to-day executive powers to Jamali, a civilian, in 2 days.

Dec. 14—The Lahore High Court releases Maulana Masood Azhar, the head of the radical Kashmiri militant group Jaish-e Mohammed; in December 2001 Maulana was placed under house arrest in the city of Bahawalpur in Punjab region but was never tried; Jaish-e Mohammed is one of two groups fighting for independence in Indian-controlled Kashmir that were blamed by the Indian government for the December 2001 attack on the Indian parliament in New Delhi that killed 14 people; one month after the attack, President Pervez Musharraf outlawed the group and ordered a crackdown on its members and seizure of its bank accounts.

2003 Events

Afghanistan

July 27—The Bush administration is reportedly readying a proposal for $1 billion in aid to Afghanistan as international donations fall short. An Afghan official complains that vio-

lence in the countryside is rampant and Taliban fighters roam freely.

Oct. 18—Government officials announce completion of a draft constitution, written by a national commission, that will be put before Afghans for public discussion before a constitutional convention scheduled for Dec. 10.

Nov. 3—The Afghan government unveils a draft constitution that proposes a strong presidential system, eliminating the position of prime minister that an advisory commission initially had recommended. The draft appears to bolster President Hamid Karzai, who hopes to win election next year to the post he now holds temporarily as a transitional leader.

Dec. 13—Approximately 500 delegates from throughout the country gather in Kabul for a grand assembly, or loya jirga, aimed at crafting a constitution for Afghanistan. Supporters of interim President Hamid Karzai, who favor a presidential system of government, must reach agreement with the supporters of powerful warlords, who favor a more decentralized parliamentary government. Delegates also are divided over women's rights and the role of Islam.

Pakistan

March 1—In the northern city of Rawalpindi, US and Pakistani intelligence agents arrest Khalid Sheik Mohammed, the Al Qaeda lieutenant who allegedly organized the September 11, 2001 terrorist attacks on the US, and 2 other suspected Al Qaeda members whom authorities identified as a Pakistani and an Arab; President Pervez Musharraf authorizes the transfer of Mohammed and the Arab suspect to a US detention center at an undisclosed location "outside Pakistan"; Mohammed also has been under indictment since 1996 in connection with a plot to blow up US airliners over the Pacific Ocean and has been linked to the kidnapping and murder of American journalist Daniel Pearl last year; Islamabad says it has handed over more than 420 Al Qaeda and Taliban suspects to US custody since the 2001 attacks.

April 30—Federal authorities in the city of Karachi capture Walid Ba'attash, a top operative of Osama bin Laden's Al Qaeda terrorist network, along with 5 Pakistani terrorist suspects. US officials believe Ba'attash, a Saudi citizen of Yemeni descent, was involved in the bombing of the USS Cole in October 2000 and in the September 11, 2001 terrorist attacks on the US.

June 2—Following local elections dominated by an alliance of religious parties, a provincial assembly votes unanimously to introduce Islamic law in Pakistan's North-West Frontier Province. The bill provides that Islamic law, or sharia, will override all other laws in local courts.

June 24—President Bush offers Pakistan a $3 billion aid package. Until two years ago, Pakistan had been under strict US sanctions for developing nuclear weapons. Following a lengthy meeting in the US with Pakistan's president, General Pervez Musharraf, Bush says the aid will be contingent on Pak-

istan's continued cooperation in the war on terrorism.

Aug. 9—Hundreds of Pakistani lawmakers and political activists greet a delegation of about 40 Indian legislators, diplomats, and journalists at a border crossing between their countries in an effort to sustain momentum for peace. India's new envoy to Pakistan presents his credentials to President Musharraf, signaling formal restoration of ties that were broken off after Pakistani-based rebels carried out a December 2001 attack on the Indian Parliament.

Dec. 14—A remote-controlled bomb explodes moments after Musharraf's motorcade passes a bridge near the capital. No one is hurt. Musharraf enraged Islamic hardliners when he backed the US-led war in Afghanistan in 2001.

Dec. 17—Musharraf offers to set aside Pakistan's 50-year-old demand to implement UN resolutions that call for both India and Pakistan to withdraw troops from Kashmir and would allow Kashmiris to decide in a vote whether to be part of India or Pakistan.

Dec. 25—The president narrowly escapes the 2nd attempt on his life in 11 days—the 4th since 2002—when 2 suicide attackers in Islamabad explode bombs as his convoy passes, killing at least 14 people and wounding 46. Musharraf vows to "cleanse the country of these extremists."

Sri Lanka

Nov. 4—President Chandrika Kumaratunga suspends Parliament and takes control of key government ministries in an apparent power struggle with Sri Lanka's technocrat prime minister, Ranil Wickremesinghe, while he is in Washington consulting with US officials. She accuses him of making too many concessions in peace talks with rebels from the Tamil ethnic minority.

Nov. 7—A political crisis that sparked fears of renewed civil war shows signs of easing as President Kumaratunga rescinds a state of emergency and calls on her political rival, the prime minister, to join her in forming a new government.

2004 Events

Afghanistan

Jan. 4—Afghan leaders approve a constitution after 3 weeks of rancorous debate. It includes a strong presidency that the country's US-backed interim president, Hamid Karzai, says is critical for uniting a country torn by 2 decades of war. The constitution creates a 2-chamber parliament, provides for equal rights for women, gives official status to minority languages, and says laws must accord with the tenets of Islam.

March 31—Afghanistan receives pledges of $4.4 billion in aid after President Karzai tells a conference of international donors that his country needs $28 billion over the next 7 years to recover from more than 2 decades of war and repression. The US pledges $2.2 billion; Europe and Japan offer the rest.

Sept. 7—An unprecedented election campaign officially begins, pitting 17 challengers against US-backed interim leader Hamid Karzai in his bid to become the country's first popularly elected president. About 10.6 million Afghans have registered to vote in the balloting scheduled for Oct. 9.

Dec. 7—Karzai is sworn in as Afghanistan's first popularly elected president. Three years after US-backed militias overthrew the Taliban government, Karzai promises to appoint a reformist cabinet and open a "new chapter" for his impoverished country.

Dec. 23—President Karzai announces a new cabinet dominated by technocrats and mostly purged of warlords who led rebel forces against the Soviet army and then the Taliban.

Bangladesh

Aug. 24—A general strike shuts down much of the country in protest against a grenade attack that killed 20 people and wounded hundreds at an opposition political rally. The opposition leader, Sheikh Hasina, blames the attack on Islamic extremists and accuses the country's government of sheltering them.

India

Jan. 12—The Bush administration says it is ready to expand high-technology cooperation with India and possibly ease export restrictions, but only after India strengthens controls to guard against re-export of sensitive technology to other countries.

Feb. 4—India announces a $5.5 billion fund to modernize its armed forces. A booming economy has helped India far outspend regional rival Pakistan on weapons systems. Recent purchases include a $1.5 billion Russian-made aircraft carrier.

May 13—Prime Minister Atal Bihari Vajpayee, whose Hindu nationalist party has led India since 1998, resigns after his ruling coalition suffers a major upset in parliamentary elections. The results are seen as a repudiation of Vajpayee's agenda of privatization, deregulation, and other economic reforms. The opposition Congress Party and its allies win 212 seats in the lower house of Parliament, compared to 180 for Vajpayee's Bharatitya Janata Party and its coalition partners.

May 18—The Italian-born Sonia Gandhi, after leading her party to an unexpected election victory over India's Hindu nationalists, surprises the nation by declining to accept the prime minister's post.

May 19—Manmohan Singh, an economist and respected economic reformer who served as finance minister from 1991 to 1996, is chosen unanimously by Congress Party lawmakers to serve as India's next prime minister.

Pakistan

Jan. 1—President Pervez Musharraf wins a vote of confidence from Pakistan's electoral college, allowing him legally to remain in office until 2007. The vote completes the transformation of the general, who seized power in a bloodless coup in 1999, into a consti-

tutionally legitimate president. Most opposition parties abstain from or boycott the vote.

Jan. 5—Musharraf meets in Islamabad with the Indian prime minister, Atal Bihari Vajpayee, boosting hopes for the start of a peace process between the nuclear-armed neighbors that have gone to war 3 times since they became independent nations in 1947.

Jan. 18—The government has detained 7 scientists and administrators in an expanding probe into allegations that Pakistanis sold nuclear-weapons information and technology to countries such as Iran, North Korea, and Libya, officials say.

Jan. 20—Pakistan bars all scientists working on its nuclear weapons program from leaving the country as it intensifies an inquiry into the sharing of nuclear technology with other countries. Pakistani experts and Western diplomats doubt whether scientists could have traded secrets abroad without the knowledge of senior military and intelligence officials.

Jan. 26—The government announces that millions of chickens in Pakistan have been infected with an influenza virus. Additional reports of large-scale chicken deaths have emerged in Burma, Laos, Bangladesh, and Saudi Arabia.

Jan. 31—The government fires Abdul Qadeer Khan, widely revered in Pakistan as the "father" of its nuclear program, from his position as scientific adviser to the prime minister.

Feb. 1—Khan confesses to having shared nuclear arms hardware and designs with North Korea, Iran, and Libya for the past decade. Opposition politicians express skepticism about official denials of any involvement by the government, military, or intelligence services.

Feb. 5—President Musharraf pardons Khan, the nation's top scientist, a day after he appears on TV to confess to and apologize for selling nuclear weapons secrets. The Bush administration praises Musharraf for breaking up the proliferation network, making little mention of his decision to pardon Khan and terminate any probe into whether the military was involved.

Feb. 22—Pakistani military officials say they are preparing, under heavy pressure from Washington, a major joint assault with US forces against Al Qaeda and a search for its leader, Osama bin Laden, in the frontier region bordering Afghanistan.

June 24—President Musharraf calls the first meeting of a new National Security Council, a top-level group created to advise the government on security and other issues. Musharraf's parliamentary opposition earlier condemned the move for reinforcing the role of the army in the country's politics.

Aug. 18—Shaukat Aziz, a former banker and finance minister, wins a parliamentary election that assures his appointment as prime minister after narrowly escaping an assassination attempt 3 weeks earlier.

Sept. 1—A report by the UN International Atomic Energy Agency says that, as early as 1995, Pakistan was providing Iran with designs for sophisticated centrifuges capable of making bomb-grade nuclear fuel.

Oct. 14—The National Assembly passes a bill allowing President Musharraf to remain as army chief, reversing his earlier promise to step down from the post.

Nov. 23—A CIA report says an arms-trafficking network based in Pakistan provided Iran's nuclear program in the 1990s with more "significant assistance" than previously realized, including designs for "advanced" weapons components.

Nov. 24—In the first visit by a Pakistani prime minister to India in 13 years, Shaukat Aziz confers in New Delhi with his Indian counterpart, Manmohan Singh. Both vow to continue the peace dialogue begun this year.

Dec. 4—US President GeorgeBush, after meeting in the White House with President Musharraf, lauds Pakistan for its hard line against terrorism and for its help in the hunt for Osama bin Laden, despite the inability of US and Pakistani troops to find the Al Qaeda leader. Bin Laden is believed to be hiding in the mountainous region along the Afghanistan-Pakistan border.

Dec. 30—Musharraf, in a televised address to the nation, explains his decision to renege on a promise to step down as army chief by the end of 2004. He accuses his political opponents of "threatening" democracy and insists he must retain the military post as well as the presidency to ensure stability.

Sri Lanka

Jan. 13—President Chandrika Kumaratunga says she privately underwent a second swearing-in ceremony in 2000, a year after she last took office, so she is entitled to serve an extra year as president, until 2006. Her announcement further complicates a political crisis stemming from her power struggle with the prime minister, Ranil Wickremasinghe.

Feb. 7—President Kumaratunga dissolves Parliament and orders new elections for April 2, escalating her rivalry with Prime Minister Ranil Wickremesinghe.

April 6—President Kumaratunga, with the support of the largest bloc in parliament after April 2 elections, swears in a new prime minister, Mahinda Rajapakse. The president was at odds with the former prime minister over concessions he made in negotiations with rebel Tamil Tigers.

About the Contributors

John Adams is Visiting Scholar at the Center for South Asian Studies, University of Virginia. He is affiliated with the Center for Middle Eastern Studies at Harvard University; Professor Emeritus, Northeastern University; and President and Chief Economist, Sawhill Associates, Chancellor, Virginia.

Samina Ahmed is the South Asia Project Director for the International Crisis Group in Islamabad, Pakistan. She is the co-editor of *Pakistan and the Bomb: Public Opinion and Nuclear Options.*

Craig Baxter is Professor Emeritus of Politics at Juniata College in Huntingdon, Pennsylvania, and a former foreign service officer who served in India and Pakistan. He has published eleven books on the history and politics of Bangladesh, India, and Pakistan. His most recent book is *Pakistan on the Brink: Politics, Economics, and Society.*

Toby F. Dalton is a project associate with the Non-Proliferation Project at the Carnegie Endowment for International Peace in Washington, D.C.

Manik De Silva is the Chief Editor of *The Island*, Sri Lanka's leading independent, English-language newspaper. He is a contributing editor to *Himal* and a contributor to the *Far Eastern Economic Review.*

Gilles Dorronsoro is Professor of Political Science, Paris I (Pantheon-Sorbonne), and the author of *Revolution Unending: Afghanistan, 1979 to the Present.* He is a member of the editorial committees of *Cultures and Conflicts* and *Central Asian Literature*. "Afghanistan's Civil War" was translated from the French by Percival Manglano.

Alexander Evans is a research associate at King's College, London. He is a regular commentator on Kashmir for BBC World Television, Reuters, AFP, and others, and is the author of numerous articles on contemporary politics in Jammu and Kashmir.

Bill Finan is the editor of *Current History*.

Sumit Ganguly is the Rabindranath Tagore Professor of Indian Cultures and Civilizations, and Professor of Political Science, at Indiana University, Bloomington. His most recent books include *Conflict Unending: India-Pakistan Tensions since 1947* and *The Crisis in Kashmir: Portents of War, Hopes of Peace*. He serves on the editorial boards of *Current History, Asian Affairs, Asian Survey*, and the *Journal of Strategic Studies*. He is also the editor of a new journal, *The India Review*. The author gratefully acknowledges support received in producing "An Opportunity for Peace in Kashmir?" from the Woodrow Wilson International Center for Scholars.

Anatol Lieven is a journalist, writer, and historian. He is a contributing correspondent for the *Washington Quarterly* and has written for *The Economist, Foreign Affairs*, and *The National Interest*, among other publications. His most recent book is *America Right or Wrong: An Anatomy of American Nationalism*. "Rebuilding Afghanistan" is adapted with permission from "Rebuilding Afghanistan: Fantasy versus Reality" (Carnegie Endowment Policy Brief no. 12, January 2002).

Pratap Bhanu Mehta is President and Chief Executive of the Centre for Policy Research in New Delhi. He was previously Visiting Professor of Government at Harvard University and Associate Professor of Government and of Social Studies at Harvard. He is also the author of *The Burdens of Democracy*.

Marina Ottaway is a senior associate in the Democracy and Rule of Law Project at the Carnegie Endowment for International Peace. She is also a lecturer in African Studies at the Nitze School for Advanced International Studies at Johns Hopkins University. Her most recent books include *Uncharted Journey: Promoting Democracy in the Middle East* (co-edited with Thomas Carothers) and *Democracy Challenged: The Rise of Semi-Authoritarianism*. "Rebuilding Afghanistan" is adapted with permission from "Rebuilding Afghanistan: Fantasy versus Reality" (Carnegie Endowment Policy Brief no. 12, January 2002).

Ahmed Rashid is a Pakistani journalist based in Lahore. He is author of the best-selling books *Taliban: Militant Islam, Oil and Fundamentalism in Central Asia* and *Jihad: The Rise of Militant Islam in Central Asia*. He has covered Pakistan, Afghanistan, and Central Asia for the past 25 years and writes for the *Far Eastern Economic Review, The Daily Telegraph*, and *The Wall Street Journal*.

Barnett R. Rubin is the Director of Studies and Senior Fellow at the Center on International Cooperation of New York University. He is the author of *The Fragmentation of Afghanistan: State Formation and Collapse in the International System* and *Blood on the Doorstep: The Politics of Preventing Violent Conflict*. "A Blueprint for Afghanistan" is adapted from a speech delivered in Tokyo at the International Symposium on Human Security.

Shalendra D. Sharma is Professor of Political Science at the University of San Francisco. He is the author of *The Asian Financial Crisis: Meltdown, Reform, and Recovery*. He also serves as a consultant for the World Bank.

David Stuligross is Visiting Professor of Politics at Oberlin College.

Robert G. Wirsing is a professor in the Regional Studies Department at the Asia-Pacific Center for Security Studies in Honolulu, Hawaii. His most recent book is *Kashmir in the Shadow of War: Regional Rivalries in a Nuclear Age*.

Miriam Young is the former executive director of the Asia Pacific Center for Justice and Peace and Senior Program Officer for the Robert F. Kennedy Center for Human Rights. "Making Peace in Sri Lanka" is adapted from "Sri Lanka's Long War," which appeared in the October 2000 issue of *Foreign Policy in Focus*.